STUDENT ATLAS OF

World Politics

Tenth Edition

John L. Allen
University of Wyoming

Christopher J. Sutton
Western Illinois University

Connect Learn Succeed™

The McGraw-Hill Companies

Connect
Learn
Succeed™

STUDENT ATLAS OF WORLD POLITICS, TENTH EDITION

This book is printed on acid-free paper.

2 3 4 5 6 7 QVS/QVS 20 19 18 17 16

MHID 0-07-802620-2
ISBN 978-0-07-802620-1
ISSN 1524-4556

Managing Editor: *Larry Loeppke*
Developmental Editor II: *Debra A. Henricks*
Senior Permissions Coordinator: *Shirley Lanners*
Marketing Specialist: *Alice Link*
Lead Project Manager: *Jane Mohr*
Design Coordinator: *Brenda A. Rolwes*
Cover Designer: *Rick D. Noel*
Buyer: *Nicole Baumgartner*
Media Project Manager: *Sridevi Palani*

Compositor: *Lachina Publishing Services*
Cover Image: © *United Nations Photo #483001*

www.mhhe.com

A Note to the Student

International politics is a drama played out on a world stage. We are not isolated from events that transpire in other parts of the world; our boundaries do not make us secure; and we ignore the conditions of political, economic, cultural, and physical geography outside those boundaries at our great peril. The maps in this atlas serve as the stage for the various scenes in this drama; the data are the building materials from which the settings are created. Just as the stage setting helps bring to life and give meaning to the actions and words of a play, so can these maps and data enhance your understanding of the vast and complex drama of global politics, including the emergence of global terrorism as a political instrument. Use this atlas in conjunction with your text on international politics or international affairs. It will help you become more knowledgeable about this international stage as well as the actors.

The maps in the *Student Atlas of World Politics*, tenth edition, are designed to introduce you to the importance of the connections between geography and world politics. In many instances, the data has been used to produce the patterns that you see on the maps. But where the data may represent absolute values (at least as reported by individual countries), the maps are generalizations based on the data. The maps are not perfect representations of reality—no maps ever are—but they do represent "models," or approximations of the real world, that should aid in your understanding of the world drama. The profiles of the world's countries and dependencies provide a "snapshot" of key demographic, cultural, and economic characteristics. Use these in concert with the maps to gain a better understanding of our world.

You will find your study of this atlas more productive in relation to your study of international politics if you examine the maps on the following pages in the context of five distinct analytical themes:

1. Location: Where Is It? This involves a focus on the precise location of places in both absolute terms (the latitude and longitude of a place) and in relative terms (the location of a place in relation to the location of other places). When you think of location, you should automatically think of both forms. Knowing something about absolute location will help you to understand a variety of features of physical geography, since such key elements are often so closely related to their position on the earth. But it is equally important to think of location in relative terms. The location of places in relation to other places is often more important in influencing social, economic, and cultural characteristics than are the factors of physical geography. The exchange of goods and services occurs between large cities at much different levels if those cities are near to each other than if they are thousands of miles apart.

2. Place: What Is It Like? This encompasses the political, economic, cultural, environmental, and other characteristics that give a place its identity. You should seek to understand the similarities and differences of places by exploring their basic characteristics. Why are some places with similar environmental characteristics so very different in economic, cultural, social, and political ways? Why are other places with such different environmental characteristics so seemingly alike in terms of their institutions, their economies, and their cultures? The place characteristics of parts of the world American students have known little about (like Afghanistan and Iraq) have now emerged as vital components of our necessary understanding of the implementation of military and political strategies.

3. Human/Environment Interactions: How Is the Landscape Shaped? This theme focuses on the ways in which people respond to and modify their environments. On the world stage, humans are not the only part of the action. The environment also plays a role in the drama of international politics. But the characteristics of the environment do not exert a controlling influence over human activities; they only provide a set of alternatives from which different cultures, in different times, make their choices. Observe the relationship between the basic elements of physical geography such as climate and terrain and the host of ways in which humans have used the land surfaces of the world. To know something of the relationship between people and the environment in the arid parts of the Old World is to begin to understand the nature of political, economic, and even religious conflicts between the inhabitants of those regions and others. The ongoing unrest in the Darfur region of Sudan or military conflict in the Congo Basin are at least partly attributable to the interaction between people and their environment.

4. Movement: How Do People Stay in Touch? This examines the transportation and communication systems that link people and places. Movement or "spatial interaction" is the chief mechanism for the spread of ideas and innovations from one place to another. It is spatial interaction that validates the old cliché, "the world is getting smaller." We find McDonald's restaurants in Tokyo and Honda automobiles in New York City because of spatial interaction. And the spread of global terrorism is, first and foremost, a process of spatial interaction. Advanced transportation and communication systems have transformed the world into which your parents were born. And the world that greets your children will be very different from your world. None of this would happen without the force of movement or spatial interaction.

5. Regions: How Is the Surface of the World Arranged and Organized? This theme, perhaps the most important for this atlas, helps to organize knowledge about the land and its people. The world consists

of a mosaic of "regions" or areas that are somehow different and distinctive from other areas. The region of Anglo-America (the United States and Canada) is, for example, different enough from the region of Western Europe that geographers clearly identify them as two unique and separate areas. Yet despite their differences, Anglo-Americans and Europeans share a number of similarities: common cultural backgrounds, comparable economic patterns, shared religious traditions, and even some shared physical environmental characteristics. Conversely, although the regions of Anglo-America and Southwestern Asia (the "Middle East") are also easily distinguished as distinctive units of the earth's surface with some shared physical environmental characteristics, the inhabitants of these two regions have fewer similarities and more differences between them than is the case with Anglo-America and Western Europe: different cultural traditions, different institutions, different linguistic and religious patterns. An understanding of both the differences and similarities between regions like Anglo-America and Europe on the one hand, or Anglo-America and Southwest Asia on the other, will help you to understand much that has happened in the human past or that is currently transpiring in the world around you. At the very least, an understanding of regional similarities and differences will help you to interpret what you read on the front page of your daily newspaper or view on the evening news report on your television set.

Not all of these themes will be immediately apparent in each of the maps in this atlas. But if you study the contents of *Student Atlas of World Politics*, tenth edition, along with the reading of your text and think about the five themes, maps and data and text will complement one another and improve your understanding of global politics. As Shakespeare said, "All the world's a stage." Your challenge is now to understand both the stage and the drama being played on it.

A Word about Data Sources

At the very outset of your study of this atlas, you should be aware of some limitations of the maps. In some instances, a map may have missing data. This may be the result of the failure of a country to report information to a central international body (like the United Nations or the World Bank). Alternatively, it may reflect shifts in political boundaries, internal or external conflicts, or changes in responsibility for reporting data, which have caused certain countries (for example, the split of Sudan into the separate states of Sudan and South Sudan) to delay their reports. Some reporting bodies include data for overseas dependencies of countries, such as French Guiana (France), Greenland (Denmark), and the Falkland Islands (United Kingdom). Not all do, however, and in such situations, the maps include data for the governing country. It is always our wish to be as up-to-date as is possible; earlier editions of this atlas were lacking more data than this one and subsequent versions will have still more data, particularly on the southeastern European countries or on African and Asian nations that are just beginning to reach a point in their economic and political development where they can consistently report reliable information. In the meantime, as events continue to restructure our world, it's an exciting time to be a student of international events!

John L. Allen
University of Wyoming

Christopher J. Sutton
Western Illinois University

What's New in This Edition

Student Atlas of World Politics, tenth edition, reflects current political, economic, demographic, and environmental change in every part of the world. This edition is the most comprehensive version yet of a book that has long been a standard in the field. Here, in one volume, are 127 thematic maps and 15 reference maps rich in details of physical and political geography. A number of new thematic maps highlight the impact of demographic stresses on political stability on a global scale. New maps have also been added in the contemporary world, political, economic, and demographic sections of the atlas. The section on current hotspots or "flashpoints" includes a number of up-to-date areas of actual or potential conflict.

Unit VII physical and political maps have been revised, and there are updates to several of the profiles of the world's countries and dependencies. The profiles contain key political, cultural, urban, and economic statistics.

This unique combination of maps and data makes the atlas an invaluable pedagogical tool. It also serves to introduce students to the five basic themes of spatial analysis:

- Location: Where Is It?
- Place: What Is It Like?
- Human/Environment Interaction: How Is the Landscape Shaped?
- Movement: How Do People Stay in Touch?
- Regions: How Is the Surface of the World Arranged and Organized?

To further enhance the learning process, an introductory section on "How to Read an Atlas" helps students evaluate and interpret map data more easily.

Concise and affordable, this up-to-date *Student Atlas of World Politics,* tenth edition, is suitable for any course dealing in current world affairs.

About the Authors

John L. Allen is emeritus professor of geography at both the University of Connecticut and the University of Wyoming. He taught at the University of Connecticut from 1967 to 2000, when he moved to the University of Wyoming as professor and chair of the Department of Geography. He retired from service at the University of Wyoming in 2007. He is a native of Wyoming and received his bachelor's degree (1963) in International Studies and his master's degree (1964) in Political Science from the University of Wyoming. In 1969 he received his Ph.D. in Geography from Clark University. His areas of special interest include human attitudes toward environmental systems, the impact of contemporary human activities on landscapes, and the historical geography of human/environment interactions. Dr. Allen is the author and editor of many scholarly books and articles as well as several other student atlases, including the best-selling *Student Atlas of World Geography*.

Christopher J. Sutton is professor of geography at Western Illinois University. Born in Virginia and raised in Illinois, he received his bachelor's degree (1988) and master's degree (1991) in Geography from Western Illinois University. In 1995 he earned his Ph.D. in Geography from the University of Denver. He is the author of numerous research articles and educational materials. A broadly trained geographer, his areas of interest include cartographic design, cultural geography, and urban transportation. After teaching at Northwestern State University of Louisiana for three years, Dr. Sutton returned to Western Illinois University in 1998, serving as chair of the Department of Geography from 2002 to 2007. Additionally, Dr. Sutton has served as president of the Illinois Geographical Society.

Acknowledgments

Robert Bednarz
Texas A & M University

Gerald E. Beller
West Virginia State College

Mark Bjelland
Gustavus Adolphus College

Kenneth L. Conca
University of Maryland

Femi Ferreira
Hutchinson Community College

Paul B. Frederic
University of Maine at Farmington

James F. Fryman
University of Northern Iowa

Michael Gold-Biss
St. Cloud State University

Herbert E. Gooch III
California Lutheran University

Lloyd E. Hudman
Brigham Young University

Edward L. Jackiewicz
Miami University of Ohio

Artimus Keiffer
Indiana University–Purdue University at Indianapolis

Richard L. Krol
Kean College of New Jersey

Jeffrey S. Lantis
The College of Wooster

Robert Larson
Indiana State University

Mark Lowry II
United States Military Academy at West Point

Max Lu
Kansas State University

Taylor E. Mack
Mississippi State University

Kenneth C. Martis
West Virginia University

Calvin O. Masilela
West Virginia University

Patrick McGreevy
Clarion University

Tyrel G. Moore
University of North Carolina at Charlotte

David J. Nemeth
The University of Toledo

Judith Otto
Framingham State University

Emmett Panzella
Point Park University

Daniel S. Papp
University System of Georgia

Lance Robinson
United States Air Force Academy

Jefferson S. Rogers
University of Tennessee at Martin

Amber Ruskell
Southeastern Community College

Barbara J. Rusnak
United States Air Force Academy

Mark Simpson
University of Tennessee at Martin

Jutta Weldes
Kent State University

Table of Contents

Unit III   Population, Health, and Human Development   75

Unit IV   The Global Economy   99

Unit V   Food and Energy   119

Unit VI   Environmental Conditions   131

Introduction: How to Read an Atlas

An atlas is a book containing maps which are "models" of the real world. By the term "model" we mean exactly what you think of when you think of a model: a representation of reality that is generalized, usually considerably smaller than the original, and with certain features emphasized, depending on the purpose of the model. A model of a car does not contain all of the parts of the original, but it may contain enough parts that it is recognizable as a car and can be used to study principles of automotive design or maintenance. A car model designed for racing, on the other hand, may contain fewer parts but would have the mobility of a real automobile. Car models come in a wide variety of types containing almost anything you can think of relative to automobiles that doesn't require the presence of a full-size car. Since geographers deal with the real world, virtually all of the printed or published studies of that world require models. Unlike a mechanic in an automotive shop, we can't roll our study subject into the shop, take it apart, and put it back together. We must use models. In other words, we must generalize our subject, and the way we do that is by using maps. Some maps are designed to show specific geographic phenomena, such as the climates of the world or the relative rates of population growth for the world's countries. We call these maps "thematic maps," and Units I through VI of this atlas contain maps of this type. Other maps are designed to show the geographic location of towns and cities and rivers and lakes and mountain ranges and so on. These are called "reference maps" and they make up many of the maps in Unit VII. All of these maps, whether thematic or reference, are models of the real world that selectively emphasize the features that we want to show on the map.

In order to read maps effectively—in other words, in order to understand the models of the world presented in the following pages—it is important for you to know certain things about maps: how they are made, using what are called *projections;* how the level of mathematical proportion of the map (or what geographers call *scale*) affects what you see; and how geographers use *generalization* techniques such as simplification and symbols where it would be impossible to draw a small version of the real world feature. In this brief introduction, then, we'll explain to you three of the most important elements of map interpretation: projection, scale, and generalization.

Map Projections

Perhaps the most basic problem in *cartography,* or the art and science of map-making, is the fact that the subject of maps—the earth's surface—is what is called by mathematicians "a non-developable surface." Since the world is a sphere (or nearly so—it's actually slightly flattened at the poles and bulges a tiny bit at the equator), it is impossible to flatten out the world or any part of its curved surface without producing some kind of distortion. This "near sphere" is represented by a geographic grid or coordinate system of lines of latitude or *parallels* that run east and west and are used to measure distance north and south on the globe, and lines of longitude or *meridians* that run north and south and are used to measure distance east and west. All the lines of longitude are half circles of equal length and they all converge at the poles. These meridians are numbered from 0 degrees (Prime or Greenwich Meridian) east and west to 180 degrees. The meridian of 0 degrees and the meridian of 180 degrees are

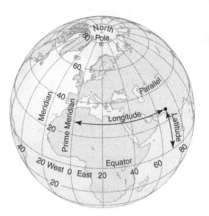

The Coordinate System

halves of the same "great circle" or line representing a plane that bisects the globe into two equal hemispheres. All lines of longitude are halves of great circles. All the lines of latitude are complete circles that are parallel to one another and are spaced equidistant on the meridians. The circumference of these circles lessens as you move north or south from the equator. Parallels of latitude are numbered from 0 degrees at the equator north and south to 90 degrees at the North and South poles. The only line of latitude that is a great circle is the equator, which equally divides the world into a northern and southern hemisphere. In the real world, all these grid lines of latitude and longitude intersect at right angles. The problem for cartographers is to convert this spherical or curved grid into a geometrical shape that is "developable"; that is, it can be flattened (such as a cylinder or cone) or is already flat (a plane). The reason the results of the conversion process are called "projections" is that we imagine a world globe (or some part of it) that is made up of wires running north-south and east-west to represent the grid lines of latitude and longitude and other wires or even solid curved plates to represent the coastlines of continents or the continents themselves. We then imagine a light source at some location inside or outside the wire globe that can "project" or cast shadows of the wires representing grid lines onto a developable surface. Sometimes the basic geometric principles of projection may be modified by other mathematical principles to yield projections that are not truly geometric but have certain desirable features. We call these types of projections "arbitrary." The three most basic types of projections are named according to the type of developable surface: cylindrical, conic, or azimuthal (plane). Each type has certain characteristic features: they may be *equal area* projections in which the size of each area on the map is a direct proportional representation of that same area in the real world but shapes are distorted; they may be *conformal* projections in which area may be distorted but shapes are shown correctly; or they may be *compromise* projections in which both shape and area are distorted but the overall picture presented is fairly close to reality. It is important to remember that all maps distort the geographic grid and continental outlines in characteristic ways. The only representation of the world that does not distort either shape or area is a globe. You can see why we must use projections—can you imagine an atlas that you would have to carry back and forth across campus that would be made up entirely of globes?

Cylindrical Projections

Cylindrical projections are drawn as if the geographic grid were projected onto a cylinder. Cylindrical projections have the advantage of having all lines of latitude as true parallels or straight lines. This makes these projections quite useful for showing geographic relationships in which latitude or distance north-south is important (many physical features, such as climate, are influenced by latitude). Unfortunately, most cylindrical-type projections distort area significantly. One of the most famous is the Mercator projection. This projection makes areas disproportionately large as you move toward the pole, making Greenland, which is actually about one-seventh the size of South America, appear to be as large as the southern continent. But the Mercator projection has the quality of conformality: landmasses on the map are true in shape and thus all coastlines on the map intersect lines of latitude and longitude at the proper angles. This makes the Mercator projection, named after its inventor, a sixteenth-century Dutch cartographer, ideal for its original purpose as a tool for navigation—but not a good projection for attempting to show some geographical feature in which areal relationship is important. Unfortunately, the Mercator projection has often been used for wall maps for schoolrooms and the consequence is that generations of American school children have been "tricked" into thinking that Greenland is actually larger than South America. Much better cylindrical-type projections are those like the Robinson projection used in this atlas that is neither equal area nor conformal but a compromise that portrays the real world much as it actually looks, enough so that we can use it for areal comparisons.

Conic Projections

Conic projections are those that are imagined as being projected onto a cone that is tangent to the globe along a standard parallel, or a series of cones tangent along several parallels or even intersecting the globe. Conic projections usually show latitude as curved lines and longitude as straight lines. They are good projections for areas with north-south extent, like the map of Europe to the right, and may be either conformal, equal area, or compromise, depending on how they are constructed. Many of the regional maps in the last map section of this atlas are conic projections.

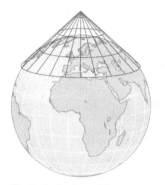

Conic Projection of Europe

Azimuthal Projections

Azimuthal projections are those that are imagined as being projected onto a plane or flat surface. They are named for one of their essential properties. An "azimuth" is a line of compass bearing, and azimuthal projections have the property of yielding true compass directions from the center of the map. This makes azimuthal maps useful for navigation purposes, particularly air navigation. But, because they distort area and shape so greatly, they are seldom used for maps designed to show geographic relationships. When they are used as illustrative rather than navigation maps, it is often in the "polar case" projection shown here, where the plane has been made tangent to the globe at the North Pole.

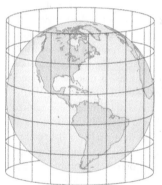

The Mercator Projection

The Robinson Projection

Azimuthal Projection of the North Polar Region

Map Scale

Since maps are models of the real world, it follows that they are not the same size as the real world or any portion of it. Every map, then, is subject to generalization, which is another way of saying that maps are drawn to certain scales. The term *scale* refers to the mathematical quality of *proportional representation,* and is expressed as a ratio between an area of the real world or the distance between places on the real world and the same area or distance on the map. We show map scale on maps in three different ways. Sometimes we simply use the proportion and write what is called a *natural scale* or representative fraction: for example, we might show on a map the mathematical proportion of 1:62,500. A map at this scale is one that is one sixty-two thousand five-hundredth the size of the same area in the real world. Other times we convert the proportion to a written description that approximates the relationship between distance on the map and distance in the real world. Since there are nearly 62,500 inches in a mile, we would refer to a map having a natural scale of 1:62,500 as having an "inch-mile" scale of "1 inch represents 1 mile." If we draw a line one inch long on this map, that line represents a distance of approximately one mile in the real world. Finally, we usually use a graphic or linear scale: a bar or line, often graduated into miles or kilometers, that shows graphically the proportional representation. A graphic scale for our 1:62,500 map might be about five inches long, divided into five equal units clearly labeled as "1 mile," "2 miles," and so on. Our examples here show all three kinds of scales.

The most important thing to keep in mind about scale, and the reason why knowing map scale is important to being able to read a map correctly, is the relationship between proportional representation and generalization. A map that fills a page but shows the whole world is much more highly generalized than a map that fills a page but shows a single city. On the world map, the city may appear as a dot. On the city map, streets and other features may be clearly seen. We call the first map, the world map, a *small-scale* map because the proportional representation is a small number. A page-size map showing the whole world may be drawn at a scale of 1:150,000,000. That is a very small number indeed—hence the term *small-scale* map even though the area shown is large. Conversely, the second map, a city map, may be drawn at a scale of 1:250,000. That is still a very small number but it is a great deal larger than 1:150,000,000! And so we'd refer to the city map as a *large scale* map, even though it shows only a small area. On our world map, geographical features are generalized greatly and many features can't even be shown at all. On the city map, much less generalization occurs—we can show specific features that we couldn't on the world map—but generalization still takes place. The general rule is that the smaller the map scale, the greater the degree of generalization; the larger the map scale, the less the degree of generalization. The only map that would not generalize would be a map at a scale of 1:1 and that map wouldn't be very handy to use. Examine the relationship between scale and generalization in the four maps on this page.

Map 1 Small Scale Map of the United States

Map 2 Map of the Northeast

Map 3 Map of Southeastern New England

Map 4 Large Scale Map of Boston, MA

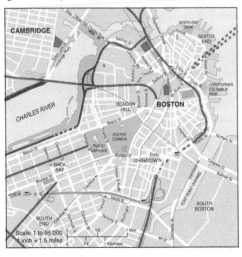

Generalization on Maps

A review of the four maps should give you some indication of how cartographers generalize on maps. One thing that you should have noticed is that the first map, that of the United States, is much simpler than the other three and that the level of *simplification* decreases with each map. When a cartographer simplifies map data, information that is not important for the purposes of the map is just left off. For example, on the first map the objective may have been to show cities over 1 million in population. To do that clearly and effectively, it is not necessary to show and label rivers and lakes. The map has been simplified by leaving those items out. The final map, on the other hand, is more complex and shows and labels geographic features that are important to the character of the city of Boston; therefore, the Charles River is clearly indicated on the map.

Another type of generalization is *classification*. Map 1 on the previous page shows cities over 1 million in population. Map 2 shows cities of several different sizes and a different symbol is used for each size classification or category. Many of the thematic maps used in this atlas rely on classification to show data. A thematic map showing population growth rates (see Map 57) will use different colors to show growth rates in different classification levels or what are sometimes called *class intervals*. Thus, there will be one color applied to all countries with population growth rates between 1.0 percent and 1.4 percent, another color applied to all countries with population growth rates between 1.5 percent and 2.1 percent, and so on. Classification is necessary because it is impossible to find enough symbols or colors to represent precise values. Classification may also be used for qualitative data, such as the national or regional origin of migrating populations. Cartographers show both quantitative and qualitative classification levels or class intervals in important sections of maps called *legends*. These legends, as in the samples that follow, make it possible for the reader of the map to interpret the patterns shown.

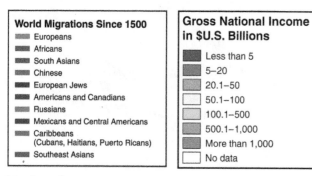

Map Legends

A third technique of generalization is *symbolization* and we've already noted several different kinds of symbols: those used to represent cities on the preceding maps, or the colors used to indicate population growth levels on Map 57. One general category of map symbols is quantitative in nature, and this category can further be divided into a number of different types. For example, the symbols showing city size on Maps 1 and 2 on the preceding page can be categorized as *ordinal* in that they show relative differences in quantities (the size of cities). A cartographer might also use lines of different widths to express the quantities of movement of people or goods between two or more points.

The color symbols used to show rates of population growth can be categorized as *interval* in that they express certain levels of a mathematical quantity (the percentage of population growth). Interval symbols are often used to show physical geographic characteristics such as inches of precipitation, degrees of temperature, or elevation above sea level. The following sample, for example, shows precipitation.

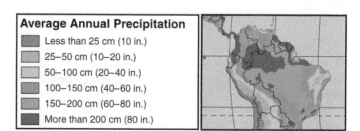

Interval Symbols

Still another type of mathematical symbolization is the *ratio* in which sets of mathematical quantities are compared: the number of persons per square mile (population density) or the growth in gross national product per capita (per person). The following map shows GDP change per capita.

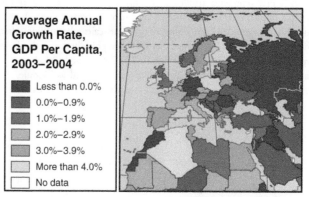

Ratio Symbols

Finally, there are a vast number of cartographic symbols that are not mathematical but show differences in the kind of information being portrayed. These symbols are called *nominal* and they range from the simplest differences, such as land and water, to more complex differences, such as those between different types of vegetation. Shapes, patterns, colors, or iconographic drawings may all be used as nominal symbols on maps.

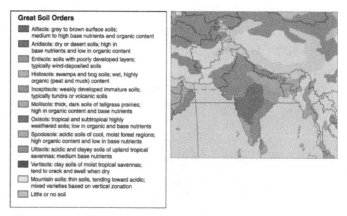

Nominal Symbols

The final technique of generalization is what cartographers refer to as *interpolation*. Here, the maker of a map may actually show more information on the map than is actually supplied by the original data. In understanding the process of interpolation it is necessary for you to visualize the quantitative data shown on maps as being three dimensional: *x* values provide geographic location along a north-south axis of the map; *y* values provide geographic location along the east-west axis of the map; and *z* values are those values of whatever data (for example, temperature) that are being shown on the map at specific points. We all can imagine a real three-dimensional surface in which the *x* and *y* values are directions and the *z* values are the heights of mountains and the depths of valleys. On a topographic map showing a real three-dimensional surface, contour lines are used to connect points of equal elevation above sea level. These contour lines are not measured directly; they are estimated by interpolation on the basis of the elevation points that are provided.

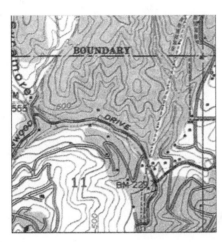

Interpolation

It is harder to imagine the statistical surface of a temperature map in which the *x* and *y* values are directions and the *z* values represent degrees of temperature at precise points. But that is just what cartographers do. And to obtain the values between two or more specific points where *z* values exist, they interpolate based on a class interval they have decided is appropriate and use *isolines* (which are statistical equivalents of a contour line) to show increases or decreases in value. The following diagram shows an example of an interpolation process. Occasionally interpolation is referred to as *induction*. By whatever name, it is one of the most difficult parts of the cartographic process.

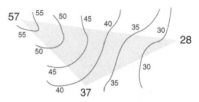

Degrees of Temperature (Celsius)
Interval = 5 degrees

And you thought all you had to do to read an atlas was look at the maps! You've now learned that it is a bit more involved than that. As you read and study this atlas, keep in mind the principles of projection, scale, and generalization (including simplification, classification, symbolization, and interpolation) and you'll do just fine. Good luck and enjoy your study of the world of maps, as well as maps of the world!

Unit I

The Contemporary World

Map 1   World Political Boundaries

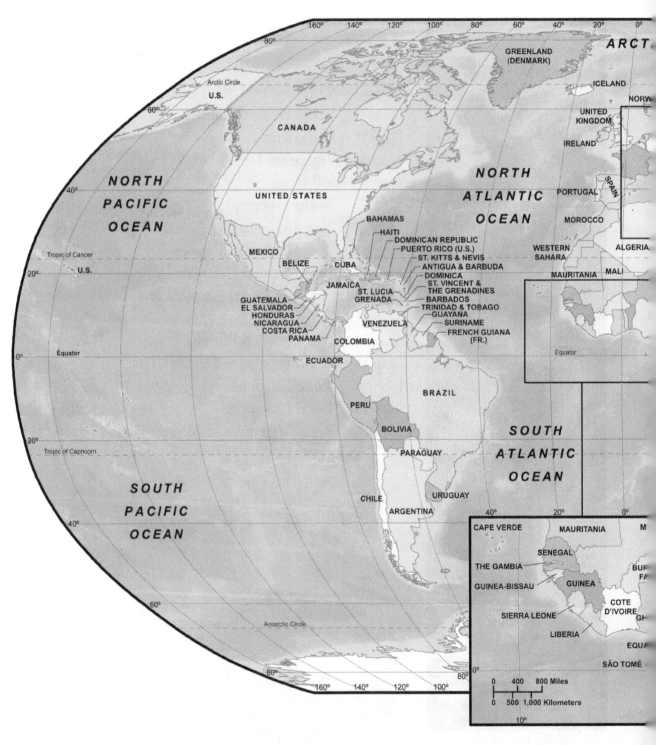

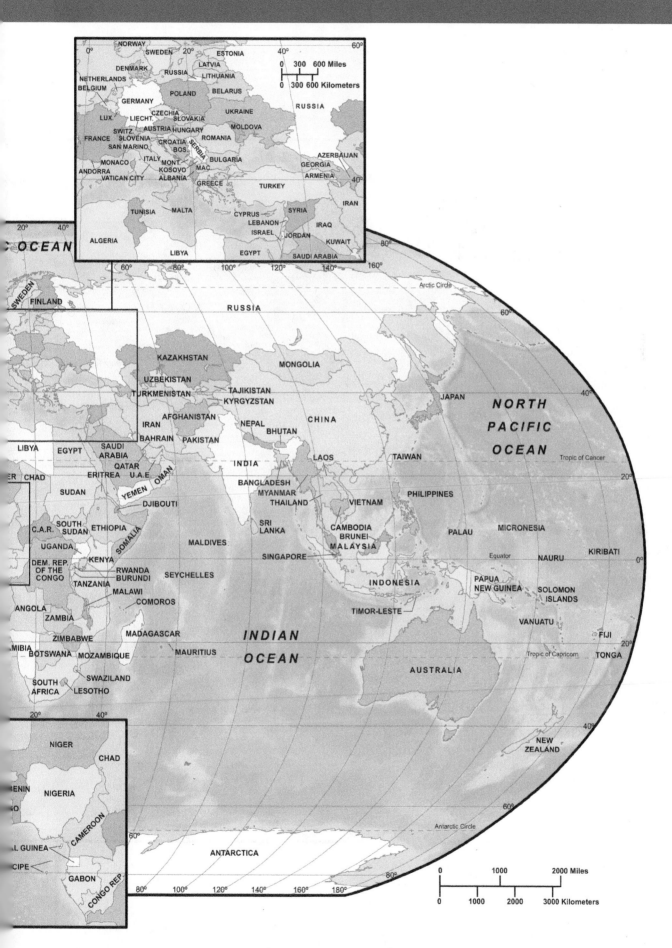

NORWAY
SWEDEN
ESTONIA
DENMARK
LATVIA
RUSSIA
LITHUANIA
NETHERLANDS
BELGIUM
POLAND
BELARUS
GERMANY
LUX.
LIECHT.
CZECHIA
SLOVAKIA
UKRAINE
RUSSIA
SWITZ.
AUSTRIA HUNGARY
MOLDOVA
FRANCE
SLOVENIA
ROMANIA
SAN MARINO
CROATIA
SERBIA
MONACO
ITALY
MONT.
BULGARIA
AZERBAIJAN
ANDORRA
KOSOVO
MAC.
GEORGIA
VATICAN CITY
ALBANIA
GREECE
ARMENIA
TURKEY
TUNISIA
MALTA
CYPRUS
SYRIA
IRAN
LEBANON
IRAQ
ALGERIA
ISRAEL
JORDAN
KUWAIT
LIBYA
EGYPT
SAUDI ARABIA

0   300   600 Miles
0   300 600 Kilometers

OCEAN

SWEDEN
FINLAND

KAZAKHSTAN
MONGOLIA
UZBEKISTAN
TURKMENISTAN
TAJIKISTAN
KYRGYZSTAN
JAPAN
AFGHANISTAN
IRAN
NEPAL
CHINA
BAHRAIN
PAKISTAN
BHUTAN
LIBYA
EGYPT
SAUDI
ARABIA
INDIA
LAOS
TAIWAN
QATAR
ERITREA
U.A.E.
OMAN
YEMEN
BANGLADESH
MYANMAR
CHAD
SUDAN
THAILAND
VIETNAM
DJIBOUTI
SRI
LANKA
CAMBODIA
PHILIPPINES
C.A.R.
SOUTH
SUDAN
ETHIOPIA
SOMALIA
MALDIVES
BRUNEI
MALAYSIA
PALAU
MICRONESIA
UGANDA
SINGAPORE
KENYA
RWANDA
BURUNDI
SEYCHELLES
NAURU
KIRIBATI
DEM. REP.
OF THE
CONGO
TANZANIA
MALAWI
INDONESIA
PAPUA
NEW GUINEA
SOLOMON
ISLANDS
ANGOLA
ZAMBIA
COMOROS
TIMOR-LESTE
VANUATU
ZIMBABWE
MADAGASCAR
FIJI
MIBIA
BOTSWANA
MOZAMBIQUE
MAURITIUS
INDIAN
OCEAN
AUSTRALIA
TONGA
SOUTH
AFRICA
SWAZILAND
LESOTHO

NORTH
PACIFIC
OCEAN

Arctic Circle
RUSSIA
Tropic of Cancer
Equator
Tropic of Capricorn

NEW
ZEALAND

Antarctic Circle

ANTARCTICA

NIGER
CHAD
ENIN
NIGERIA
CAMEROON
GUINEA
CIPE
GABON
CONGO REP.

0   1000   2000 Miles
0 1000 2000 3000 Kilometers

-3-

Map 2   World Physical Features

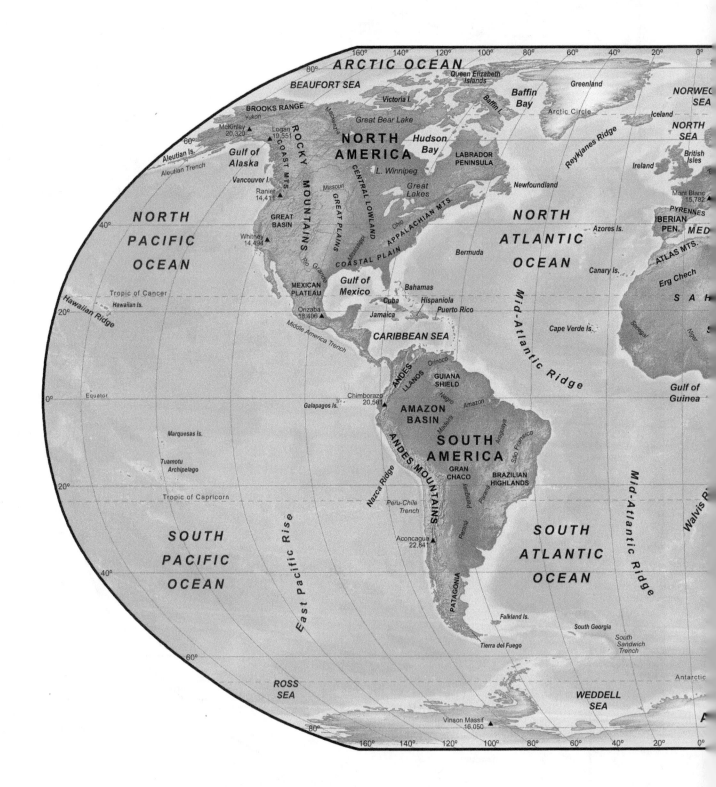

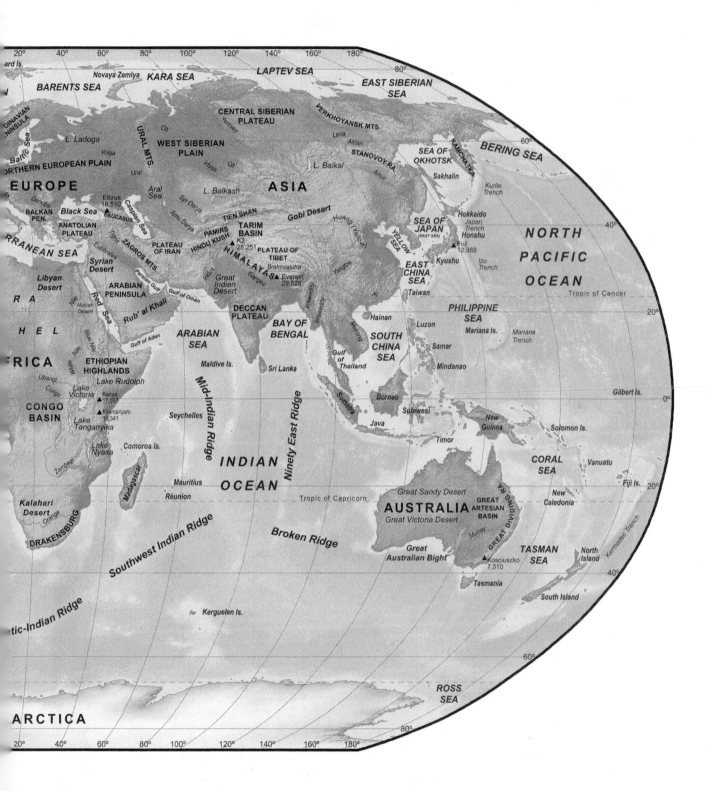

20° 40° 60° 80° 100° 120° 140° 160° 180°

BARENTS SEA
Novaya Zemlya   KARA SEA   LAPTEV SEA   EAST SIBERIAN SEA
CENTRAL SIBERIAN PLATEAU   VERKHOYANSK MTS.
DINAVIAN
-NINSULA
L. Ladoga   Ob   WEST SIBERIAN PLAIN   Lena   BERING SEA
Baltic Sea   URAL MTS.   Volga   Yenisey   STANOVOY RA.   SEA OF OKHOTSK   KAMCHATKA
Ural   Irtysh   Ob   L. Baikal   Aldan   Amu   Sakhalin
ORTHERN EUROPEAN PLAIN
EUROPE   Aral Sea   L. Balkash   ASIA   Kurile Trench
Elbrus 18,510   Syr Darya   TIEN SHAN   Gobi Desert   Huang (Yellow)   Hokkaido   Japan Trench   NORTH
BALKAN PEN.   Black Sea   CAUCASUS   Caspian Sea   Amu Darya   PAMIRS   TARIM BASIN   Honshu
ANATOLIAN PLATEAU   Tigris   ZAGROS MTS.   PLATEAU OF IRAN   HINDU KUSH   K2 28,251   PLATEAU OF TIBET   SEA OF JAPAN (EAST SEA)   Fuji 12,388   PACIFIC
RRANEAN SEA   Euphrates   HIMALAYAS   Everest 29,028   Yangtze   Kyushu   Izu Trench   OCEAN
Syrian Desert   Persian Gulf   Indus   Brahmaputra   EAST CHINA SEA
RA   Libyan Desert   Nile   Red Sea   ARABIAN PENINSULA   Gulf of Oman   Great Indian Desert   Ganges   Xi   Taiwan   Tropic of Cancer
Nubiah Desert   Rub' al Khali   DECCAN PLATEAU   YELLOW SEA   PHILIPPINE SEA
HEL   Blue Nile   Gulf of Aden   ARABIAN SEA   BAY OF BENGAL   Hainan   Luzon   Mariana Is.   Mariana Trench
RICA   White Nile   ETHIOPIAN HIGHLANDS   Maldive Is.   Sri Lanka   SOUTH CHINA SEA   Samar
Ubangi   Lake Rudolph   Gulf of Thailand   Mindanao   Gilbert Is.
Congo   Lake Victoria   Kenya 17,057   Mid-Indian Ridge   Seychelles   Sumatra   Borneo   Sulawesi
CONGO BASIN   Kilimanjaro 19,341   Lake Tanganyika   Ninety East Ridge   Java   Timor   New Guinea   Solomon Is.
Lake Nyasa   Comoros Is.   INDIAN   CORAL SEA   Vanuatu
Zambezi   Madagascar   Mauritius   OCEAN   Fiji Is.
Kalahari Desert   Orange   Réunion   Tropic of Capricorn   Great Sandy Desert   GREAT ARTESIAN BASIN   New Caledonia
DRAKENSBURG   Southwest Indian Ridge   Broken Ridge   AUSTRALIA   Great Victoria Desert   Murray   TASMAN SEA   North Island
Great Australian Bight   Kosciuszko 7,310
tic-Indian Ridge   Kerguelen Is.   Tasmania   South Island

ARCTICA

ROSS SEA

20° 40° 60° 80° 100° 120° 140° 160° 180°

80°
60°
40°
20°
0°
20°
40°
60°
80°

Map 3 World Climate Regions

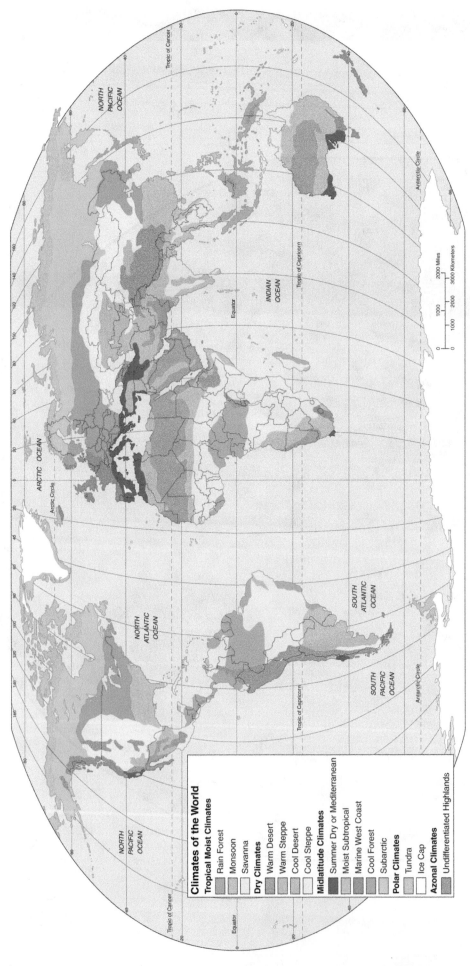

Of the world's many physical geographic features, climate (the long-term average of such weather conditions as temperature and precipitation) is the most important. It is climate that conditions the types of natural vegetation patterns and the types of soil that will exist in an area. It is also climate that determines the availability of our most precious resource: water. From an economic standpoint, the world's most important activity is agriculture; no other element of physical geography is more important for agriculture than climate.

Map 4 Vegetation Types

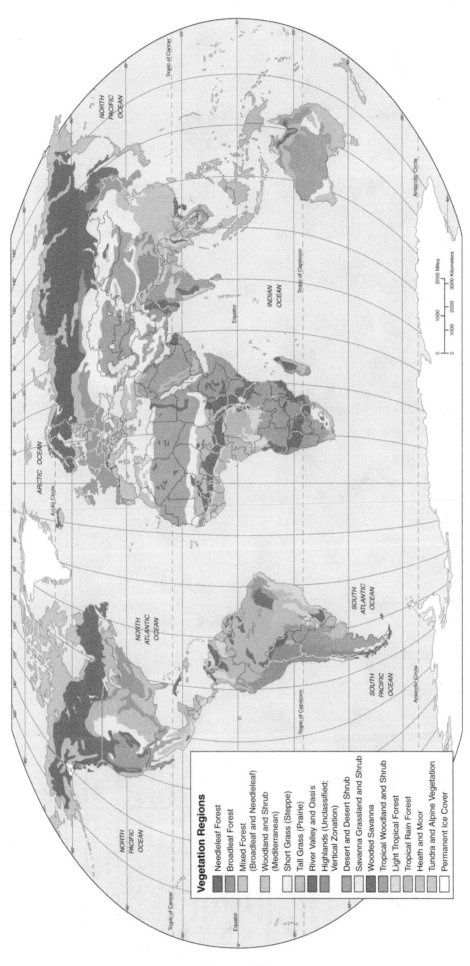

Vegetation Regions

- Needleleaf Forest
- Broadleaf Forest
- Mixed Forest (Broadleaf and Needleleaf)
- Woodland and Shrub (Mediterranean)
- Short Grass (Steppe)
- Tall Grass (Prairie)
- River Valley and Oasis
- Highlands (Unclassified; Vertical Zonation)
- Desert and Desert Shrub
- Savanna Grassland and Shrub
- Wooded Savanna
- Tropical Woodland and Shrub
- Light Tropical Forest
- Tropical Rain Forest
- Heath and Moor
- Tundra and Alpine Vegetation
- Permanent Ice Cover

Vegetation is the most visible consequence of the distribution of temperature and precipitation. The global pattern of vegetative types or "habitat classes" and the global pattern of climate are closely related and make up one of the great global spatial correlations. But not all vegetation types are the consequence of temperature and precipitation or other climatic variables. Many types of vegetation in many areas of the world are the consequence of human activities, particularly the grazing of domesticated livestock, burning, and forest clearance. This map shows the pattern of natural or "potential" vegetation, or vegetation as it might be expected to exist without significant human influences, rather than the actual vegetation that results from a combination of environmental and human factors.

-7-

Map **5**   Soil Orders

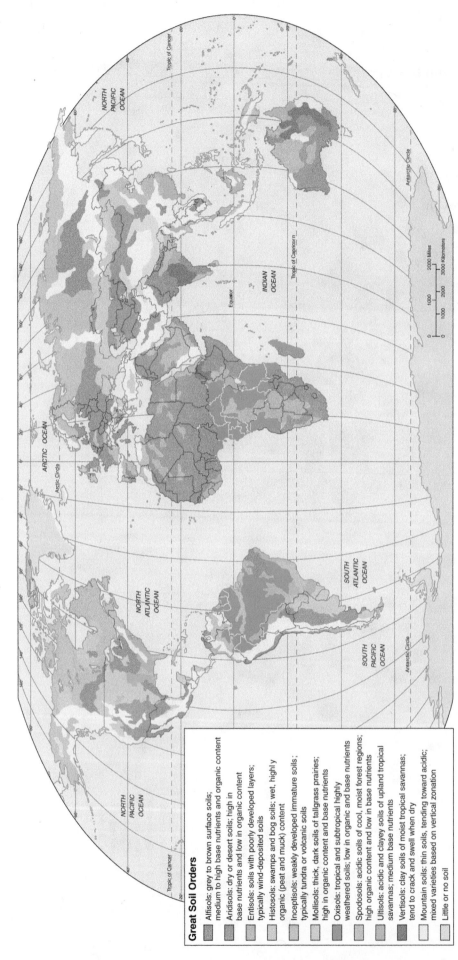

Great Soil Orders

Alfisols: grey to brown surface soils; medium to high base nutrients and organic content

Aridisols: dry or desert soils; high in base nutrients and low in organic content

Entisols: soils with poorly developed layers; typically wind-deposited soils

Histosols: swamps and bog soils; wet, highly organic (peat and muck) content

Inceptisols: weakly developed immature soils; typically tundra or volcanic soils

Mollisols: thick, dark soils of tallgrass prairies; high in organic content and base nutrients

Oxisols: tropical and subtropical highly weathered soils; low in organic and base nutrients

Spodosols: acidic soils of cool, moist forest regions; high organic content and low in base nutrients

Ultisols: acidic and clayey soils of upland tropical savannas; medium base nutrients

Vertisols: clay soils of moist tropical savannas; tend to crack and swell when dry

Mountain soils: thin soils, tending toward acidic; mixed varieties based on vertical zonation

Little or no soil

The characteristics of soil are one of the three primary physical geographic factors, along with climate and vegetation, that determine the habitability of regions for humans. In particular, soils influence the kinds of agricultural uses to which land is put. Since soils support the plants that are the primary producers of all food in the terrestrial food chain, their characteristics are crucial to the health and stability of ecosystems. Two types of soil are shown on this map: zonal soils, the characteristics of which are based on climatic patterns; and azonal soils, such as alluvial (water-deposited) or aeolian (wind-deposited) soils, the characteristics of which are derived from forces other than climate. However, many of the azonal soils, particularly those dependent upon drainage conditions, appear over areas too small to be readily shown on a map of this scale. Thus, almost none of the world's swamp or bog soils appear on this map.

Map 6 World Topography

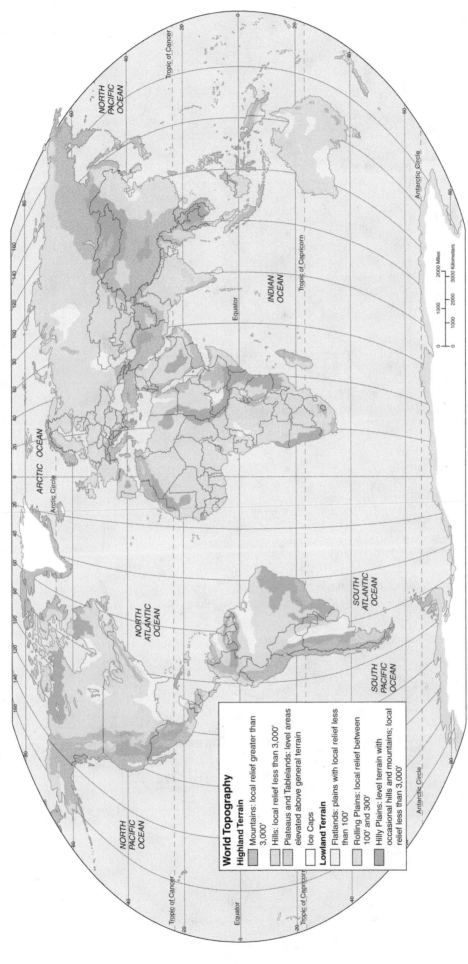

World Topography

Highland Terrain

- Mountains: local relief greater than 3,000'
- Hills: local relief less than 3,000'
- Plateaus and Tablelands: level areas elevated above general terrain
- Ice Caps

Lowland Terrain

- Flatlands: plains with local relief less than 100'
- Rolling Plains: local relief between 100' and 300'
- Hilly Plains: level terrain with occasional hills and mountains; local relief less than 3,000'

Second only to climate as a conditioner of human activity—particularly in agriculture and in the location of cities and industry—is topography or terrain. It is what we often call *landforms*. A comparison of this map with the map of land use (Map 10) will show that most of the world's productive agricultural zones are located in lowland regions. Where large regions of agricultural productivity are found, we tend to find urban concentrations and, with cities, industry. There is also a good spatial correlation between the map of landforms and the map showing the distribution and density of the human population (Map 13). Normally, the world's landforms shown on this map are the result of extremely gradual primary geologic activity, such as the long-term movement of crustal plates (sometimes called continental drift). This activity occurs over hundreds of millions of years. Also important is the more rapid (but still slow by human standards) geomorphological or erosional activity of water, wind, and glacial ice, and waves, tides, and currents. Some landforms may be produced by abrupt or cataclysmic events, such as a major volcanic eruption or a meteor strike, but these are relatively rare and their effects are usually too minor to show up on a map of this scale.

Map 7 Plate Tectonics

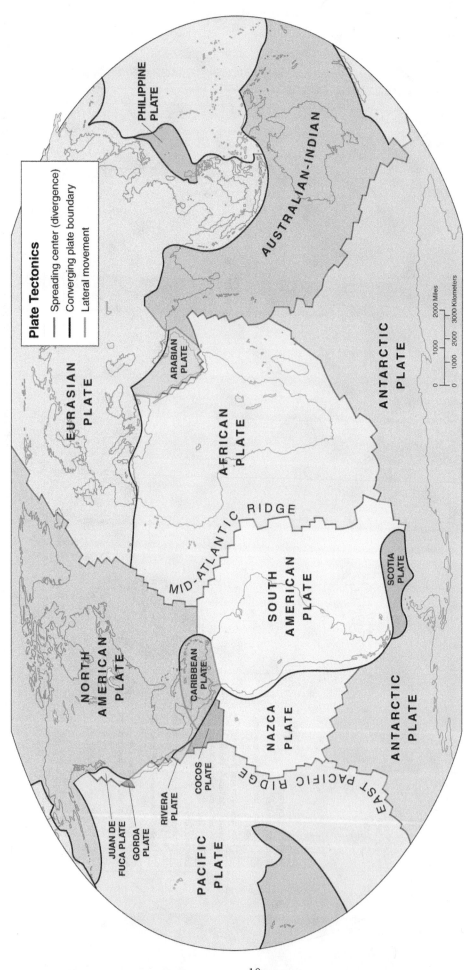

Plate Tectonics

—— Spreading center (divergence)
—— Converging plate boundary
—— Lateral movement

PHILIPPINE PLATE

AUSTRALIAN–INDIAN PLATE

EURASIAN PLATE

ARABIAN PLATE

AFRICAN PLATE

ANTARCTIC PLATE

MID-ATLANTIC RIDGE

NORTH AMERICAN PLATE

CARIBBEAN PLATE

SOUTH AMERICAN PLATE

SCOTIA PLATE

NAZCA PLATE

ANTARCTIC PLATE

EAST PACIFIC RIDGE

COCOS PLATE

RIVERA PLATE

JUAN DE FUCA PLATE

GORDA PLATE

PACIFIC PLATE

0   1000   2000   3000 Kilometers
0   1000   2000 Miles

An understanding of the forces that shape the primary features of the earth's surface—the continents and ocean basins—requires a view of the earth's crust as fragments or "lithospheric plates" that shift position relative to one another. There are three dominant types of plate movement: *convergence*, in which plates move together, compressing former ocean floor or continental rocks together to produce mountain ranges, or producing mountain ranges through volcanic activity if one plate slides beneath another; *divergence*, in which the plates move away from one another, producing rifts in the earth's crust through which molten material wells up to produce new sea floors and mid-oceanic ridges; and *lateral shift*, in which plates move horizontally relative to one another, causing significant earthquake activity. All the major forms of these types of shifts are extremely slow and take place over long periods of geologic time. The movement of crustal plates, or what is known as "plate tectonics," is responsible for the present shape and location of the continents but is also the driving force behind some much shorter-term earth phenomena like earthquakes and volcanoes.

Map 8 World Ecological Regions

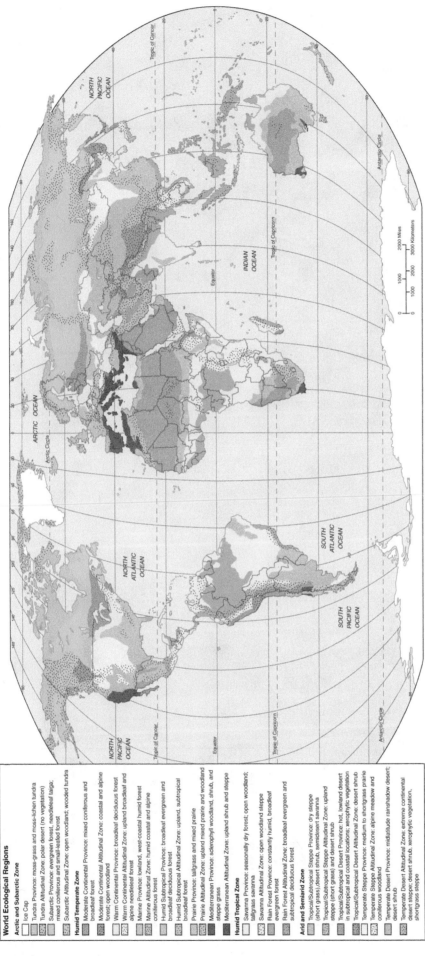

World Ecological Regions

Arctic and Subarctic Zone

Ice Cap

Tundra Province: moss-grass and moss-lichen tundra

Tundra Altitudinal Zone: polar desert (no vegetation)

Subarctic Province: evergreen forest, needleleaf taiga; mixed coniferous and small-leafed forest

Subarctic Altitudinal Zone: open woodland, wooded tundra

Humid Temperate Zone

Moderate Continental Province: mixed coniferous and broadleaf forest

Moderate Continental Altitudinal Zone: coastal and alpine forest; open woodland

Warm Continental Province: broadleaf deciduous forest

Warm Continental Altitudinal Zone: upland broadleaf and alpine needleleaf forest

Marine Province: lowland, west-coastal humid forest

Marine Altitudinal Zone: humid coastal and alpine coniferous forest

Humid Subtropical Province: broadleaf evergreen and broadleaf deciduous forest

Humid Subtropical Altitudinal Zone: upland, subtropical broadleaf forest

Prairie Province: tallgrass and mixed prairie

Prairie Altitudinal Zone: upland mixed prairie and woodland

Mediterranean Province: scleorophyll woodland, shrub, and steppe grass

Mediterranean Altitudinal Zone: upland shrub and steppe

Humid Tropical Zone

Savanna Province: seasonally dry forest; open woodland; tallgrass savanna

Savanna Altitudinal Zone: open woodland steppe

Rain Forest Province: constantly humid, broadleaf evergreen forest

Rain Forest Altitudinal Zone: broadleaf evergreen and subtropical deciduous forest

Arid and Semiarid Zone

Tropical/Subtropical Steppe Province: dry steppe (short grass), desert shrub, semidesert savanna

Tropical/Subtropical Steppe Altitudinal Zone: upland steppe (short grass) and desert shrub

Tropical/Subtropical Desert Province: hot, lowland desert in subtropical and coastal locations; xerophytic vegetation

Tropical/Subtropical Desert Altitudinal Zone: desert shrub

Temperate Steppe Province: medium to shortgrass prairie

Temperate Steppe Altitudinal Zone: alpine meadow and coniferous woodland

Temperate Desert Province: midlatitude rainshadow desert; desert shrub

Temperate Desert Altitudinal Zone: extreme continental desert steppe; desert shrub, xerophytic vegetation, shortgrass steppe

Ecology is the study of the relationships between living organisms and their environmental surroundings. Ecological regions are distinctive areas within which unique sets of organisms and environments are found. Within each ecological region, a particular combination of vegetation, wildlife, soil, water, climate, and terrain defines that region's habitability, or ability to support life, including human life. Like climate and landforms, ecological relationships are crucial to the existence of agriculture, the most basic of our economic activities, and important for many other kinds of economic activity as well.

-11-

Map 9 World Natural Hazards

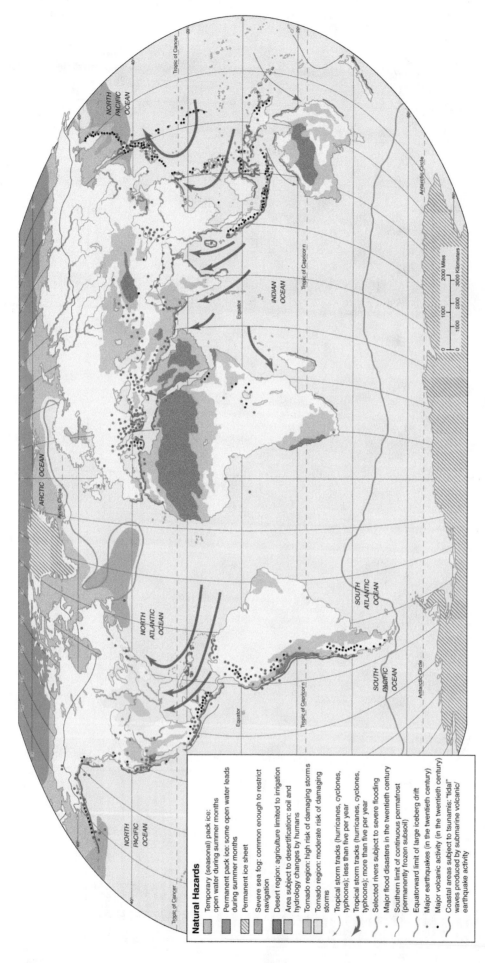

Natural Hazards

Temporary (seasonal) pack ice: open water during summer months

Permanent pack ice: some open water leads during summer months

Permanent ice sheet

Severe sea fog: common enough to restrict navigation

Desert region: agriculture limited to irrigation

Area subject to desertification: soil and hydrology changes by humans

Tornado region: high risk of damaging storms

Tornado region: moderate risk of damaging storms

Tropical storm tracks (hurricanes, cyclones, typhoons): less than five per year

Tropical storm tracks (hurricanes, cyclones, typhoons): more than five per year

Selected rivers subject to severe flooding

Major flood disasters in the twentieth century

Southern limit of continuous permafrost (permanently frozen subsoil)

Equatorward limit of large iceberg drift

Major earthquakes (in the twentieth century)

Major volcanic activity (in the twentieth century)

Coastal areas subject to tsunamis: "tidal" waves produced by submarine volcanic/earthquake activity

Unlike other elements of physical geography, natural hazards are unpredictable. There are certain regions, however, where the probability of the occurrence of a particular natural hazard is high. This map shows regions affected by major natural hazards at rates that are higher than the global norm. Persistent natural hazards may undermine the utility of an area for economic purposes. Some scholars suggest that regions of environmental instability may be regions of political instability as well.

Map 10 Land Use Patterns of the World

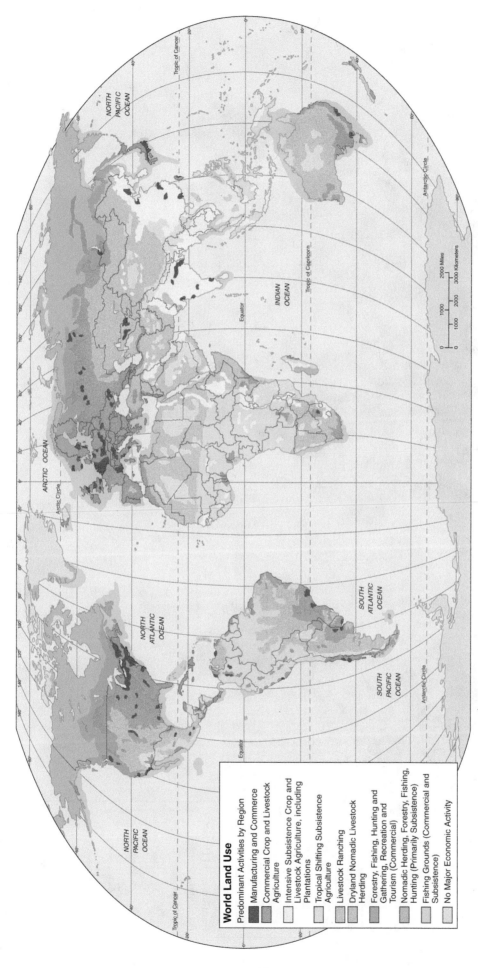

World Land Use

Predominant Activities by Region

- Manufacturing and Commerce
- Commercial Crop and Livestock Agriculture
- Intensive Subsistence Crop and Livestock Agriculture, including Plantations
- Tropical Shifting Subsistence Agriculture
- Livestock Ranching
- Dryland Nomadic Livestock Herding
- Forestry, Fishing, Hunting and Gathering, Recreation and Tourism (Commercial)
- Nomadic Herding, Forestry, Fishing, Hunting (Primarily Subsistence)
- Fishing Grounds (Commercial and Subsistence)
- No Major Economic Activity

Many of the major land use patterns of the world (such as urbanization, industry, and transportation) are relatively small in area and are not easily seen on maps, but the most important uses people make of the earth's surface have more far-reaching effects. This map illustrates, in particular, the variations in primary land uses (such as agriculture) for the entire world. Note the differences between land use patterns in the more developed countries of the middle latitude zones and the less developed countries of the tropics.

Map 11   Urbanization

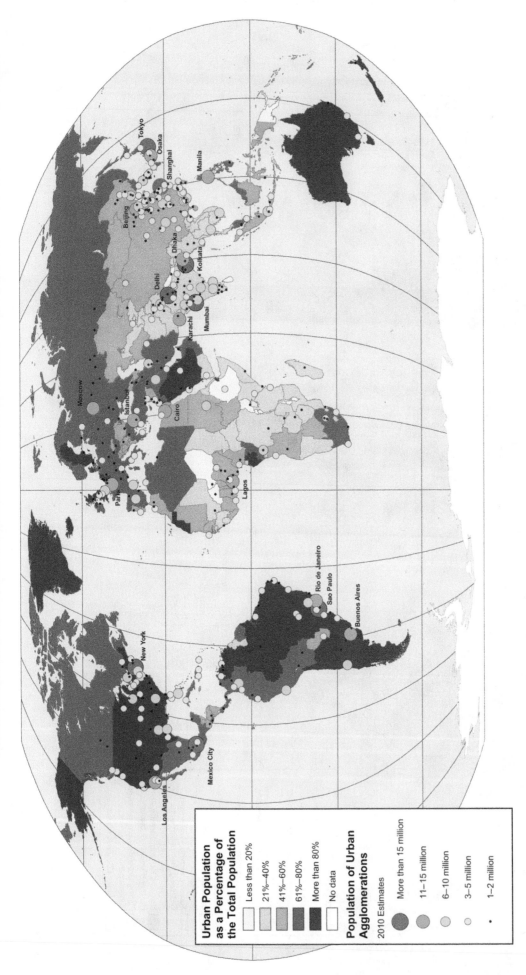

Urban Population as a Percentage of the Total Population

- Less than 20%
- 21%–40%
- 41%–60%
- 61%–80%
- More than 80%
- No data

Population of Urban Agglomerations

2010 Estimates

- More than 15 million
- 11–15 million
- 6–10 million
- 3–5 million
- 1–2 million

The degree to which a region's population is concentrated in urban areas is a major indicator of a number of things: the potential for environmental impact, the level of economic development, and the problems associated with human concentrations. Urban dwellers are rapidly becoming the norm among the world's people, and rates of urbanization are increasing worldwide, with the greatest increases in urbanization taking place in developing regions. Whether in developed or developing countries, those who live in cities exert an influence on the environment, politics, economics, and social systems that goes far

beyond the confines of the city itself. Acting as the focal points for the flow of goods and ideas, cities draw resources and people not just from their immediate hinterland but from the entire world. This process creates far-reaching impacts as resources are extracted, converted through industrial processes, and transported over great distances to metropolitan regions. The significance of urbanization can be most clearly seen in North America where, in spite of vast areas of relatively unpopulated land, well over 90 percent of the population lives in urban areas.

Map 12   Transportation Patterns

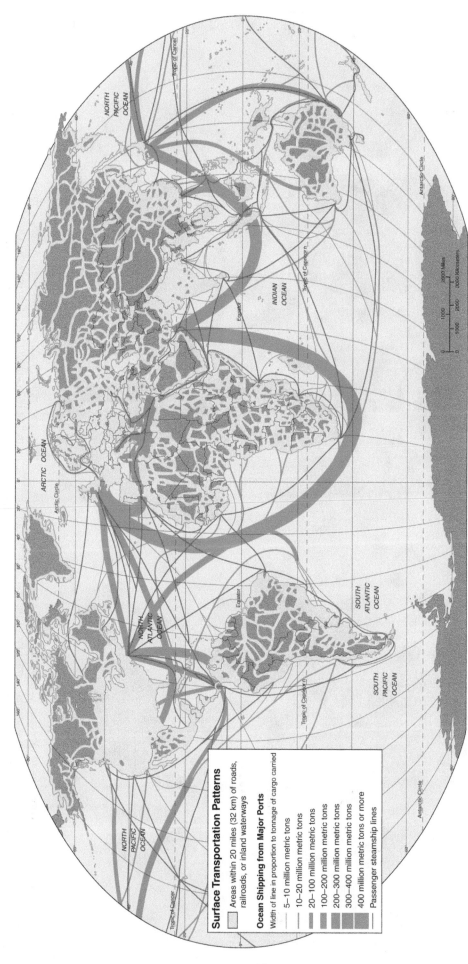

Surface Transportation Patterns

☐ Areas within 20 miles (32 km) of roads, railroads, or inland waterways

Ocean Shipping from Major Ports

Width of line in proportion to tonnage of cargo carried

5–10 million metric tons

10–20 million metric tons

20–100 million metric tons

100–200 million metric tons

200–300 million metric tons

300–400 million metric tons

400 million metric tons or more

Passenger steamship lines

As a form of land use, transportation is second only to agriculture in its coverage of the earth's surface and is one of the clearest examples in the human world of a *network*, a linked system of lines allowing flows from one place to another. The global transportation network and its related communication web are responsible for most of the *spatial interaction*, or movement of goods, people, and ideas between places. As the chief mechanism of spatial interaction, transportation is linked firmly with the concept of a shrinking world and the development of a global community and economy. Because transportation systems require significant modification of the earth's surface, transportation is also responsible for massive alterations in the quantity and quality of water, for major soil degradations and erosion, and (indirectly) for the air pollution that emanates from vehicles utilizing the transportation system. In addition, as improved transportation technology draws together places on the earth that were formerly remote, it allows people to impact environments a great distance away from where they live.

Map 13 World Population Density

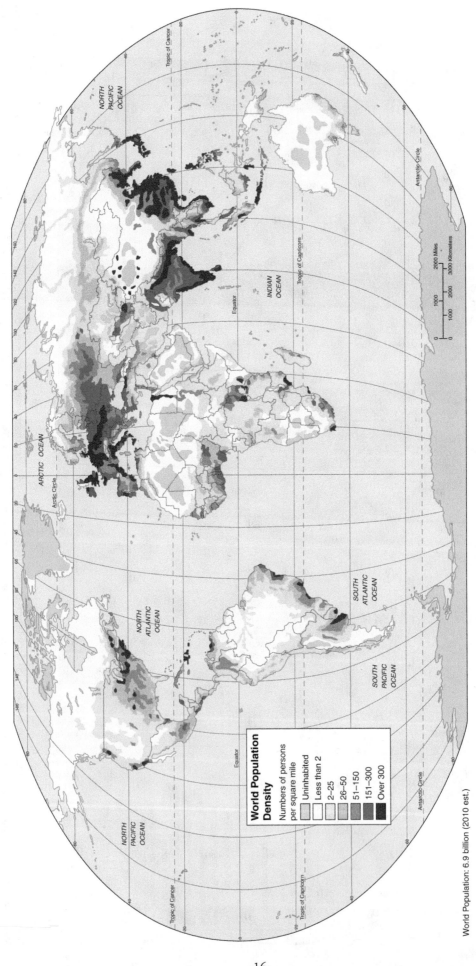

World Population: 6.9 billion (2010 est.)

World Population Density

Numbers of persons per square mile

- Uninhabited
- Less than 2
- 2–25
- 26–50
- 51–150
- 151–300
- Over 300

No feature of human activity is more reflective of environmental conditions than where people live. In the areas of densest populations, a mixture of natural and human factors has combined to allow maximum food production, maximum urbanization, and maximum centralization of economic activities. Three great concentrations of human population appear on the map—East Asia, South Asia, and Europe—with a fourth, lesser concentration in eastern North America. One of these great population clusters—South Asia—is still growing rapidly and is expected to become even more densely populated during the twenty-first century. The other concentrations are likely to remain about as they now appear. In Europe and North America, this is the result of economic development that has caused population growth to level off during the last century. In East Asia, population has also begun to grow more slowly. In the case of Japan and the Koreas, this is the consequence of economic development; in the case of China, it is the consequence of government intervention in the form of strict family planning. The areas of future high density (in addition to those already existing) are likely to be in Middle and South America and Africa, where population growth rates are well above the world average.

Map 14 World Religions

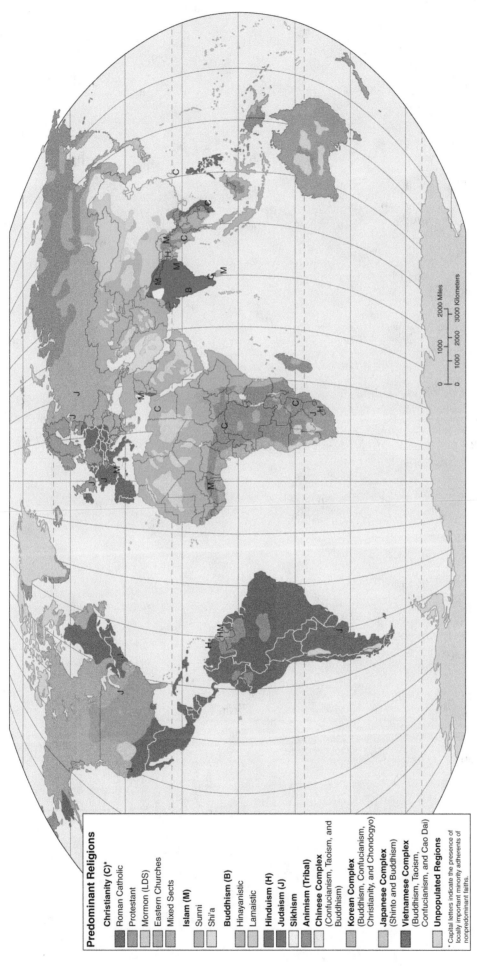

Predominant Religions

Christianity (C)*
- Roman Catholic
- Protestant
- Mormon (LDS)
- Eastern Churches
- Mixed Sects

Islam (M)
- Sunni
- Shi'a

Buddhism (B)
- Hinayanistic
- Lamaistic

Hinduism (H)

Judaism (J)

Sikhism

Animism (Tribal)

Chinese Complex
(Confucianism, Taoism, and Buddhism)

Korean Complex
(Buddhism, Confucianism, Christianity, and Chondogyo)

Japanese Complex
(Shinto and Buddhism)

Vietnamese Complex
(Buddhism, Taoism, Confucianism, and Cao Dai)

Unpopulated Regions

* Capital letters indicate the presence of locally important minority adherents of nonpredominant faiths.

0   1000   2000 Miles
0   1000   2000   3000 Kilometers

Religious adherence is one of the fundamental defining characteristics of culture. A depiction of the spatial distribution of religions is, therefore, as close as we can come to a map of cultural patterns. More than just a set of behavioral patterns having to do with worship and ceremony, religion is an important conditioner of how people treat one another and the environments that they occupy. In many areas of the world, the ways in which people make a living, the patterns of occupation that they create on the land, and the impacts that they make on ecosystems are the direct consequence of their adherence to a religious faith.

Map 15 World Languages

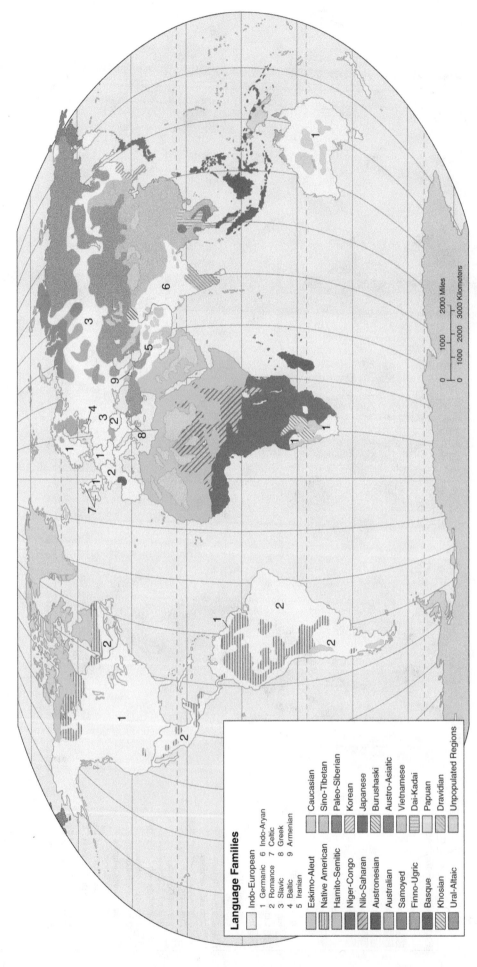

Language Families

Indo-European

1 Germanic	6 Indo-Aryan
2 Romance	7 Celtic
3 Slavic	8 Greek
4 Baltic	9 Armenian
5 Iranian	

Eskimo-Aleut
Native American
Hamito-Semitic
Niger-Congo
Nilo-Saharan
Austronesian
Australian
Samoyed
Finno-Ugric
Basque
Khoisan
Ural-Altaic

Caucasian
Sino-Tibetan
Paleo-Siberian
Korean
Japanese
Burushaski
Austro-Asiatic
Vietnamese
Dai-Kadai
Papuan
Dravidian
Unpopulated Regions

Like religion, language is an important defining characteristic of culture. It is perhaps the most durable of all cultural traits. Even after centuries of exposure to other languages or of conquest by speakers of other languages, the speakers of a specific tongue will often retain their own linguistic identity. As a geographic element, language helps us to locate areas of potential conflict, particularly in regions where two or more languages overlap.

Many, if not most, of the world's conflict zones are areas of linguistic diversity. Language also provides clues that enable us to chart the course of human migrations, as shown in the distribution of Indo-European languages. And it helps us to understand some of the reasons behind important historical events; linguistic identity differences played an important part in the disintegration of the U.S.S.R.

Map 16 World Migrations in Modern Times

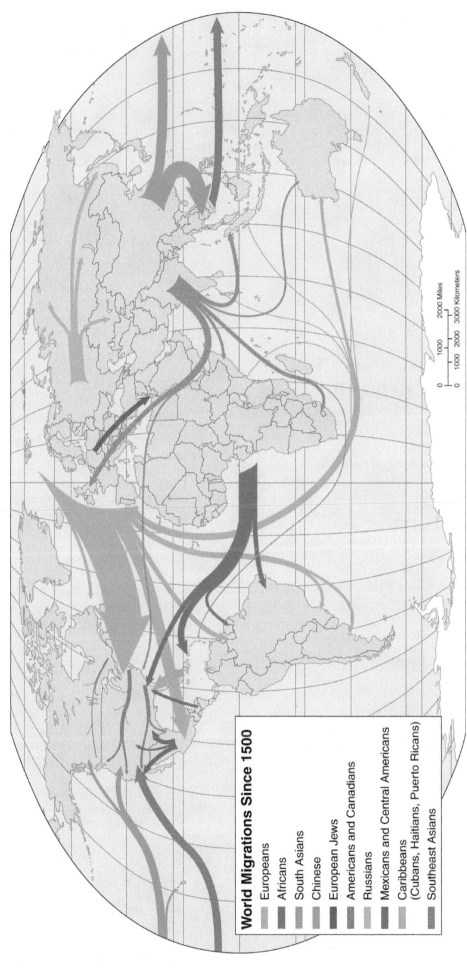

World Migrations Since 1500

- Europeans
- Africans
- South Asians
- Chinese
- European Jews
- Americans and Canadians
- Russians
- Mexicans and Central Americans
- Caribbeans (Cubans, Haitians, Puerto Ricans)
- Southeast Asians

0   1000   2000 Miles
0 1000 2000 3000 Kilometers

Migration has had a significant effect on world geography, contributing to cultural change and development, to the diffusion of ideas and innovations, and to the complex mixture of people and cultures found in the world today. Internal migration occurs within the boundaries of a country; external migration is movement from one country or region to another. Over the last 50 years, the most important migrations in the world have been internal, largely the rural-to-urban migration that has been responsible for the recent rise of global urbanization. Prior to the mid-twentieth century, three types of external migrations were most important: voluntary, most often in search of better economic conditions and opportunities; involuntary or forced, involving people who have been driven from their homelands by war, political unrest, or environmental disasters, or who have been transported as slaves or prisoners; and imposed, not entirely forced but which conditions make highly advisable. Human migrations in recorded history have been responsible for major changes in the patterns of languages, religions, ethnic composition, and economies. Particularly during the last 500 years, migrations of both the voluntary and involuntary or forced type have literally reshaped the human face of the earth.

-19-

Unit II

States: The Geography of Politics and Political Systems

Map 17   Political Boundary Types

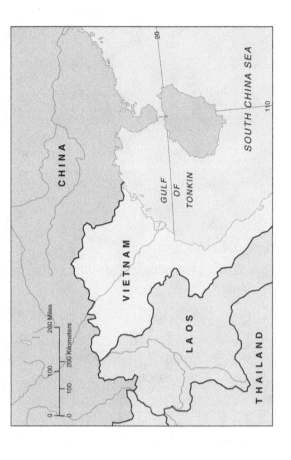

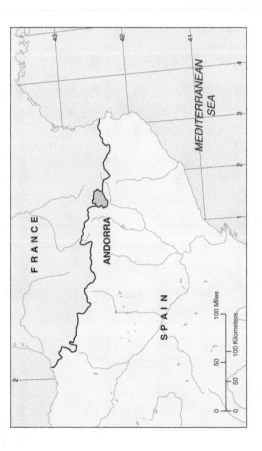

Antecedent: Antecedent boundaries are those that existed as part of the cultural landscape before the establishment of political territories. The boundary between Spain and France is the crest of the Pyrenees Mountains, long a cultural and linguistic barrier and a region of sparse population that is reflected on population density maps even at the world scale.

Subsequent: Subsequent boundaries are those that develop along with the cultural landscape of a region, part of a continuing evolution of political territory to match cultural region. The border region between Vietnam and China has developed over thousands of years of adjustment of territory between the two different cultural realms. Following the end of the Vietnam War, a lengthy border conflict between Vietnam and China suggests that the process is not yet completed.

Map 17   Political Boundary Types

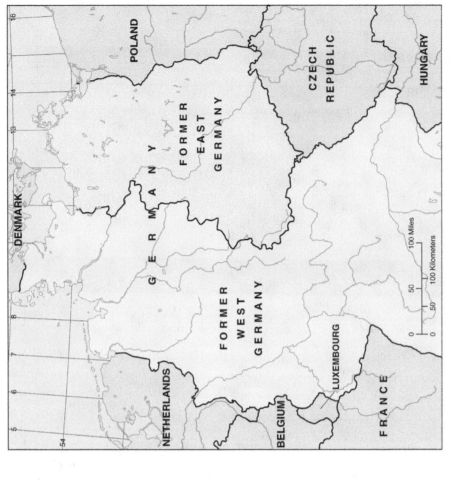

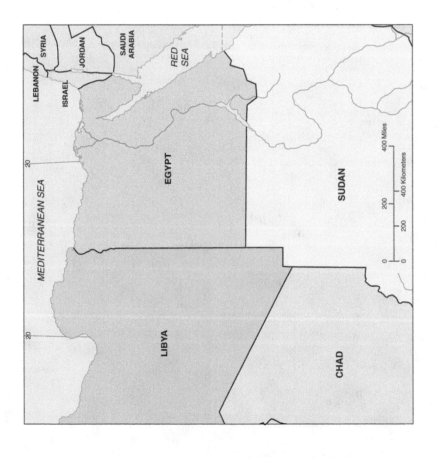

Relict: A relict boundary is like a relict landscape. The boundary between the former North and South Vietnam, along the Ben Hai River, is an example of a relict boundary. So too is the dividing line between the former Federal Republic of Germany (West Germany) and the German Democratic Republic (East Germany). Germany has been unified since 1990, with reintegration of the former Communist East into the West German economy happening progressively and more rapidly than expected. Nevertheless, there are still significant and visible differences between the urban German west and the rural east, between a progressive and modern economic landscape and a deteriorating one.

Superimposed: Superimposed boundaries are drawn arbitrarily across a uniform or homogenous cultural landscape. These boundaries often result from the occupation of territory by an expansive settlement process (see, for example, many of the boundaries of the western states in the United States) or from the process whereby colonial powers divided territory to suit their own needs rather than those of the indigenous population. The borders of Egypt, Libya, and Sudan meet in the center of a uniform cultural and physical region, artificially dividing what (from a natural and human perspective) is unified.

Map 18   Political Systems

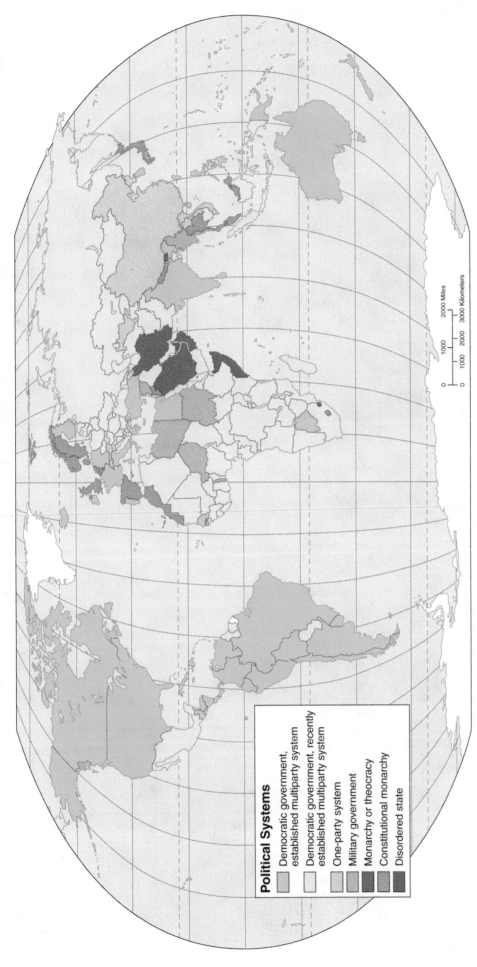

Political Systems

- Democratic government, established multiparty system
- Democratic government, recently established multiparty system
- One-party system
- Military government
- Monarchy or theocracy
- Constitutional monarchy
- Disordered state

0   1000   2000 Miles
0 1000 2000 3000 Kilometers

World political systems have changed dramatically during the last decade and may change even more in the future. The categories of political systems shown on the map are subject to some interpretation: established multiparty democracies are those in which elections by secret ballot with adult suffrage are and have been long-term features of the political landscape; recently established multiparty democracies are those in which the characteristic features of multiparty democracies have only recently emerged. The former Soviet satellites of Eastern Europe and the republics that formerly constituted the U.S.S.R. are in this category; so are states in emerging regions that are beginning to throw off the single-party rule that often followed the violent upheavals of the immediate postcolonial governmental transitions. The other categories are more or less obvious. One-party systems are states where

single-party rule is constitutionally guaranteed or where a one-party regime is a fact of political life. Monarchies are countries with heads of state who are members of a royal family. In a constitutional monarchy, such as the United Kingdom and the Netherlands, the monarchs are titular heads of state only. Theocracies are countries in which rule is within the hands of a priestly or clerical class; today, this means primarily fundamentalist Islamic countries such as Iran. Military governments are frequently organized around a junta that has seized control of the government from civil authority; such states are often technically transitional, that is, the military claims that it will return the reins of government to civil authority when order is restored. Finally, disordered states are countries so beset by civil war or widespread ethnic conflict that no organized government can be said to exist within them.

-25-

Map 19   The Emergence of the State

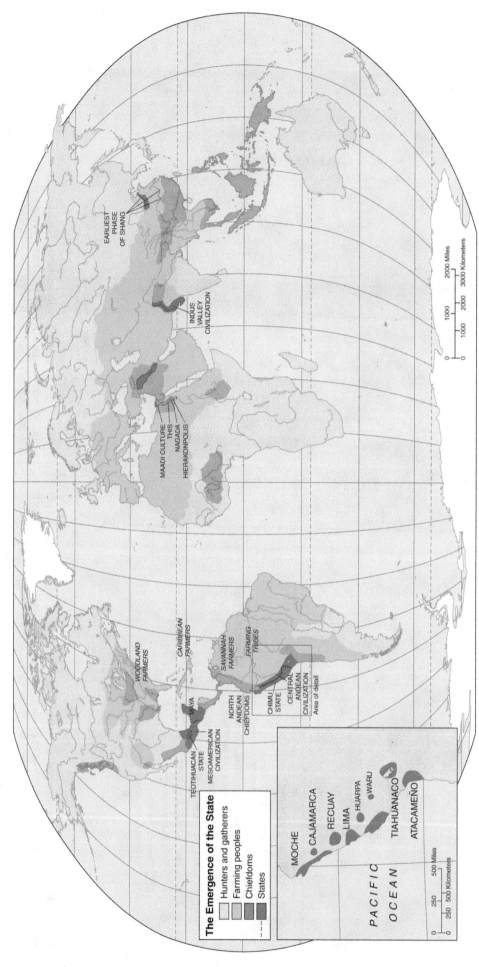

Agriculture is the basis of the development of the state, a form of complex political organization. Geographers and anthropologists believe that agriculture allowed for larger concentrations of population. Farmers do not need to be as mobile as hunters and gatherers to make a living, and people living sedentarily can have larger families than those constantly on the move. Ideas about access to land and ownership also change as people develop the social and political hierarchies that come with the transition from a hunting-gathering society to an agricultural one. Social stratification based on wealth and power creates different classes or groups, some of which no longer work the land. An agricultural surplus supports those who perform other functions for society, such as artisans and craftspeople, soldiers and police, priests and kings. Thus, over time, egalitarian hunters and gatherers shifted to state-level societies in some parts of the world. The first true states are shown in the rust-colored areas of this map.

-26-

Map 20 Organized States and Chiefdoms, A.D. 1500

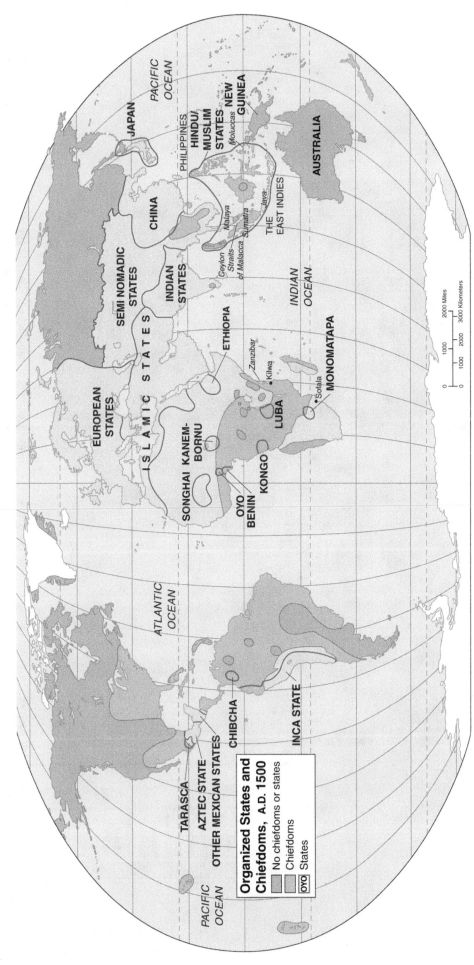

Map 20 Organized States and Chiefdoms, A.D. 1500

As Europeans began to expand outward through exploration and settlement from the late fifteenth to eighteenth centuries, it was inevitable that they would find the complex political organizations of chiefdoms and states in many different parts of the world. Both chiefdoms and states are large-scale forms of political organization in which some people have privileged access to land, power, wealth, and prestige. Chiefdoms are kin-based societies in which wealth is distributed from upper to lower classes. States are organized on the basis of socioeconomic classes, headed by a centralized government that is led by an elite class. States in non-European areas included, just as they did in Europe, full-time bureaucracies and specialized subsystems for such activities as military action, taxation, operation of state religions, and social control. In many of the colonial regions of the world after the fifteenth century, Europeans actually found it easier to gain control of organized states and chiefdoms because those populations were already accustomed to some form of institutionalized central control.

Map 21 European Colonialism, 1500–2000

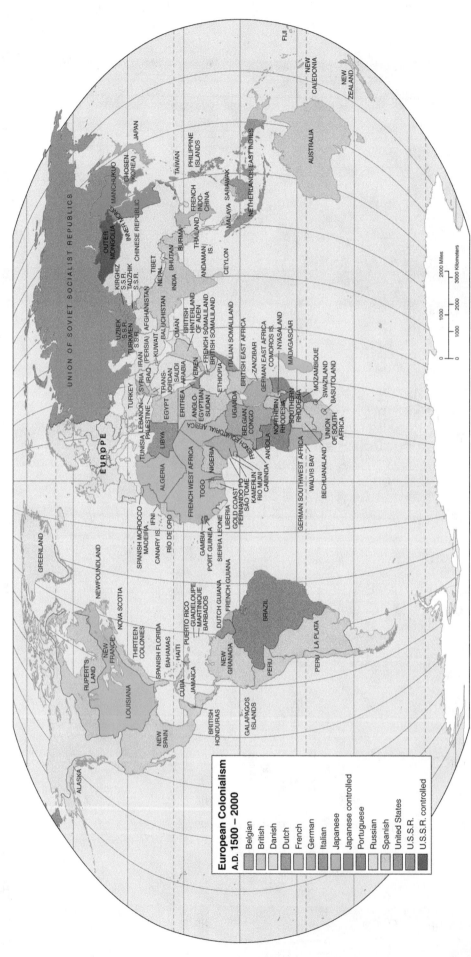

European Colonialism
A.D. 1500 – 2000

- Belgian
- British
- Danish
- Dutch
- French
- German
- Italian
- Japanese
- Japanese controlled
- Portuguese
- Russian
- Spanish
- United States
- U.S.S.R.
- U.S.S.R. controlled

European nations have controlled many parts of the world during the last 500 years. The period of European expansion began when European explorers sailed the oceans in search of new trading routes and ended after World War II when many colonies in Africa and Asia gained independence. The process of colonization was very complex but normally involved the acquisition, extraction, or production of raw materials (including minerals, forest products, products from the sea, agricultural products, and animal furs/pelts) from the areas being controlled by the European colonial power in exchange for items of European manufacture. The concept of colonial dependency implied an economic structure in which the European country obtained raw materials from the colonial country in exchange for those manufactured items upon which populations in the colonial areas quickly came to depend. The colors on this map represent colonial control at its maximum extent and do not take into account shifting colonial control. In North America, for example, "New France" became British territory and "Louisiana" became Spanish territory after the Seven Years' (French and Indian) War.

-28-

Map 22 Federal and Unitary States

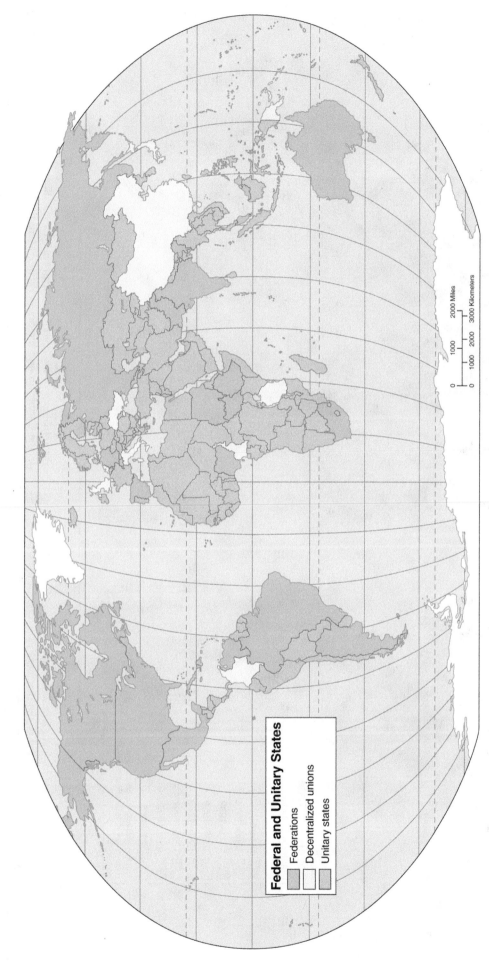

Federal and Unitary States

- Federations
- Decentralized unions
- Unitary states

0   1000   2000 Miles
0   1000   2000   3000 Kilometers

Countries vary greatly in the degree to which the national government makes all decisions or certain matters are left to governments of subdivisions. In federal states, each subdivision (state, province, and so on) has its own capital, and certain aspects of life are left to the subdivisions to manage. For example, in the United States, motor vehicle and marriage/divorce laws are powers for states rather than the federal government. Federal systems are suited to large countries with a diversity of cultures. They easily accommodate new territorial subdivisions, which can take their places among those already a part of the country. In unitary states, major decisions come from the national capital, and subdivisions administer those decisions. Unitary systems are best suited to small states with a relatively homogeneous ethnic and cultural makeup. Some countries, the decentralized unions, have a mix of systems—for example, provinces that follow the dictates of the central government and other subdivisions that have more autonomy.

Map 23 Sovereign States: Duration of Independence

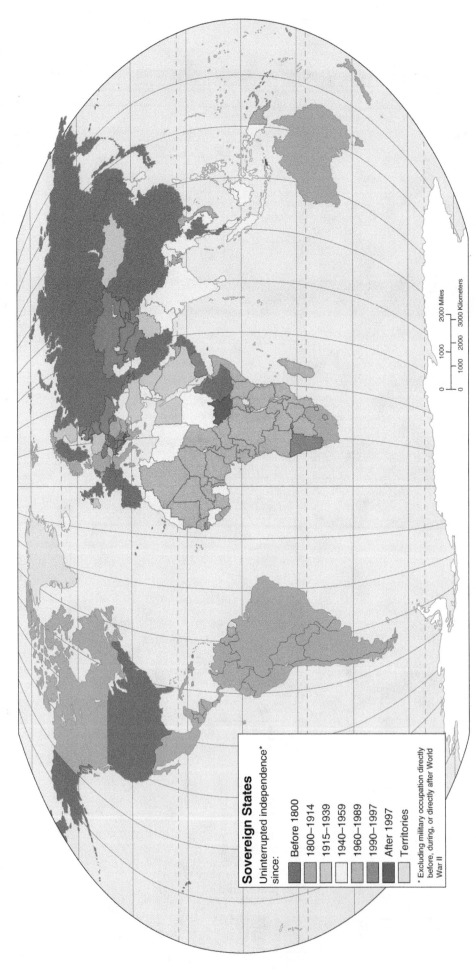

Sovereign States

Uninterrupted independence*
since:

Before 1800
1800–1914
1915–1939
1940–1959
1960–1989
1990–1997
After 1997
Territories

* Excluding military occupation directly before, during, or directly after World War II

Most countries of the modern world, including such major states as Germany and Italy, became independent after the beginning of the nineteenth century. Of the world's current countries, only 27 were independent in 1800. Following 1800, there have been five great periods of national independence. During the first of these (1800–1914), most of the mainland countries of the Americas achieved independence. During the second period (1915–1939), the countries of Eastern Europe emerged as independent entities. The third period (1940–1959) includes World War II and the years that followed, when independence for African and Asian nations that had been under control of colonial powers first began to occur. During the fourth period (1960–1989), independence came to the remainder of the colonial African and Asian nations, as well as to former colonies in the Caribbean and the South Pacific. More than half of the world's countries came into being as independent political entities during this period. During the last decade of the twentieth century, the breakup of the existing states of the U.S.S.R., Yugoslavia, and Czechoslovakia created 22 countries where only three had existed before. Since 2000, Timor-Leste (East Timor), Montenegro, Kosovo, and South Sudan have joined the ranks of the independent states. While Kosovo's sovereignty has been recognized by the United States, fewer than half of the world's states have followed suit and Kosovo does not have membership in the United Nations.

0   1000   2000 Miles
0   1000   2000   3000 Kilometers

-30-

Map 24 The United Nations

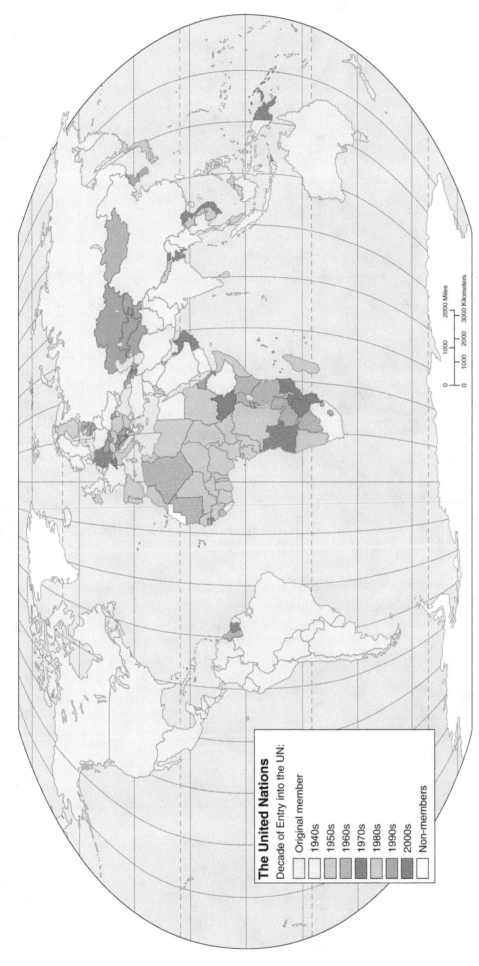

The United Nations
Decade of Entry into the UN:

- Original member
- 1940s
- 1950s
- 1960s
- 1970s
- 1980s
- 1990s
- 2000s
- Non-members

0 1000 2000 Miles
0 1000 2000 3000 Kilometers

The United Nations was formed in 1945 after World War II to maintain international peace and security and to promote cooperation involving economic, social, cultural, and humanitarian problems. Originally consisting of 51 member states, the organization has grown to 193 member states, the most recently admitted being South Sudan, which joined in July 2011. Most of the African continent and the smaller Caribbean states entered the UN during the 1960s and 1970s following the end of European colonial rule. The 1990s saw the entry of several countries following the dissolution of the U.S.S.R. and the breakup of Yugoslavia.

China was represented by the government of the Republic of China at the creation of the United Nations. Following the Communist victory during the Chinese Civil War, the government fled to the island of Taiwan. UN representation was maintained by the Republic of China government until 1971 when the government of the People's Republic of China (mainland China) was recognized as the representative of China to the organization. Western Sahara is not a member of the UN as its sovereignty status is in dispute. Much of the territory of Western Sahara is controlled by Morocco. Kosovo declared its independence in 2008, which was recognized by the United States and 59 other countries. As of 2009, its entry into the UN has been blocked by Russia, which has not recognized its independence from Serbia. The Holy See (Vatican City) and Palestine hold status as observer.

-31-

Map 25   United Nations Regions and Sub-Regions

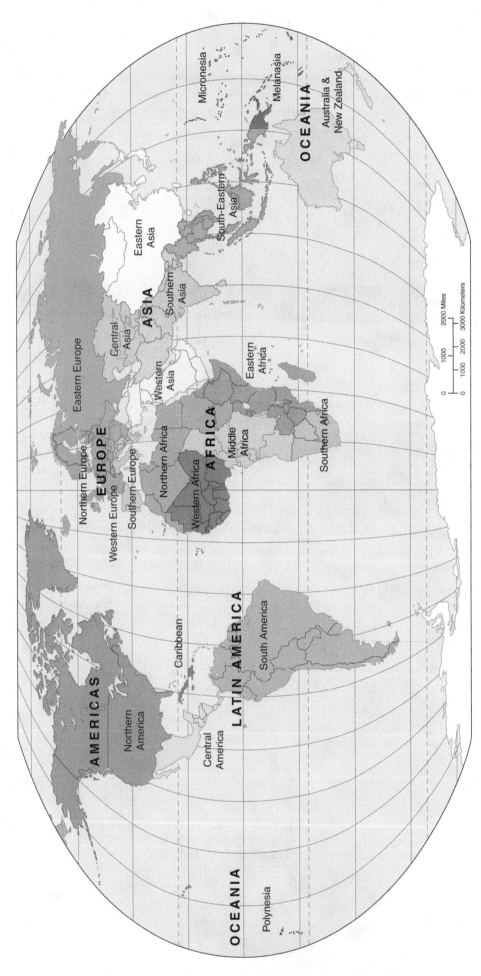

Where in the world is a country? At first, the response to that question seems fairly straightforward: China is in Asia, Angola is in Africa, and so on. The more one learns about the world, however, the more one finds that not everyone groups the world's countries the same way, nor do they use standard terminology. For example, is Russia in Europe? Is it in Asia? Is it in both? Some terms commonly used in Western culture tend not to be applicable in a global context. Using "Middle East" to describe the countries

of the Arabian Peninsula and the eastern Mediterranean makes sense when viewing the world from the United Kingdom, but one would be hard-pressed to characterize these countries as "East" or in the "Middle" of countries to the east if one were in Japan. The map above presents the classification of the world's countries by the United Nations. How well do the names of the regions and sub-regions conform to the names with which you are familiar?

Map 26 Is It a Country?

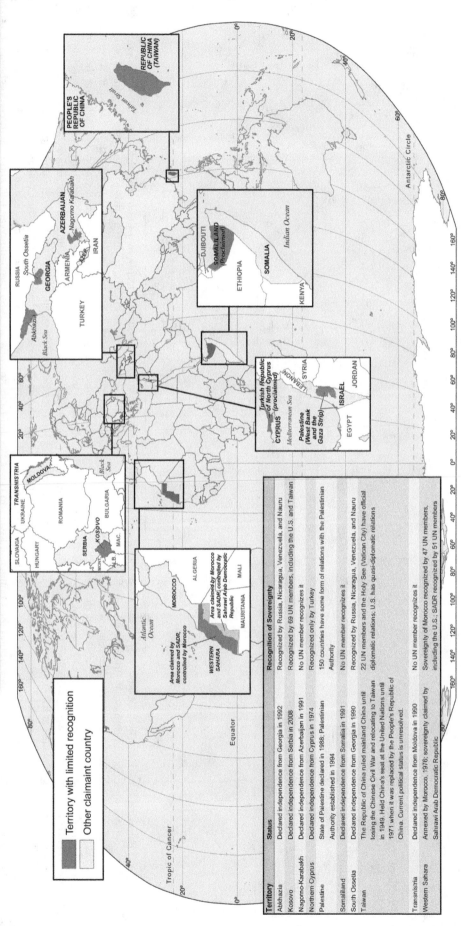

Legend:
- Territory with limited recognition
- Other claimant country

Territory	Status	Recognition of Sovereignty
Abkhazia	Declared independence from Georgia in 1992	Recognized by Russia, Nicaragua, Venezuela, and Nauru
Kosovo	Declared independence from Serbia in 2008	Recognized by 69 UN members, including the U.S. and Taiwan
Nagorno-Karabakh	Declared independence from Azerbaijan in 1991	No UN member recognizes it
Northern Cyprus	Declared independence from Cyprus in 1974	Recognized only by Turkey
Palestine	State of Palestine declared in 1988; Palestinian Authority established in 1994	150 countries have some form of relations with the Palestinian Authority
Somaliland	Declared independence from Somalia in 1991	No UN member recognizes it
South Ossetia	Declared independence from Georgia in 1990	Recognized by Russia, Nicaragua, Venezuela, and Nauru
Taiwan	The Republic of China ruled mainland China until losing the Chinese Civil War and relocating to Taiwan in 1949. Held China's seat at the United Nations until 1971 when it was replaced by the People's Republic of China. Current political status is unresolved.	22 UN members and the Holy See (Vatican City) have official diplomatic relations; U.S. has quasi-diplomatic relations
Transnistria	Declared independence from Moldova in 1990	No UN member recognizes it
Western Sahara	Annexed by Morocco, 1976; sovereignty claimed by Saharawi Arab Democratic Republic	Sovereignty of Morocco recognized by 47 UN members, including the U.S.; SADR recognized by 51 UN members

When a group of people within a territory declares independence, does that territory become a country? The short answer is "it depends." This question begs a follow-up question: What makes a country a country? The criteria defining a country, or, more appropriately, a *state*, are fairly straightforward. To begin with, a state must have territory and a resident population. There must be political, economic, and social organization. A state possesses *sovereignty*. Generally, sovereignty can be thought of as having complete control over one's territory and possessing the right to defend oneself against external aggression. Finally, a state is *recognized* as a country by other states. Today, that recognition generally is manifested by entry into the United Nations (Map 24). One cannot overstate the importance of international recognition, because it does not always happen automatically or quickly. For example, international recognition and subsequent entry of Macedonia into the UN was delayed because of objections by Greece to the name of the new country. Even though it is a member of the UN, Israel is not recognized as a state by several UN members. The map above illustrates ten examples of territories that possess varying levels of international recognition of their sovereignty. None of the territories is a member of the UN, although the Republic of China (Taiwan) held China's seat in the UN until 1971, and the Palestine Liberation Organization was granted observer status to the UN in 1974. Some of the territories have declared independence but have received no recognition (Somaliland, Transnistria) or limited recognition (Abkhazia, Nagorno-Karabakh, South Ossetia, Turkish Republic of North Cyprus). Kosovo has been recognized by 69 countries, including the United States, but not by Serbia, Russia, China, and several other Asian and African states. In the case of Taiwan, it never declared independence from mainland China. Rather, it views itself as the legitimate government of all of China, while the People's Republic of China views it as a breakaway province. A handful of countries have official diplomatic relations with the Republic of China (Taiwan). Much of the rest of the world, including the United States, has quasi-diplomatic relations with the island.

Map 27 Political Realms: Regional Changes, 1945–2003

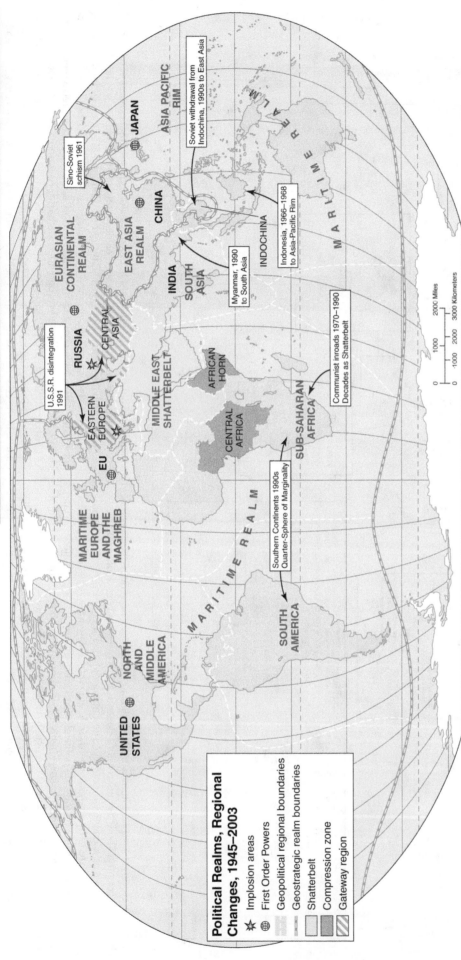

Political Realms, Regional Changes, 1945–2003

- ✩ Implosion areas
- ⊕ First Order Powers
- Geopolitical regional boundaries
- Geostrategic realm boundaries
- Shatterbelt
- Compression zone
- Gateway region

Labels on map:

UNITED STATES

NORTH AND MIDDLE AMERICA

MARITIME REALM

SOUTH AMERICA

MARITIME EUROPE AND THE MAGHREB

EU

EASTERN EUROPE

U.S.S.R. disintegration 1991

RUSSIA

CENTRAL ASIA

EURASIAN CONTINENTAL REALM

Sino-Soviet schism 1961

JAPAN

ASIA PACIFIC RIM

CHINA

EAST ASIA REALM

INDIA

SOUTH ASIA

MIDDLE EAST SHATTERBELT

AFRICAN HORN

CENTRAL AFRICA

SUB-SAHARAN AFRICA

Southern Continents 1990s Quarter-Sphere of Marginality

Communist inroads 1970–1990 Decades as Shatterbelt

INDOCHINA

Myanmar, 1990 to South Asia

Indonesia, 1966–1968 to Asia-Pacific Rim

Soviet withdrawal from Indochina, 1990s to East Asia

MARITIME REALM

Miles: 0 1000 2000
Kilometers: 0 1000 2000 3000

The Cold War following World War II shaped the major outlines of today's geopolitical relations. The Cold War included three phases. In the first, from 1945–1956, the Maritime Realm established a ring around the Continental Eurasian Realm in order to prevent its expansion. This phase included the Korean War (1950–1953), the Berlin Blockade (1948), the Truman Doctrine and Marshall Plan (1947), and the founding of NATO (1949) and the Warsaw Pact (1955). Most of the world fell within one of the two realms: the Maritime time (dominated by the United States) or the Eurasian Continental Realm (dominated by the U.S.S.R.). The U.S.S.R. sought to establish a ring of satellite states to protect it from a repeat of the invasions of World War II. The United States and other Maritime Realm states, in turn, sought to establish a ring of allies around the Continental Realm to prevent its expansion. South Asia was politically independent, but under pressure from both realms. During the second phase (1957–1979), Communist forces from the Continental

Eurasian Realm penetrated deeply into the Maritime Realm. The Berlin Wall went up in 1961, Soviet missiles in Cuba ignited a crisis in 1962, and the United States became increasingly involved in the war in Vietnam (late 1960s). The U.S.S.R. sought increased political and military presence along important waterways including those in the Middle East, Southeast Asia, and the Caribbean. These regions became especially dangerous shatterbelts. The third phase (1980–1989) saw the retreat of Communist power from the Maritime Realm. China, after ten years of radical Communism and chaos of the Cultural Revolution (1966–1976), broke away from the Continental Eurasian Realm to establish a new East Asian realm. Soviet influence declined in the Middle East, Sub-Saharan Africa, and Latin America. In 1989 the Berlin Wall fell, and Eastern Europe began to establish democratic governments. In the 1990s the U.S.S.R., Yugoslavia, and Czechoslovakia broke apart into 22 independent states.

-34-

Map 28   European Boundaries, 1914–1949

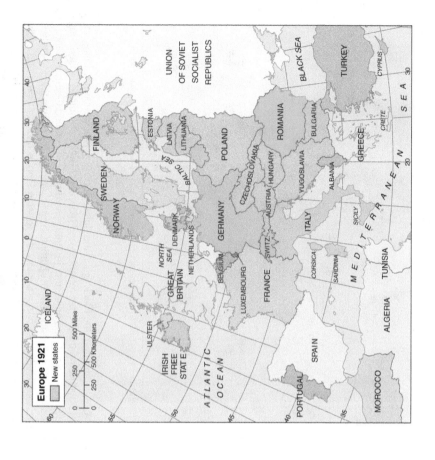

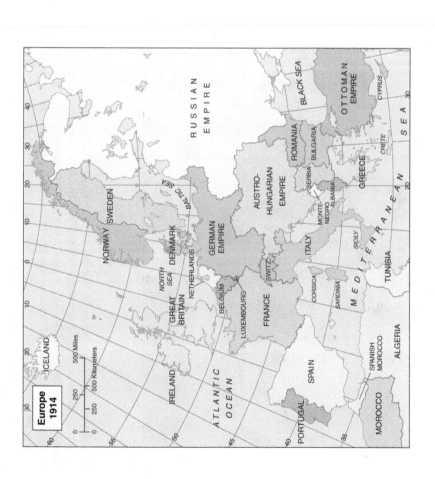

In 1914, on the eve of the First World War, Europe was dominated by the United Kingdom and France in the west, the German Empire and the Austro-Hungarian Empire in central Europe, and the Russian Empire in the east. Battle lines for the conflict that began in 1914 were drawn when the United Kingdom, France, and the Russian Empire joined together as the Triple Entente. In the view of the Germans, this coalition was designed to encircle Germany and its Austrian ally, which, along with Italy, made up the Triple Alliance. The German and Austrian fears were heightened in 1912–1914 when a Russian-sponsored "Balkan League" pushed the Ottoman Turkish Empire from Europe, leaving behind the weak and

mutually antagonistic Balkan states Serbia and Montenegro. In August 1914, Germany and Austria-Hungary attacked in several directions and World War I began. Four years later, after massive loss of life and destruction, the Central European empires were defeated. The victorious French, English, and Americans (who had entered the war in 1917) restructured the map of Europe in 1919, carving nine new states out of the remains of the German and Austro-Hungarian empires and the westernmost portions of the Russian Empire. By the end of the war, the Russian Empire was deep in the revolution that deposed the czar and brought the Communists to power in a new Union of Soviet Socialist Republics.

Map 28 European Boundaries, 1914–1949

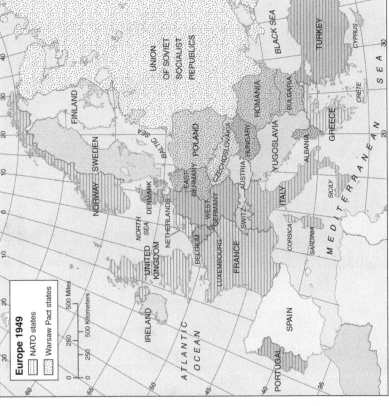

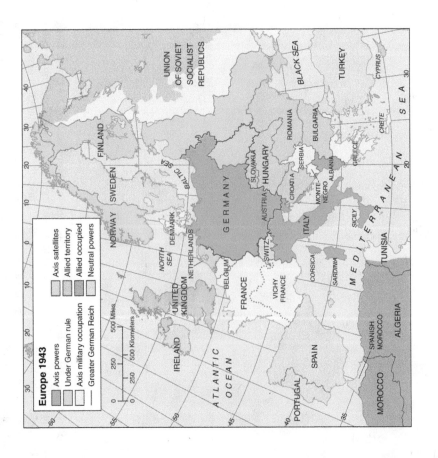

When the victorious Allies redrew the map of Central and Eastern Europe in 1919, they caused as many problems as they were trying to solve. The interval between the First and Second World Wars was really just a lull in a long war that halted temporarily in 1918 and erupted once again in 1939. Defeated Germany, resentful of the terms of the 1918 armistice and 1919 Treaty of Versailles and beset by massive inflation and unemployment at home, overthrew the Weimar republican government in 1933 and installed the National Socialist (Nazi) party led by Adolf Hitler in Berlin. Hitler quickly began making good on his promises to create a "thousand year realm" of German influence by annexing Austria and the Czech region of Czechoslovakia and allying Germany with a fellow fascist state in Mussolini's Italy. In September 1939 Germany launched the lightning-quick combined infantry, artillery, and armor attack known as *der Blitzkrieg* and took Poland to the east and, in quick succession, the Netherlands, Belgium, and France to the west. By 1943 the greater German Reich extended from the Russian Plain

to the Atlantic and from the Black Sea to the Baltic. But the Axis powers of Germany and Italy could not withstand the greater resources and manpower of the combined United Kingdom–United States–U.S.S.R.–led Allies and, in 1945, Allied armies occupied Germany. Once again, the lines of the Central and Eastern European map were redrawn. This time, a strengthened U.S.S.R. took back most of the territory the Russian Empire had lost at the end of the First World War. Germany was partitioned into four occupied sectors (English, French, American, and Russian) and later into two independent countries, the Federal Republic of Germany (West Germany) and the German Democratic Republic (East Germany). Although the U.S.S.R.'s territory stopped at the Polish, Hungarian, Czechoslovakian, and Romanian borders, the Eastern European countries (Poland, East Germany, Czechoslovakia, Hungary, Romania, Yugoslavia, Albania, and Bulgaria) became Communist between 1945 and 1948 and were separated from the West by the Iron Curtain.

*The Warsaw Pact was not formally established until 1955 but it was a de facto organization prior to that.

Map 29 An Age of Bipolarity: The Cold War ca. 1970

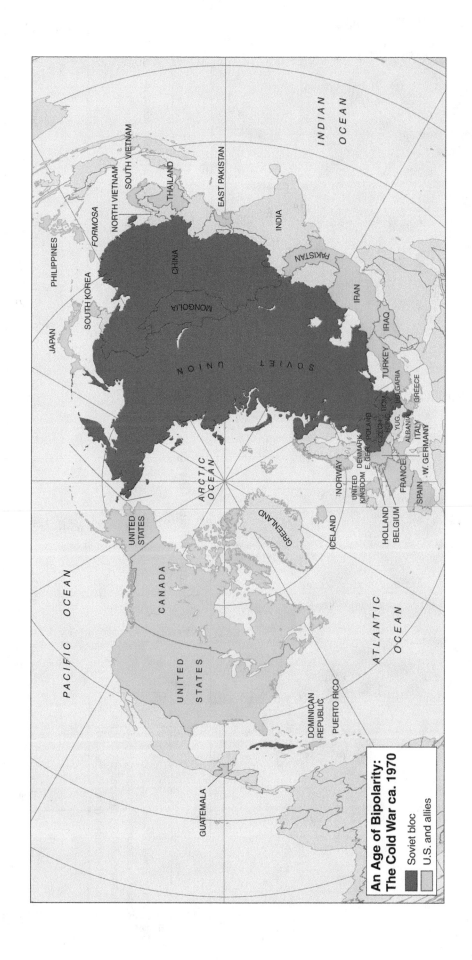

**An Age of Bipolarity:
The Cold War ca. 1970**

◼ Soviet bloc
◻ U.S. and allies

Following the Second World War, the world was divided into two armed camps led by the United States and the U.S.S.R. The U.S.S.R. and its allies, the Warsaw Pact countries, feared a U.S.-led takeover of the Eastern European countries that became Soviet satellites after the war and the replacing of a socialist political and economic system with a liberal one. The United States and its allies, the NATO (North Atlantic Treaty Organization) countries, equally feared that the U.S.S.R. would overrun Western Europe. Both sides sought to defend themselves by building up massive military arsenals. The United States, adopting an international geopolitical strategy of containment, sought to ring the U.S.S.R. with a string of allied countries and military bases that would prevent Soviet expansion in any direction. The levels of spending on military hardware contributed to the devolution of the U.S.S.R., and the obsolescence of alliances and military bases in an age of advanced guidance and delivery systems made the U.S. military containment less necessary. Following a peak in the early 1960s, the Cold War gradually became less significant and the age of bipolar international power essentially ended with the dissolution of the U.S.S.R. in 1991.

Map 30   Europe: Political Changes, 1989–2012

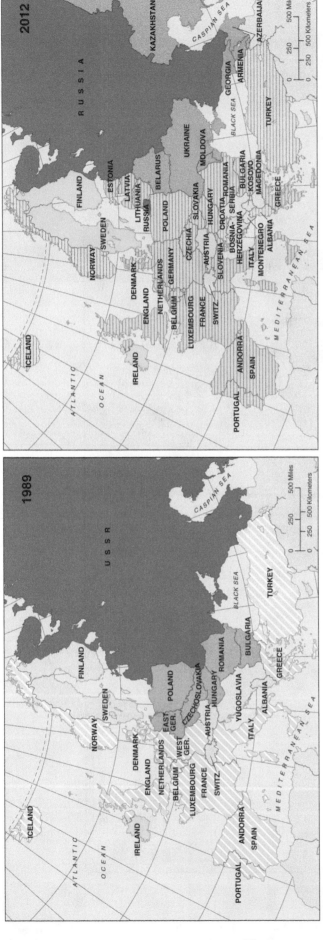

Europe: Political Changes, 1989–2012

2012

- Former republics of the U.S.S.R., now independent countries
- Russian Federation
- NATO countries
- European Union (formerly the EC)

1989

- Union of Soviet Socialist Republics
- Warsaw Pact countries (excluding the U.S.S.R.)
- North Atlantic Treaty Organization countries
- European Community (formerly the EEC)

During the last decade of the twentieth century, one of the most remarkable series of political geographic changes of the last 500 years took place. The bipolar east-west structure that had characterized Europe's political geography since the end of the Second World War altered in the space of a very few years. In the mid-1980s, as Soviet influence over Eastern and Central Europe weakened, those countries began to turn to the capitalist West. Between 1989, when the country of Hungary was the first Soviet satellite to open its borders to travel, and 1991, when the U.S.S.R. dissolved into 15 independent countries, abrupt change in political systems occurred. Seven countries formed out of the former Yugoslavia beginning in 1991, culminating with Kosovo's 2008 declaration of independence. The result is a new map of Europe that includes a number of countries not present on the map of 1989. These countries have emerged as the result of reunification, separation, or independence from the former U.S.S.R. and Yugoslavia. The new political structure has been accompanied by growing economic cooperation.

-38-

Map 31   The European Union, 2011

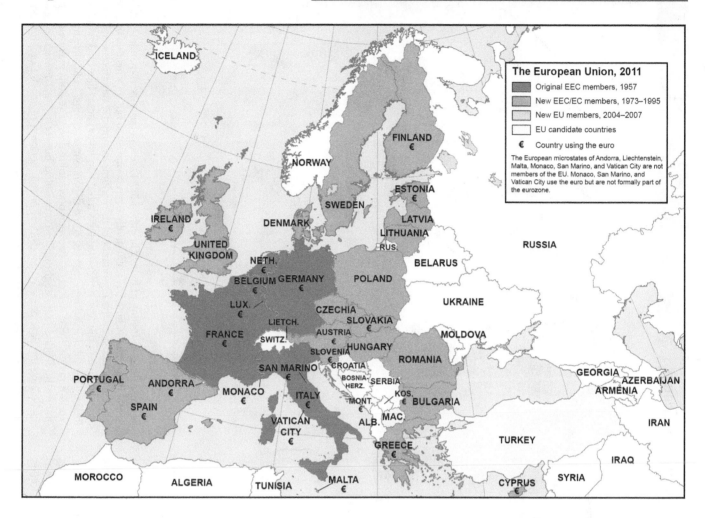

The European Union, 2011

- Original EEC members, 1957
- New EEC/EC members, 1973–1995
- New EU members, 2004–2007
- EU candidate countries
- € Country using the euro

The European microstates of Andorra, Liechtenstein, Malta, Monaco, San Marino, and Vatican City are not members of the EU. Monaco, San Marino, and Vatican City use the euro but are not formally part of the eurozone.

After World War II, a number of European leaders became convinced that the only way to secure a lasting peace between their countries was to unite them economically and politically. The first attempts at this were made in 1951, when the European Coal and Steel Community (ECSC) was set up, with six members: Belgium, West Germany, Luxembourg, France, Italy, and the Netherlands. The ECSC was such a success that, within a few years, these same six countries decided to go further and integrate other sectors of their economies. In 1957 they signed the Treaties of Rome, creating the European Atomic Energy Community (EURATOM) and the European Economic Community (EEC). The member states set about removing trade barriers between them and forming a "common market." The six original members were joined in the common market of the EEC by Denmark, Ireland, and the United Kingdom in 1973, followed by Greece in 1981 and Spain and Portugal in 1986. In 1992 the 12 countries of the EEC signed the Treaty of Maastricht, which introduced new forms of cooperation between the member state governments—particularly in defense and legal systems—and created the European Union (EU). The original 12 EU members were joined by Austria, Finland, and Sweden in 1995. In 2004, ten new members joined the EU: Cyprus, the Czech Republic, Estonia, Hungary, Latvia, Lithuania, Malta, Poland, Slovakia, and Slovenia; Bulgaria and Romania joined three years later. In 2011, Croatia, Iceland, Macedonia, Montenegro, and Turkey all were candidates for membership. The EU has worked toward the dropping of trade barriers and labor migration barriers among member countries, along with economic and political cooperation in a number of areas. The "eurozone" consists of 17 of the 27 EU member states that have adopted the euro as their official currency. The euro is also the currency of six European states that are not members of the EU. Additionally, 23 countries have currencies that are directly pegged to the euro.

Map 32   The Geopolitical World at the Beginning of the Twenty-First Century

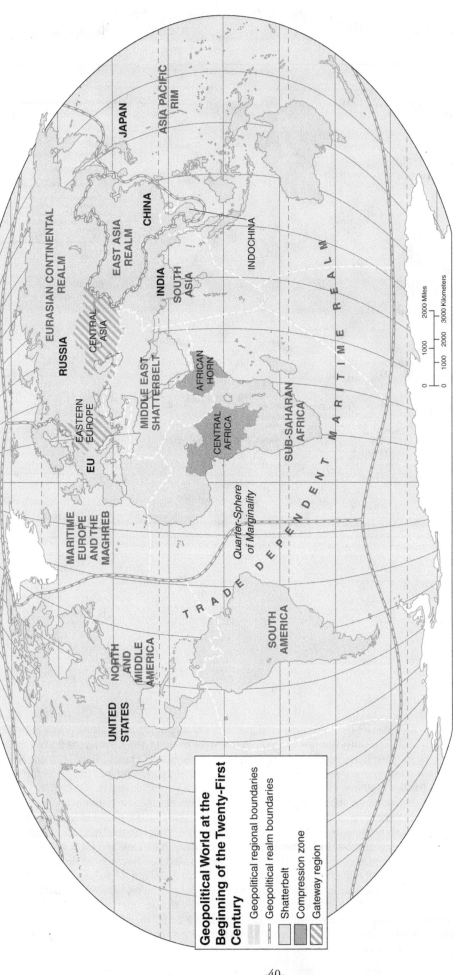

Geopolitical World at the Beginning of the Twenty-First Century

Geopolitical regional boundaries
Geopolitical realm boundaries
Shatterbelt
Compression zone
Gateway region

UNITED STATES

NORTH AND MIDDLE AMERICA

MARITIME EUROPE AND THE MAGHREB

EU

EASTERN EUROPE

RUSSIA

CENTRAL ASIA

EURASIAN CONTINENTAL REALM

EAST ASIA REALM

CHINA

JAPAN

ASIA PACIFIC RIM

MIDDLE EAST SHATTERBELT

AFRICAN HORN

CENTRAL AFRICA

INDIA

SOUTH ASIA

INDOCHINA

SUB-SAHARAN AFRICA

TRADE DEPENDENT MARITIME REALM

Quarter-Sphere of Marginality

SOUTH AMERICA

0   1000   2000   3000 Kilometers
0   1000   2000 Miles

In the geostrategic structure of the world, the largest territorial units are realms. They are shaped by circulation patterns that link people, goods, and ideas. Realms are shaped by maritime and continental influences. Today's Atlantic and Pacific Trade-Dependent Maritime Realm has been shaped by international exchange over the oceans and their interior seas as mercantilism, capitalism, and industrialization gave rise to maritime-oriented states and to economic and political colonialism. The world's leading trading and economic powers are part of this realm. The Eurasian Continental Realm, centered around Russia, is inner-oriented, less influenced by outside economic or cultural forces, and politically closed, even after the fall of Communism. Expansion of NATO in Europe has increased its feeling of being "hemmed in." East Asia has mixed maritime and continental influences. China has traditionally been continental, but reforms that began in the late 1970s increased the importance of its maritime-oriented southern coasts. Even so, its trade volume is still low, and it maintains a hold on inland areas like Tibet and Xinjiang. Realms are subdivided into regions, some dependent on others, as South America is on North America. Regions located between powerful realms or regions may be shatterbelts (internally divided and caught up in competition between Great Powers) or gateways (facilitating the flow of ideas, goods, and people between regions). Compression zones are areas of conflict, but they are not contested by major powers.

-40-

Map 33   Democracy on the Rise

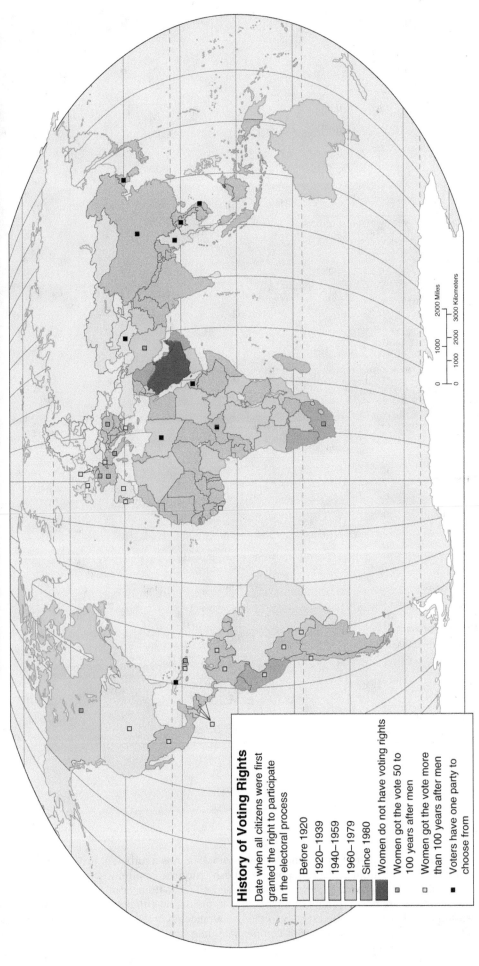

History of Voting Rights

Date when all citizens were first granted the right to participate in the electoral process

- Before 1920
- 1920–1939
- 1940–1959
- 1960–1979
- Since 1980
- Women do not have voting rights

☐ Women got the vote 50 to 100 years after men

☐ Women got the vote more than 100 years after men

■ Voters have one party to choose from

In 1800 most of the world's people were ruled by a monarch—sometimes with a constitution and sometimes with a parliament, but a monarch, nevertheless. Few monarchs remain and where they do, their role is largely that of a figurehead than of an actual ruler. For all the veneration given to, say, Queen Elizabeth II of the United Kingdom, whoever is prime minister in that government has enormously more power—and the prime minister is elected by a constituency. But having elected leaders as opposed to hereditary rulers is not the only criterion for identifying a democracy. Suffrage, or who possesses the right to vote, ought to be universal (it is worth noting that in the United States—one of the world's oldest democracies—black men possessed the right to vote more than a half century before white women). Elections should be competitive: A true democracy can rarely exist without multiple political parties with equal access to the electorate. Elections must also be free from internal or external coercion or corruption. And, in true democracies, there are a number of other identifying components such as a free press, an advanced legal system in which laws rather than men rule, and a respect for human rights. By these more rigorous standards perhaps only two-thirds of the countries on this map are true, Western-style liberal democracies. But that is a great deal better (unless, of course, you are a monarchist) than the situation in 1800. What explains the rise of democratic systems? Most experts point to such things as higher levels of economic development and greater literacy among populations. Even more important, however, is globalization and the shrinking of the world through increased communication systems. People who live in democracies tend to have certain advantages not possessed by those who do not. In a world of low or no barriers to interpersonal and interregional information flows, this fact is hard to hide. Isolated countries (North Korea is a case-in-point) are more likely to be autocratic than democratic and the future for truly democratic governance would seem bright.

-41-

Map 34 The Middle East: Territorial Changes, 1918–Present

Territorial Changes in the Middle East, World War I to present

- Ottoman Empire to World War I
- British control
- French control
- Kurdish homelands
- International boundaries in 1994

LEBANON AND SYRIA
Ottoman Empire to 1920
French (1920–1944)
Independent 1944

CYPRUS from
Ottoman Empire to
British control 1878
Independent 1960

ISRAEL
Ottoman Empire to 1920
UK (1920–1948)

LIBYA
Ottoman Empire
to 1911

Italian colony
(1911–1943)

UK–French
Protectorate
(1943–1951)

EGYPT
Ottoman Empire to 1885
UK Protectorate
(1885–1936)

IRAQ
UK (1920–1932)

JORDAN
Ottoman Empire
to 1920
UK (1920–1946) Hejaz Nedj
(to 1926)

IRAN
(named Persia
until 1935)

KUWAIT
UK (1899–1961)

BAHRAIN
UK (1861–1971)

OMAN

U.A.E.
UK (1820s–1971)

QATAR
UK 1868–1971

King Saud
expanded territory
(1901–1936)

Asir
(1917–1934)

YEMEN
(Independent
1918)

OMAN
UK
(1891–1971)

YEMEN
UK 1868–1971
Independent as (South) Yemen 1967
Merged with (North) Yemen 1990

Suez
Canal
British
control
to 1956

INSET

ISRAELI
SECURITY
ZONE

GOLAN
HEIGHTS

WEST
BANK

GAZA

SINAI PENINSULA

The Middle East, encompassing the northeastern part of Africa and southwestern Asia, has a turbulent history. In the last century alone, many of the region's countries have gone from being ruled by the Turkish Ottoman Empire, to being dependencies of the United Kingdom or France, to being independent. Having experienced the Crusades and colonial domination by European powers, the region's predominantly Islamic countries are now resentful of interference in the region's affairs by countries with a European and/or Christian heritage. The tension between Israel (settled largely in the late nineteenth and twentieth centuries by Jews of predominantly European background) and its neighbors is a matter of European–Middle Eastern cultural stress as well as a religious conflict between Islamic Arab culture and Judaism.

Map 35   Africa: Colonialism to Independence

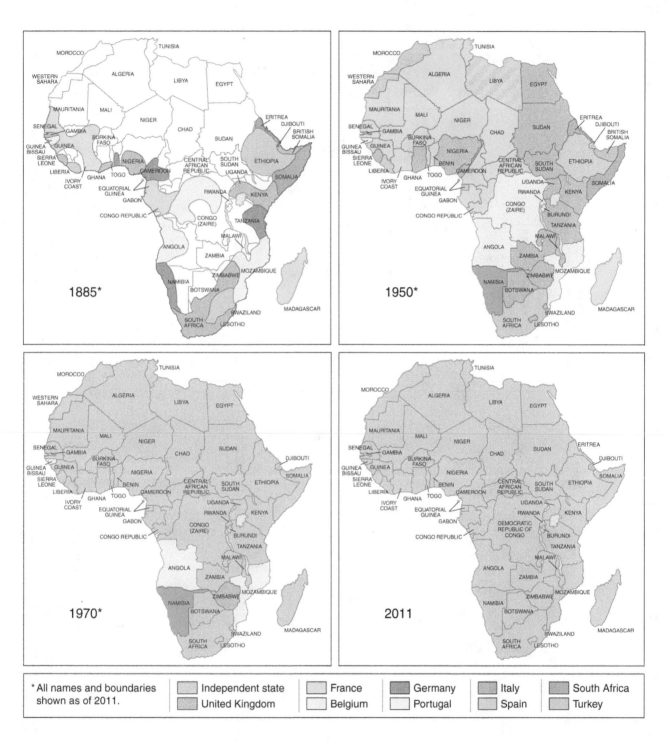

| * All names and boundaries shown as of 2011. | Independent state | France | Germany | Italy | South Africa |
| | United Kingdom | Belgium | Portugal | Spain | Turkey |

In few parts of the world has the transition from colonialism to independence been as abrupt as on the African continent. Most African states did not become colonies until the nineteenth century and did not become independent until the twentieth, nearly all of them after World War II. Much of the colonial power in Africa is social and economic. The African colony provided the mother country with raw materials in exchange for marginal economic returns, and many African countries still exist in this colonial dependency relationship. An even more important component of the colonial legacy of Europe in Africa is geopolitical. When the world's colonial powers joined at the Conference of Berlin in 1884, they divided up Africa to fit their own needs, drawing boundary lines on maps without regard for terrain or drainage features, or for tribal/ethnic linguistic, cultural, economic, or political borders. Traditional Africa was enormously disrupted by this process. After independence, African countries retained boundaries that are legacies of the colonial past; and African countries today are beset by internal problems related to tribal and ethnic conflicts, the disruption of traditional migration patterns, and inefficient spatial structures of market and supply.

Map 36 South Africa: Black Homelands and Post-Apartheid Provinces

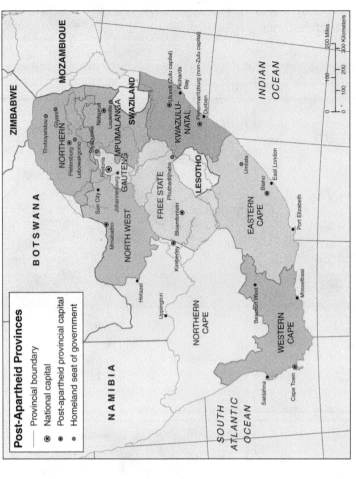

Post-Apartheid Provinces
- Provincial boundary
- ⊛ National capital
- ◉ Post-apartheid provincial capital
- ● Homeland seat of government

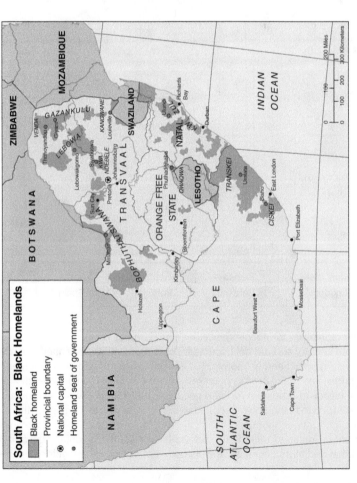

South Africa: Black Homelands
- Black homeland
- Provincial boundary
- ⊛ National capital
- ● Homeland seat of government

After their defeat by the British in the Boer War (1899–1902), the Dutch-descended Afrikaners negotiated with the British for greater powers in South Africa. Eventually, they became the most powerful group and imposed "separate development" or *apartheid* on the country. African (and other minority) populations would live completely separated from white South Africans. Millions were forced to relocate to the ancestral areas, where "homelands" that would be declared "independent" were set up for them. The amounts and quality of the land were completely insufficient to support the populations assigned

to them, and many of the "homelands" were fragmented as well. Thousands of black Africans flocked to the black "townships" around major cities, looking for work. Here, they were foreigners in their own land. After the fall of *apartheid* in 1994, the "homelands" were abolished, and South Africa's political geography was reorganized, with each new province centered around its dominant ethnic group. These provinces now serve as subdivisions within the country without restrictions by race or ethnicity on where people can live. This organization was important in the peaceful transfer to majority rule.

-44-

Map 37 Asia: Colonialism to Independence, 1930–2007

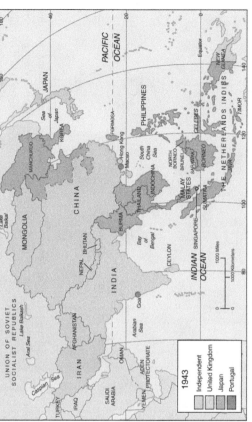

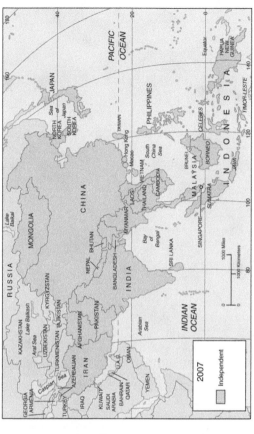

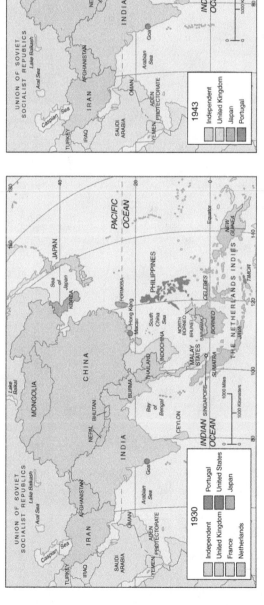

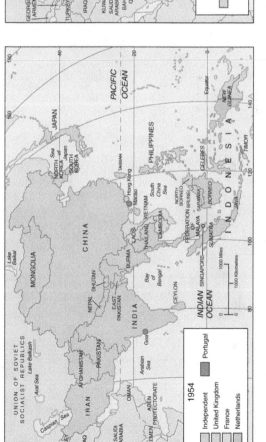

Asian countries, like those in Africa, have recently emerged from a colonial past. With the exception of China, Japan, and Thailand, virtually all Asian nations were until not long ago under the colonial control of the United Kingdom, France, Spain, the Netherlands, or the United States. For a short period of time between 1930 and 1945, Japan itself was a colonial power with considerable territories on the Asian mainland. The unraveling of colonial control in Asia, particularly in South and Southeast Asia, has precipitated internal conflicts in the newly independent states that make up a significant part of the political geography of the region. The last vestiges of European colonialism in Asia disappeared with the cession of Hong Kong (1997) and Macao (1999) to China.

Map 38 Global Distribution of Minority Groups

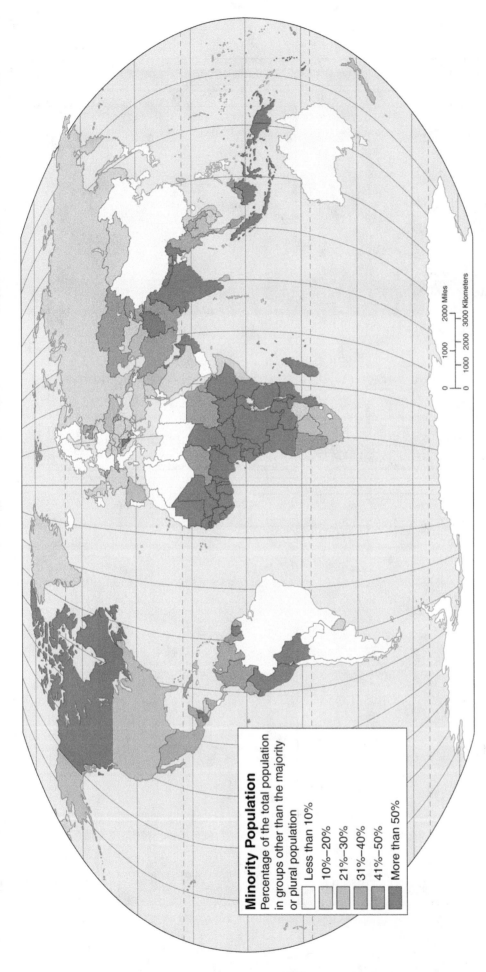

Minority Population

Percentage of the total population in groups other than the majority or plural population

- Less than 10%
- 10%–20%
- 21%–30%
- 31%–40%
- 41%–50%
- More than 50%

The presence of minority ethnic, national, or racial groups within a country's population can add a vibrant and dynamic mix to the whole. Plural societies with a high degree of cultural and ethnic diversity should, according to some social theorists, be among the world's most healthy. Unfortunately, the reality of the situation is quite different from theory or expectation. The presence of significant minority populations played an important role in the disintegration of the U.S.S.R.; the continuing existence of minority populations within the new states formed from former Soviet republics threatens the viability and stability of those young political units. In Africa, national boundaries were drawn by colonial powers without regard for the geographical distribution of ethnic groups, and the continuing tribal conflicts that have resulted hamper both economic and political development. Even in the most highly developed regions of the world, the presence of minority ethnic populations poses significant problems: witness the separatist movement in Canada, driven by the desire of some French-Canadians to be independent of the English majority, and the continuing ethnic conflict between Flemish-speaking and Walloon-speaking Belgians. This map, by arraying states on a scale of homogeneity to heterogeneity, indicates areas of existing and potential social and political strife.

Map 39 Linguistic Diversity

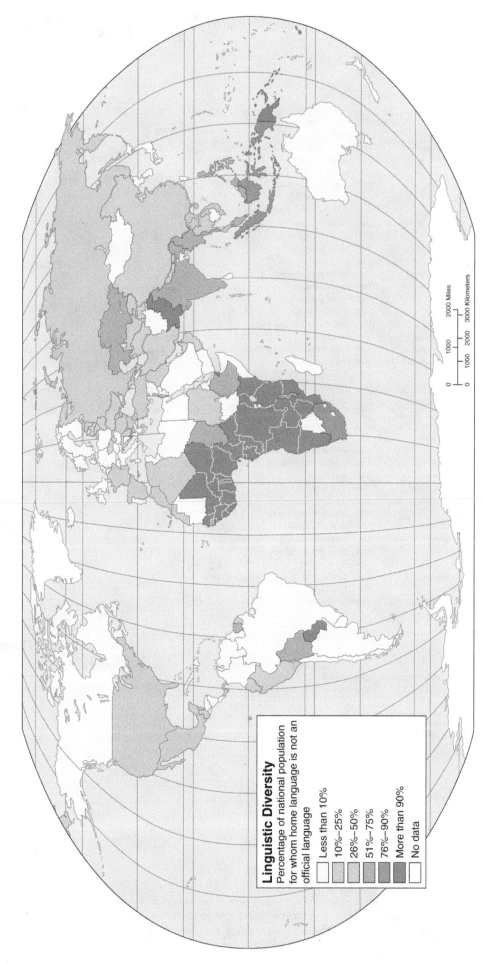

Linguistic Diversity
Percentage of national population for whom home language is not an official language

- Less than 10%
- 10%–25%
- 26%–50%
- 51%–75%
- 76%–90%
- More than 90%
- No data

Of the world's approximately 6,000 languages, fewer than 100 are official languages, those designated by a country as the language of government, commerce, education, and information. This means that for much of the world's population, the language that is spoken in the home is different from the official language of the country of residence. The world's former colonial areas in Middle and South America, Africa, and South and Southeast Asia stand out on the map as regions in which there is significant disparity between home languages and official languages. To complicate matters further, for most of the world's population, the primary international languages of trade and tourism (French and English) are neither home nor official languages. China is a special case, as the official language is the written form of Chinese while several spoken Chinese dialects (such as Mandarin and Cantonese, most of them mutually unintelligible) are recognized as official languages. The formal language of government and business is Mandarin.

Map 40   International Conflicts in the Post–World War II World

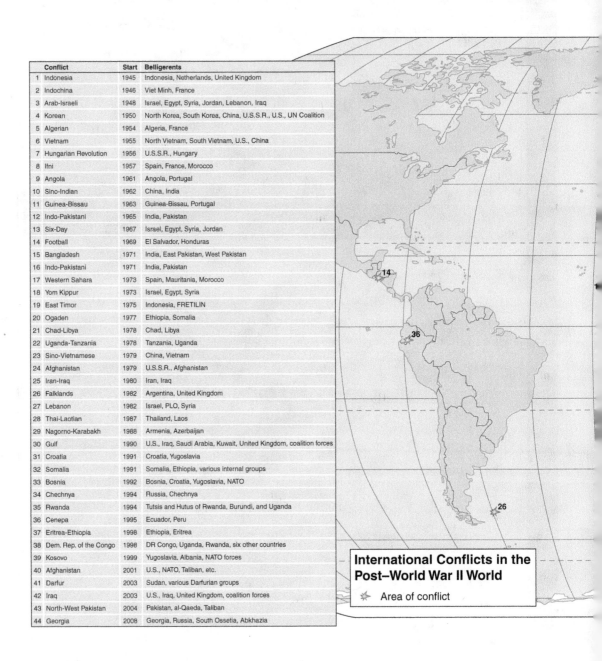

	Conflict	Start	Belligerents
1	Indonesia	1945	Indonesia, Netherlands, United Kingdom
2	Indochina	1946	Viet Minh, France
3	Arab-Israeli	1948	Israel, Egypt, Syria, Jordan, Lebanon, Iraq
4	Korean	1950	North Korea, South Korea, China, U.S.S.R., U.S., UN Coalition
5	Algerian	1954	Algeria, France
6	Vietnam	1955	North Vietnam, South Vietnam, U.S., China
7	Hungarian Revolution	1956	U.S.S.R., Hungary
8	Ifni	1957	Spain, France, Morocco
9	Angola	1961	Angola, Portugal
10	Sino-Indian	1962	China, India
11	Guinea-Bissau	1963	Guinea-Bissau, Portugal
12	Indo-Pakistani	1965	India, Pakistan
13	Six-Day	1967	Israel, Egypt, Syria, Jordan
14	Football	1969	El Salvador, Honduras
15	Bangladesh	1971	India, East Pakistan, West Pakistan
16	Indo-Pakistani	1971	India, Pakistan
17	Western Sahara	1973	Spain, Mauritania, Morocco
18	Yom Kippur	1973	Israel, Egypt, Syria
19	East Timor	1975	Indonesia, FRETILIN
20	Ogaden	1977	Ethiopia, Somalia
21	Chad-Libya	1978	Chad, Libya
22	Uganda-Tanzania	1978	Tanzania, Uganda
23	Sino-Vietnamese	1979	China, Vietnam
24	Afghanistan	1979	U.S.S.R., Afghanistan
25	Iran-Iraq	1980	Iran, Iraq
26	Falklands	1982	Argentina, United Kingdom
27	Lebanon	1982	Israel, PLO, Syria
28	Thai-Laotian	1987	Thailand, Laos
29	Nagorno-Karabakh	1988	Armenia, Azerbaijan
30	Gulf	1990	U.S., Iraq, Saudi Arabia, Kuwait, United Kingdom, coalition forces
31	Croatia	1991	Croatia, Yugoslavia
32	Somalia	1991	Somalia, Ethiopia, various internal groups
33	Bosnia	1992	Bosnia, Croatia, Yugoslavia, NATO
34	Chechnya	1994	Russia, Chechnya
35	Rwanda	1994	Tutsis and Hutus of Rwanda, Burundi, and Uganda
36	Cenepa	1995	Ecuador, Peru
37	Eritrea-Ethiopia	1998	Ethiopia, Eritrea
38	Dem. Rep. of the Congo	1998	DR Congo, Uganda, Rwanda, six other countries
39	Kosovo	1999	Yugoslavia, Albania, NATO forces
40	Afghanistan	2001	U.S., NATO, Taliban, etc.
41	Darfur	2003	Sudan, various Darfurian groups
42	Iraq	2003	U.S., Iraq, United Kingdom, coalition forces
43	North-West Pakistan	2004	Pakistan, al-Qaeda, Taliban
44	Georgia	2008	Georgia, Russia, South Ossetia, Abkhazia

International Conflicts in the Post–World War II World

✳ Area of conflict

The Korean War and the Vietnam War dominated the post–World War II period in terms of international military conflict. But numerous smaller conflicts have taken place, with fewer numbers of belligerents and with fewer battle and related casualties. These smaller international conflicts have been mostly territorial conflicts, reflecting the continual readjustment of political boundaries and loyalties brought about by the end of colonial empires and the dissolution of the U.S.S.R. Many of these conflicts were not wars in the more traditional sense,

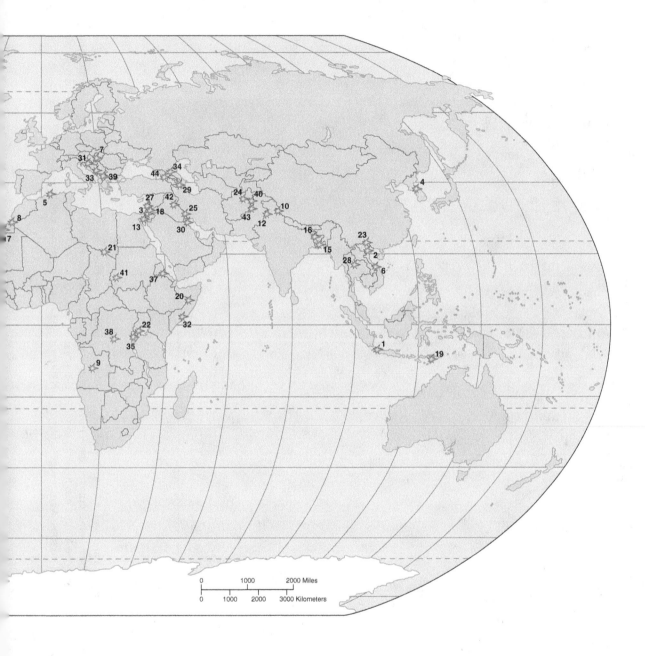

in which two or more countries formally declare war on one another, severing diplomatic ties and devoting their entire national energies to the war effort. Rather, many of these conflicts were and are undeclared wars, sometimes fought between rival groups within the same country with outside support from other countries. The aftermath of the September 11, 2001, terrorist attacks on the United States indicate the dawn of yet another type of international conflict, namely a "war" fought between traditional nation-states and non-state actors.

Map 41 World Refugees: Country of Origin

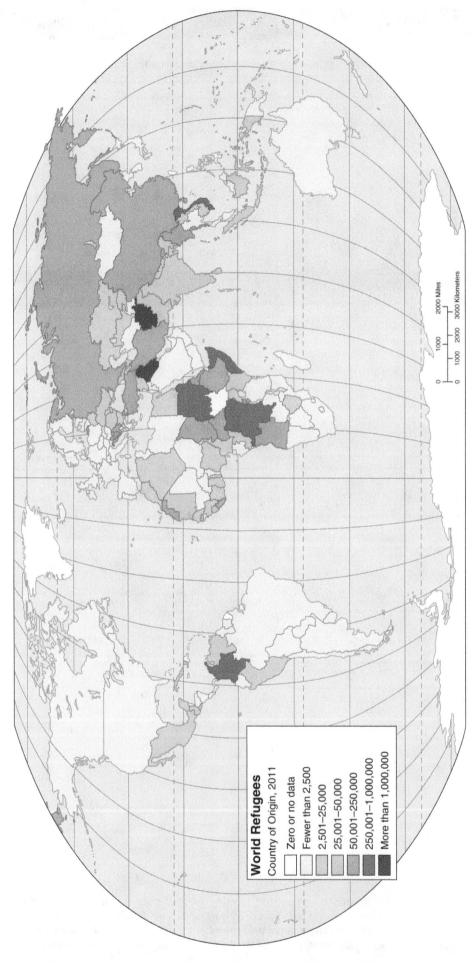

World Refugees
Country of Origin, 2011

- Zero or no data
- Fewer than 2,500
- 2,501–25,000
- 25,001–50,000
- 50,001–250,000
- 250,001–1,000,000
- More than 1,000,000

0   1000   2000 Miles
0   1000   2000   3000 Kilometers

Refugees are persons who have been driven from their homes and seek refuge in another country. While there are many reasons why people flee their home country, the vast majority are fleeing armed conflict. In such cases, there may be a mass exodus from the country involving tens or perhaps hundreds of thousands of persons. Most refugees flee into neighboring countries. Because armed conflict is oftentimes short-lived, the number of refugees in the world changes from year to year, sometimes substantially. The refugee population is recognized by international agencies and is monitored by the United Nations High Commissioner for Refugees (UNHCR).

Map 42 World Refugees: Host Country

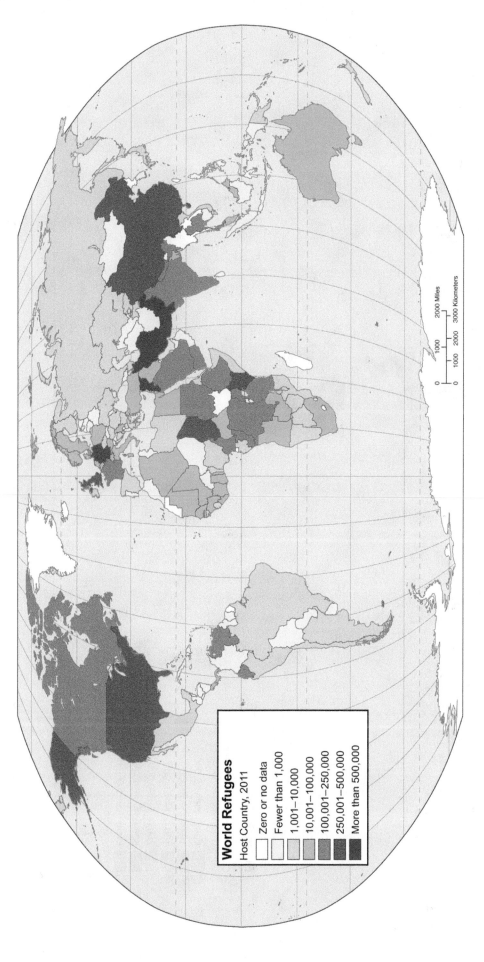

World Refugees

Host Country, 2011

- Zero or no data
- Fewer than 1,000
- 1,001–10,000
- 10,001–100,000
- 100,001–250,000
- 250,001–500,000
- More than 500,000

When refugees flee their country, they most commonly flee to a neighboring country, and not every country is equally equipped to handle such an influx of persons. During such times, international agencies often financially reward the countries of refuge for their willingness to take in externally displaced persons. For most of the host countries, the challenge of hosting a large refugee population is a short-term problem. As we have seen in recent decades, the burden of hosting massive numbers refugees can be a destabilizing force for the country of refuge.

Map 43   Internally Displaced Persons

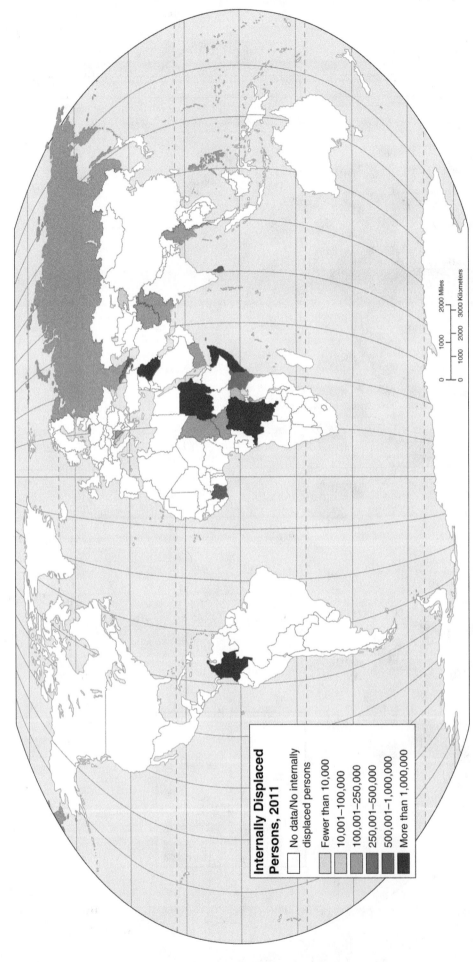

Internally Displaced Persons, 2011

☐ No data/No internally displaced persons

Fewer than 10,000

10,001–100,000

100,001–250,000

250,001–500,000

500,001–1,000,000

More than 1,000,000

0   1000   2000 Miles

0   1000   2000   3000 Kilometers

Internally displaced persons (IDPs) are those who flee their homes because of conflict, persecution, or disaster and seek refuge in another location within their country. With the exception of not leaving their country, they are essentially the same as refugees. International organizations offer the same assistance to internally displaced persons as is provided to refugees. The actual number of IDPs is more difficult to assess than refugee data. Not only do IDP populations fluctuate, there likely are a large number of displaced persons who flee to the larger cities in the countries rather than to the camps established by international relief organizations. In early 2009, the countries with the greatest number of IPDs were Colombia, Iraq, Democratic Republic of the Congo, Somalia, and Sudan.

Map 44   Post–Cold War International Alliances

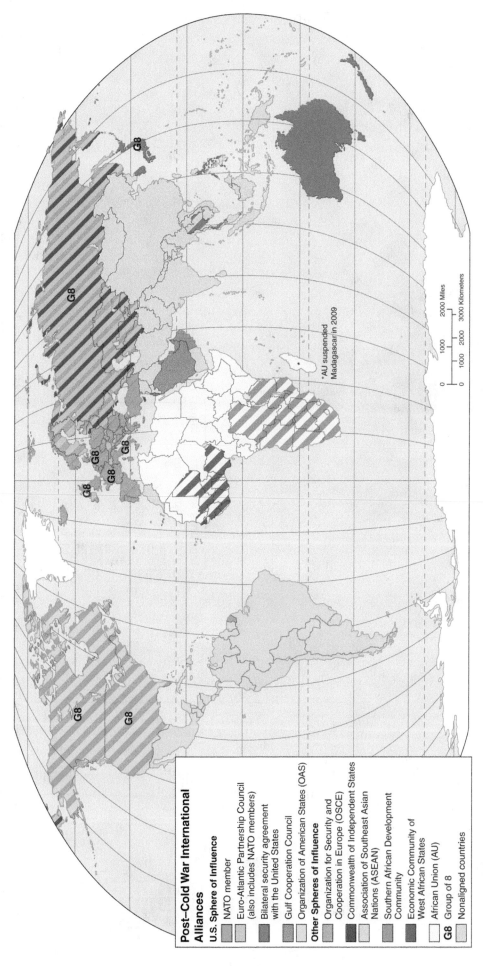

Post–Cold War International Alliances

U.S. Sphere of Influence

- NATO member
- Euro-Atlantic Partnership Council (also includes NATO members)
- Bilateral security agreement with the United States
- Gulf Cooperation Council
- Organization of American States (OAS)

Other Spheres of Influence

- Organization for Security and Cooperation in Europe (OSCE)
- Commonwealth of Independent States
- Association of Southeast Asian Nations (ASEAN)
- Southern African Development Community
- Economic Community of West African States
- African Union (AU)
- **G8** Group of 8
- Nonaligned countries

*AU suspended Madagascar in 2009

0   1000   2000 Miles
0   1000   2000   3000 Kilometers

When the Warsaw Pact dissolved in 1992, the North Atlantic Treaty Organization (NATO) was left as the only major military alliance in the world. Some former Warsaw Pact members (Czechia, Hungary, and Poland) have joined NATO, and others are petitioning for entry. The bipolar division of the world into two major military alliances is over, at least temporarily, leaving the United States alone as the world's dominant political and military power. But other international alliances, such as the Commonwealth of Independent States (including most of the former republics of the U.S.S.R.), will continue to be important. It may well be that during the first few decades of the twenty-first century, economic alliances will begin to overshadow military ones in their relevance for the world's peoples.

Map 45 The Political Geography of a Global Religion: The Islamic World

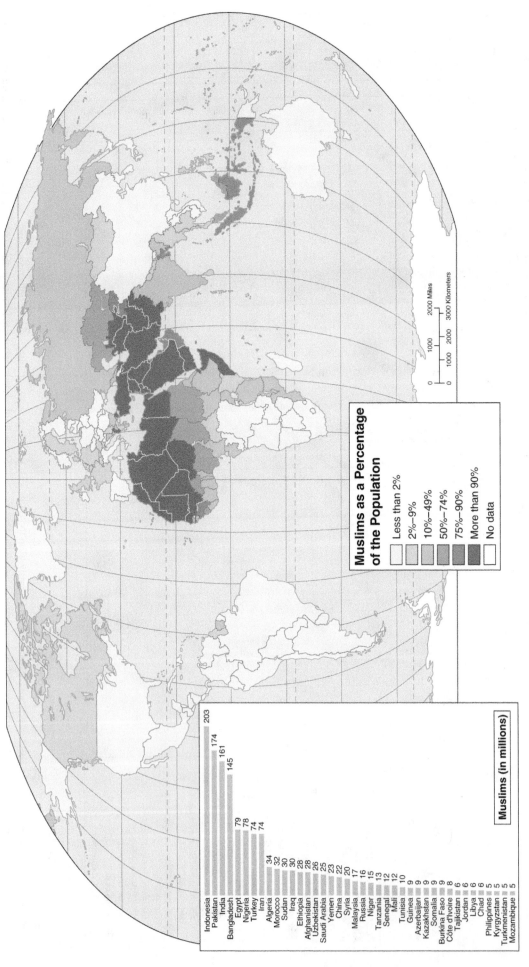

Muslims as a Percentage of the Population

- Less than 2%
- 2%–9%
- 10%–49%
- 50%–74%
- 75%–90%
- More than 90%
- No data

Muslims (in millions)

Country	Muslims
Indonesia	203
Pakistan	174
India	161
Bangladesh	145
Egypt	79
Nigeria	78
Turkey	74
Iran	74
Algeria	34
Morocco	32
Sudan	30
Iraq	30
Ethiopia	28
Afghanistan	28
Uzbekistan	26
Saudi Arabia	25
Yemen	23
China	22
Syria	20
Malaysia	17
Russia	16
Niger	15
Tanzania	13
Senegal	12
Mali	12
Tunisia	10
Guinea	9
Azerbaijan	9
Kazakhstan	9
Somalia	9
Burkina Faso	9
Côte d'Ivoire	8
Tajikistan	6
Jordan	6
Libya	6
Chad	6
Philippines	5
Kyrgyzstan	5
Turkmenistan	5
Mozambique	5

Islam, as a religion, does not promote conflict. The term *jihad*, often mistranslated to mean "holy war," in fact refers to the struggle to find God and to promote the faith. In spite of the beneficent nature of Islamic teachings, the tensions between Muslims and adherents of other faiths often flare into warfare. A comparison of this map with the map of international conflict will show a disproportionate number of wars in that portion of the world where Muslims are either majority or significant minority populations. The reasons for this are based more in the nature of government, culture, and social structure than in the tenets of the faith of Islam. Nevertheless, the spatial correlations cannot be ignored. Similarly, terrorist incidents falling considerably short of open armed warfare are spatially consistent with the distribution of Islam and even more consistent with the presence of Islamic fundamentalism or "Islamism," which tends to be less tolerant and more aggressive than the mainstream of the religion. Terrorism is also consistent with those areas where the legacy of colonialism or the persistent presence of non-Islamic cultures intrudes into the Islamic world.

Map 46   Countries with Nuclear Weapons

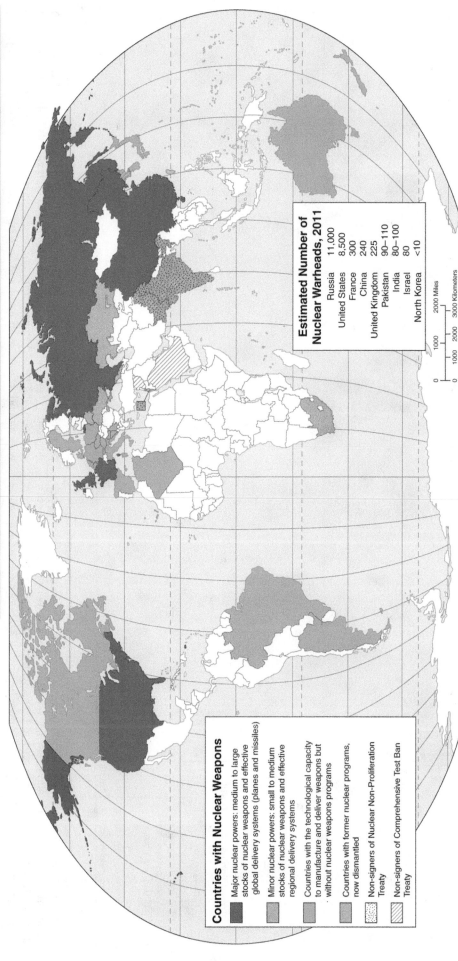

Countries with Nuclear Weapons

- Major nuclear powers: medium to large stocks of nuclear weapons and effective global delivery systems (planes and missiles)
- Minor nuclear powers: small to medium stocks of nuclear weapons and effective regional delivery systems
- Countries with the technological capacity to manufacture and deliver weapons but without nuclear weapons programs
- Countries with former nuclear programs, now dismantled
- Non-signers of Nuclear Non-Proliferation Treaty
- Non-signers of Comprehensive Test Ban Treaty

Estimated Number of Nuclear Warheads, 2011

Russia	11,000
United States	8,500
France	300
China	240
United Kingdom	225
Pakistan	90–110
India	80–100
Israel	80
North Korea	<10

Since 1980, the number of countries possessing the capacity to manufacture and deliver nuclear weapons has grown dramatically, increasing the chances of accidental or intentional nuclear exchanges. In addition to the traditional nuclear powers of the United States, Russia, China, the United Kingdom, and France, must now be added Israel, India, and Pakistan as countries that, without possessing the large stocks of weapons of the major powers, nor the extensive delivery systems of the United States and Russia, still have effective regional (and possibly global) delivery systems and medium stocks of warheads. Countries such as Kazakhstan, Ukraine, Georgia, and Belarus that were created out of what had been the U.S.S.R. did have some nuclear capacity in the 1991–1995 period but have since had all nuclear weapons removed from their territories. North Korea has recently announced the re-suspension of its nuclear weapons programs, although it may possess a small stock of nuclear warheads along with the capacity to deliver those weapons regionally. Iran has announced nuclear ambitions and recently tested delivery systems. Until the overthrow of the Baathist regime of Saddam Hussein in 2003, Iraq also had nuclear ambitions. The proliferation of nuclear states threatens global security, and the objective of the Nuclear Non-Proliferation Treaty was to reduce the chances for expanding nuclear arsenals worldwide. This treaty has been partially successful in that a number of countries in the developed world certainly have the capacity to manufacture and deliver nuclear weapons but have chosen not to do so. These countries include Canada, European countries other than the United Kingdom and France, South Korea, Japan, Australia, and New Zealand, and Brazil and Argentina in South America. On the other side of the coin, the still-possible intent of North Korea to emerge as a nuclear power may force countries such as South Korea and Japan to re-think their positions as non-nuclear countries.

Map 47   Size of Armed Forces

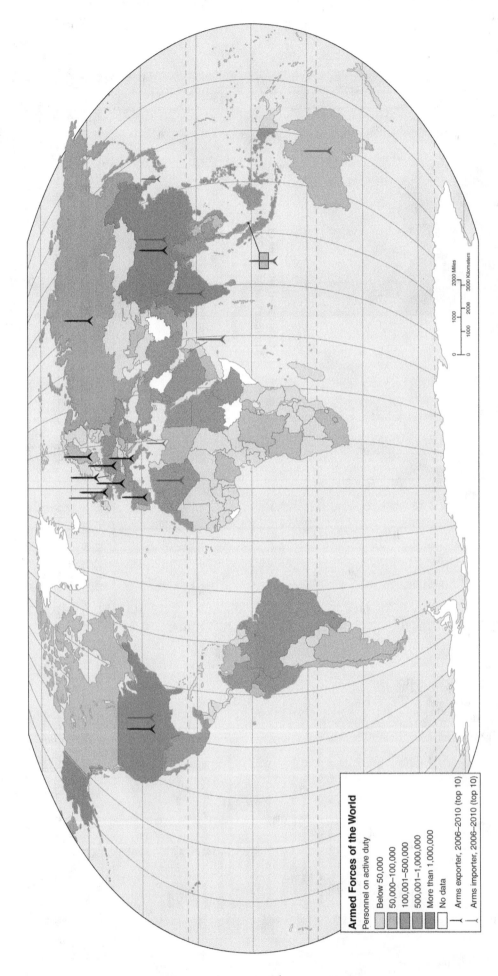

Armed Forces of the World

Personnel on active duty

- Below 50,000
- 50,000–100,000
- 100,001–500,000
- 500,001–1,000,000
- More than 1,000,000
- No data

⊢ Arms exporter, 2006–2010 (top 10)
⊢ Arms importer, 2006–2010 (top 10)

While the size of a country's armed forces is still an indicator of national power on the international scene, it is no longer as important as it once was. The increasing high technology of military hardware allows smaller numbers of military personnel to be more effective. There are some countries, such as China, with massive numbers of military personnel but with relatively limited military power because of a lack of modern weaponry. Additionally, the use of rapid transportation allows personnel to be deployed about the globe or any region of it quickly; this also increases the effectiveness of highly trained and well-armed smaller military units. Nevertheless, the world is still a long way from the predicted "push-button warfare" that many experts have long anticipated. Indeed, the pattern of the last few years has been for most military conflicts to involve ground troops engaged in fairly traditional patterns of operation. Even with its high-tech "unmanned" weaponry, the United States carries out most of its military operations during wartime with ground infantry, with naval and air support, using conventional weaponry. Thus, while the size of a country's armed forces may not be as important as it once was, it is still a major factor in measuring the ability of nations to engage successfully in armed conflict.

Map 48 Military Expenditures as a Percentage of Gross National Product

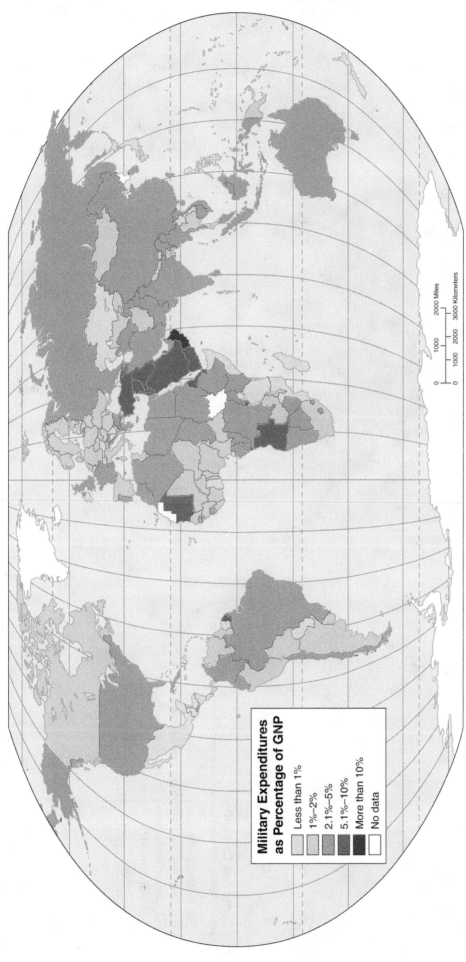

Military Expenditures as Percentage of GNP

- Less than 1%
- 1%–2%
- 2.1%–5%
- 5.1%–10%
- More than 10%
- No data

0   1000   2000 Miles

0   1000 2000 3000 Kilometers

Many countries devote a significant proportion of their total central governmental expenditures to defense: weapons, personnel, and research and development of military hardware. A glance at the map reveals that there are a number of regions in which defense expenditures are particularly high, reflecting the degree of past and present political tension between countries. The clearest example is the Middle East. The steady increase in military expenditures by developing countries is one of the most alarming (and least well-known) worldwide defense issues. Where the end of the Cold War has meant a substantial

reduction of military expenditures for the countries in North America and Europe and for Russia, in many of the world's developing countries military expenditures have risen between 15 percent and 20 percent per year for the past few years, averaging out to 7.5 percent per year for the past quarter-century. Even though many developing countries still spend less than 5 percent of their gross national product on defense, these funds could be put to different uses in such human development areas as housing, land reform, health care, and education.

Map 49   Abuse of Public Trust

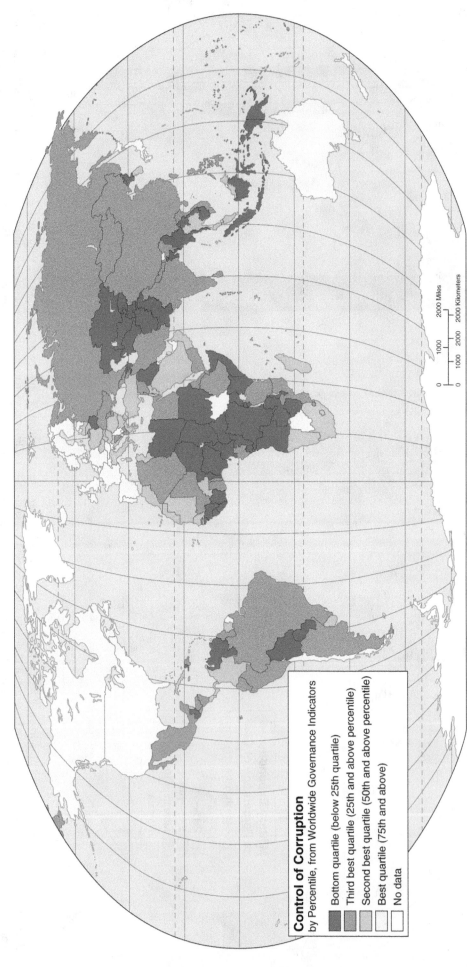

Control of Corruption
by Percentile, from Worldwide Governance Indicators

- Bottom quartile (below 25th quartile)
- Third best quartile (25th and above percentile)
- Second best quartile (50th and above percentile)
- Best quartile (75th and above)
- No data

0   1000   2000 Miles

0   1000   2000   2000 Kilometers

Abusing the public trust is simply another way of saying "corruption in government." In many parts of the world, corruption in the government is not an aberration but a way of life. Normally, although not always, governmental corruption is an indication of a weak and ineffective government, one that negatively affects such public welfare issues as public health, sanitation, education, and the provision of social services. It also tends to impact the cost of doing business and, thereby, drives away the foreign capital so badly needed in many African and Asian countries for economic development. Corruption is not automatic in poor countries, nor are rich countries free from it. But there is a general correlation between abuse of the public trust and lower levels of per capita income—excepting such countries as the Baltic states and Chile that have reached high standards of governance without joining the ranks of the wealthy countries. Studies by the World Bank have shown that countries that address issues of corruption and clean up the operations of their governments increase national incomes as much as four or five times. In those countries striving to attain governments that function according to a rule of law—rather than a rule of abusing the public trust—such important demographic measures as child mortality drop by as much as 75 percent. Clearly, good government and good business and higher incomes and better living conditions for the general public all go hand in hand.

Map 50 The Perception of Corruption

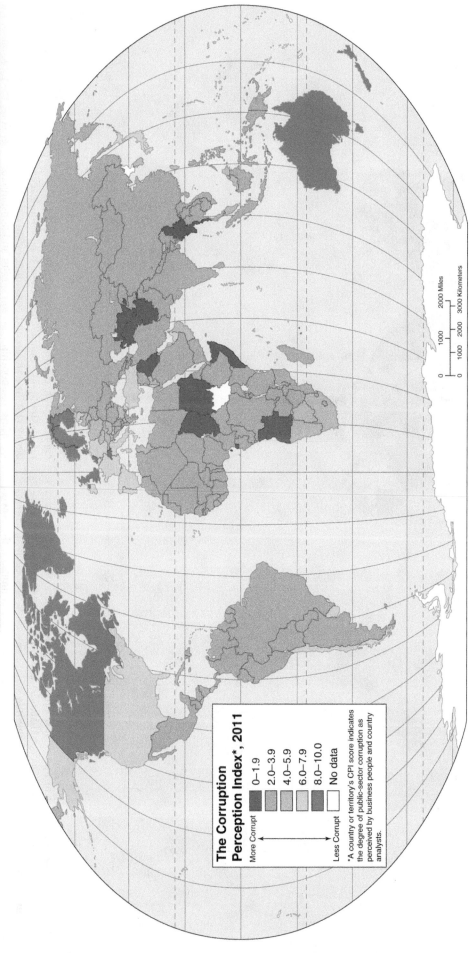

The Corruption Perception Index*, 2011

More Corrupt ← → Less Corrupt

- 0–1.9
- 2.0–3.9
- 4.0–5.9
- 6.0–7.9
- 8.0–10.0
- No data

*A country or territory's CPI score indicates the degree of public-sector corruption as perceived by business people and country analysts.

0 1000 2000 Miles
0 1000 2000 3000 Kilometers

A country's Corruption Perception Index is based on analyses by business executives who work with a country's government or whose company does business within the country evaluated; in addition, the CPI is contributed to by analysts from press sources, international organizations, and others whose jobs are involved in the gathering of intelligence on foreign areas. A glance at the map tells us things that we might have easily intuited: Iraq, Afghanistan, Sudan, Somalia, Myanmar, and other disrupted or failed states or military dictatorships fall into the range of "more corrupt." At the same time, Northern and Western European governments with stable parliamentary democracies and high standards of living are, as we might expect, among the least corrupt. But why should the United States fall into a middle-range category, along with Mediterranean, Central, and Eastern European countries on the CPI scale? Have U.S. governmental actions and/or business dealings over the last few years reduced our international reputation? It would be tempting to think so. Non-U.S. analysts are not stupid, and when such large percentages of American tax dollars devoted to the Iraq war end up in either American or Iraqi private hands, without discernible benefit, that fact registers with those analysts. The great Scottish poet Robert Burns wrote "Oh, would some Power the gift give us, to see ourselves as others see us" (translated from the Scottish). This may not be a bad plea for American officials to make. It is simply not good enough, in a country that supposedly governs itself by the rule of law, to say, "Well, we're not seen as corrupt as Somalia or Myanmar." It would also be self-defeating to dismiss these perceptions as unimportant. How a country is seen by others is often a very important factor in how that country is dealt with by others.

-59-

Map 51 Political and Civil Liberties

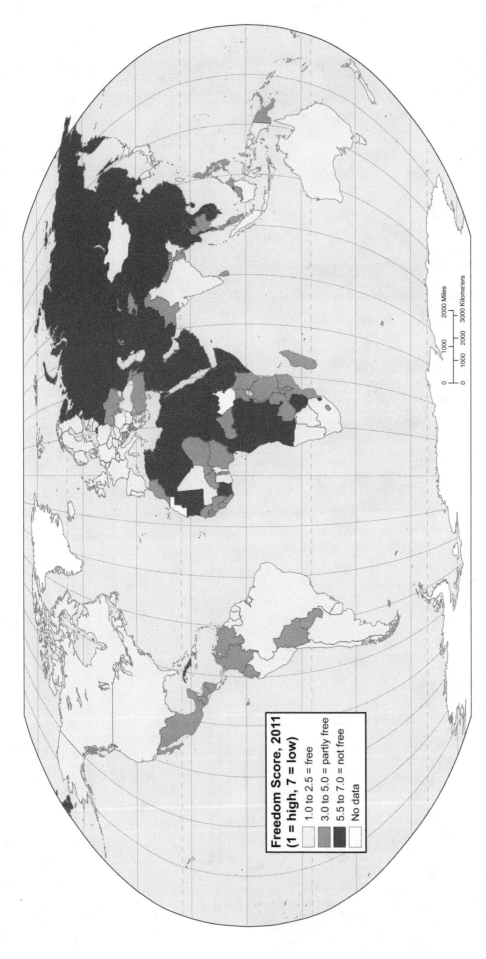

**Freedom Score, 2011
(1 = high, 7 = low)**
- 1.0 to 2.5 = free
- 3.0 to 5.0 = partly free
- 5.5 to 7.0 = not free
- No data

0   1000   2000 Miles
0   1000   2000   3000 Kilometers

Although measures of political and civil liberty are somewhat difficult to obtain and assess, there are some generally accepted standards that can be evaluated: open elections and competitive political parties, the rule of law, freedoms of speech and press, judicial systems separate from other branches of government, and limits on the power of elected or appointed governmental officials. Interestingly, there appear to be correlations between "degrees of freedom" and such other characteristics of a state as per capita wealth, environmental quality, and healthy economic growth—characteristics that may be mutually contradictory. There is no empirical evidence of a causal link between democratic institutions and consumption; on the other hand, there is clear evidence of a positive relationship between wealth and consumption. Therefore, the three variables are closely correlated and should be used in assessing the nature of the state in any part of the world.

Map 52 Human Rights Abuse

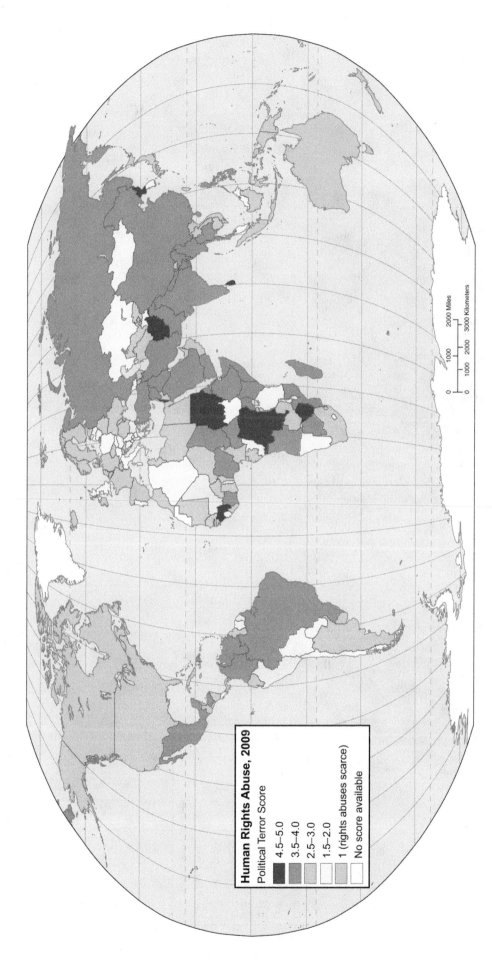

Human Rights Abuse, 2009

Political Terror Score

- 4.5–5.0
- 3.5–4.0
- 2.5–3.0
- 1.5–2.0
- 1 (rights abuses scarce)
- No score available

The Political Terror Score measures levels of political violence and terror that a country experiences in a particular year. The score is calculated using data from the U.S. State Department Country Reports on Human Rights and yearly country reports from Amnesty International. At the lowest end of the scale, torture or political murder are scarce and the rule of law dominates. Higher scores indicate increasing pervasiveness of human rights abuses. At the highest level, a country's entire population is affected by political terror, genocide, or other crimes against humanity. Countries with high scores typically are dictatorships or totalitarian states whose leaders oftentimes carry out political terror through secret police forces or death squads. In many politically unstable countries, the Political Terror Scale may fluctuate from year to year. In the early 2000s countries like Liberia, Colombia, and Rwanda ranked much higher than in 2009. Conversely, Central African Republic, Thailand, and Kenya have seen increases in the score since the early 2000s. Afghanistan, Democratic Republic of the Congo, Guinea, and Zimbabwe have had very high scores since the turn of the century.

Map 53 Women's Rights

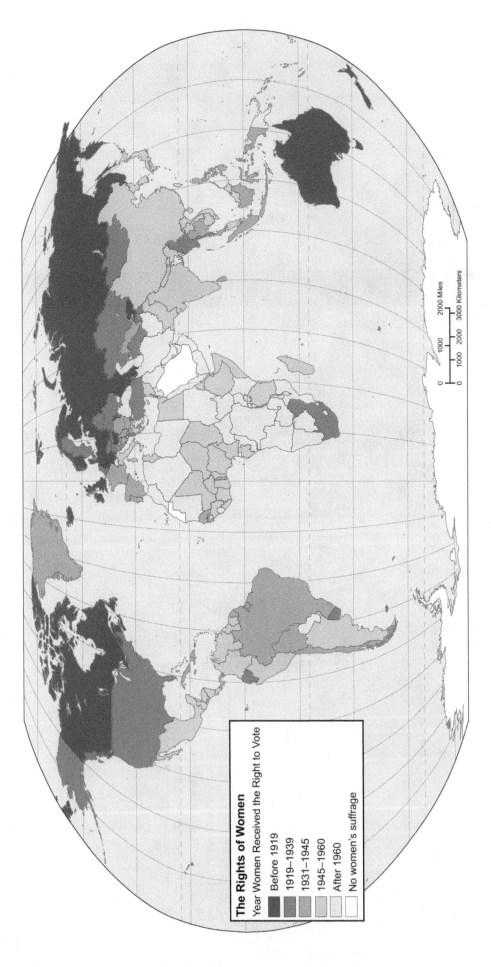

The Rights of Women

Year Women Received the Right to Vote

- Before 1919
- 1919–1939
- 1931–1945
- 1945–1960
- After 1960
- No women's suffrage

0   1000   2000 Miles

0   1000   2000   3000 Kilometers

The "rights" referred to in this map refer primarily to the right to vote. But where women have the right to vote in free elections, the other fundamental rights tend to become available as well: the right to own property, the right to an education, the right to leave a domestic alliance without fear of retribution, or the right to be treated as a human being rather than property. But the time lag between women receiving the right to vote and their attainment of other fundamental human rights does not occur immediately or, in many cases, even relatively quickly. On the map, the most recent countries to grant suffrage to women are in Africa and Southwest Asia. In these regions, women still do not have access to many of the basic rights of what we would consider to be a civilized life. And, of course, there are still areas where women cannot vote: Kuwait, for example. Neither men nor women are allowed to vote in Brunei, Saudi Arabia, United Arab Emirates, or Western Sahara.

-62-

Map 54 Capital Punishment

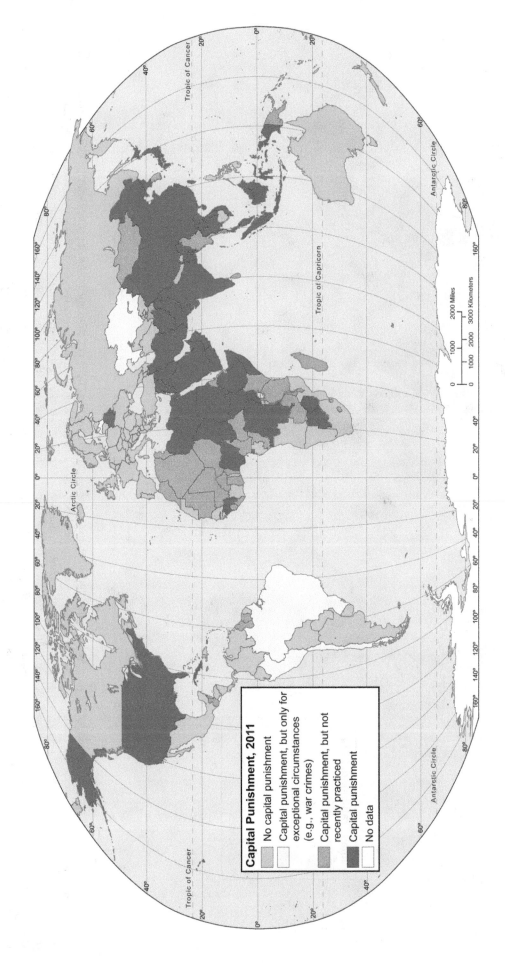

Capital Punishment, 2011

- No capital punishment
- Capital punishment, but only for exceptional circumstances (e.g., war crimes)
- Capital punishment, but not recently practiced
- Capital punishment
- No data

The most basic human right is life itself. More than half the countries of the world have abolished capital punishment by law or in practice. In some of these countries, capital punishment remains on the books, but no one has been executed in so long that in practice, capital punishment can be considered abolished. A few countries retain capital punishment only for crimes committed in extraordinary circumstances, such as military law. About three countries per year have abolished capital punishment in the last decade. Some states in the United States retain capital punishment; in others it has been abolished.

Map 55   Human Trafficking

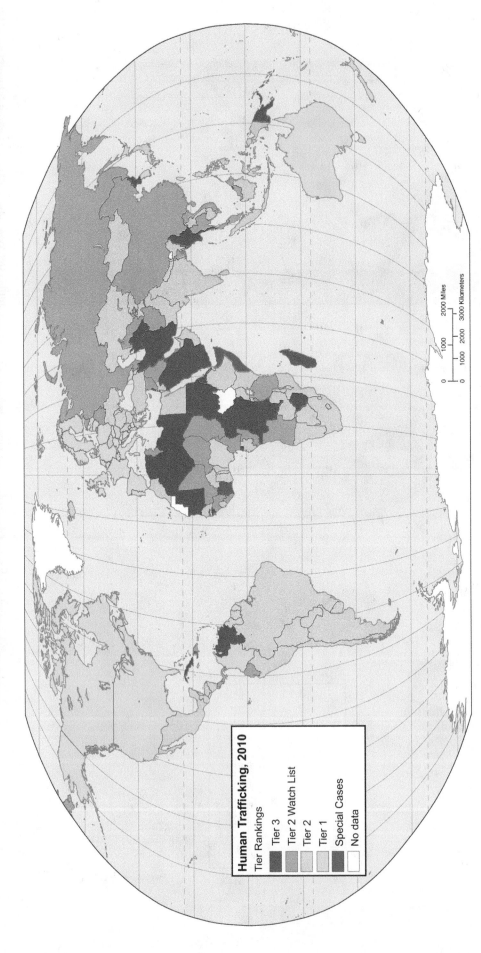

Human Trafficking, 2010

Tier Rankings

- Tier 3
- Tier 2 Watch List
- Tier 2
- Tier 1
- Special Cases
- No data

0   1000   2000 Miles
0   1000   2000   3000 Kilometers

Human trafficking is trade of human beings for the purposes of compelling them to service against their will. The term is broad and can include many activities, such as forced labor, sex trafficking, bonded labor (when a person uses services to pay off a loan), involuntary domestic servitude, forced child labor, child soldiers, and child sex trafficking. In 2000, the United Nations adopted the Protocol to Prevent, Suppress and Punish Trafficking in Persons, Especially Women and Children in an attempt to prevent and combat trafficking in persons. To date, 117 countries have adopted the protocol. That same year the United States passed the Victims of Trafficking and Violence Protection Act, which was reauthorized in 2003 as the Trafficking Victims Protection Act (TVPA). The U.S. State Department ranks the countries of the world based on the degree to which they meet standards of TVPA and places the countries

into three tiers. Tier 1 countries are those that comply with the TVPA minimum standards. Tier 2 countries do not fully comply with the TVPA's minimum standards, but are making significant efforts to bring themselves into compliance with those standards. Tier 3 countries do not fully comply with the minimum standards and are not making significant efforts to do so. The State Department places some of the Tier 2 countries on a Watch List. In these countries, the absolute number of victims of severe forms of trafficking is very significant or is significantly increasing, or there is a failure to provide evidence of increasing efforts to combat severe forms of trafficking in persons from the previous year. Three countries have been identified as "Special Cases"—countries without government infrastructure to effectively prevent human trafficking, either because of civil war (Somalia and Côte d'Ivoire) or natural disaster (Haiti).

Map 56 Flashpoints 2012

Map 56a

Fewer than 100
101–500
501–1,000
1,001–2,000
2,001–4,000
More than 4,000

Drug-Related Homicides 2006–2012

Mexico: Although drug-related crime has been present in Mexico for decades, the last few years have seen a dramatic increase in narco-related violence. The surge in violence came as a result of Mexican drug cartels supplanting Colombian drug cartels for control of illegal drug trafficking into the United States. These cartels have become heavily armed and not only are capable of battling government troops, but also have targeted police officers, politicians, journalists, and entertainers for kidnapping and murder. Although there have been many drug cartels operating in Mexico, power recently has begun to consolidate among those operating in the cities of Ciudad Juaréz and Tijuana as well as the states of Michoacán, Sinaloa, and Tamaulipas. Mexico ranks in the top ten most dangerous countries for journalists to work in and, in 2006, it ranked behind only Iraq for this dubious honor. The Mexican newspaper *Reforma* estimates that more than 27,000 persons died in drug-related violence between 2006 and 2010. All of this presents problems both for Mexico and for the United States. At nearly 2,000 miles in length, the border between Mexico and the United States is the most frequently crossed international border in the world, and border cities have been the most violent. Given the likelihood of continued demand for foreign narcotics in the United States into the future, narco-related violence, and the ever-increasing attention to U.S.-Mexican border issues, Mexico will likely continue to be a flashpoint for the foreseeable future.

Map 56c

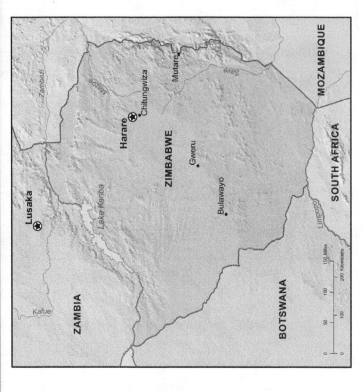

Map 56b

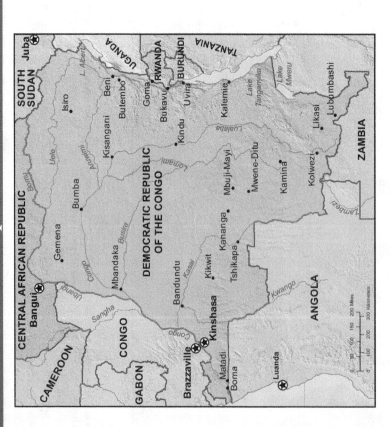

Dem. Rep. Congo: The war in the Democratic Republic of the Congo (formerly Zaire) has preoccupied United Nations and African diplomats since 1999. Troops from Zimbabwe, Angola, Sudan, Chad, and Namibia joined with the president of the Congo, Laurent Kabila, against his former allies Rwanda, Burundi, and Uganda, which each backed several separate Congolese rebel groups. The origins of the conflict lie in the overthrow of longtime dictator Mobutu Sese Seko by Kabila's army in 1997 after a year of civil war. Kabila's failure to call elections or stabilize the country's economy led to further rounds of rebellion in the huge but fractious nation—rebellion supported by the economic and military assistance of neighboring Rwanda, Burundi, and Uganda. After Kabila's assassination in 2001 and the succession of his son, Joseph, to the presidency, accord seemed to have been reached, and the various conflicting parties agreed to withdraw troops in 2002. But in early 2003, new fighting flared along the country's eastern border, threatening a new and broadened war and the addition of more deaths to the 3.9 million since 1998. Diplomats called the conflict "Africa's first world war." With fighting continuing in the east, fears are that the Congo conflict could destabilize the entire southern half of the continent, leading to massive refugee flows and abject poverty.

Zimbabwe: When Zimbabwe achieved independence in 1980, Robert Mugabe assumed leadership of the country—a position he has held ever since. In 2000, Mugabe instituted a highly controversial land reform program, appropriating white-owned farms and giving them to tribal leaders. A country that had Africa's highest literacy rate and was one of the continent's leaders in agricultural production, Zimbabwe quickly deteriorated into conditions of abject poverty and famine. Hyperinflation was rampant in the early 2000s, peaking at a rate of over 11 million percent and bringing the country to the brink of economic collapse. Elections held in 2008 left Mugabe's chief rival, Morgan Tsvangirai, with the largest number of votes, but he did not receive enough votes to prevent a run-off election. Before that election could be held, Tsvangirai withdrew from the race, claiming (quite probably with some justification) that his supporters had been threatened with beatings, imprisonment, murder, and torture and that he did not wish to subject them to those dangers. In 2009, Tsvangirai was sworn in as prime minister, part of a power-sharing agreement with Mugabe—at least on paper—in which he and Mugabe would combine their forces to try to lead the country out of its economic chaos and medical crisis created by a cholera epidemic. Although Zimbabwe does not have the tribal conflicts that beset so many African nations (most Zimbabweans are Shona), the feelings between the supporters of the two rival political factions run deeply enough that, if the power-sharing arrangement does not work and the economy continues to deteriorate, the country could be plunged into a civil war.

Map 56d

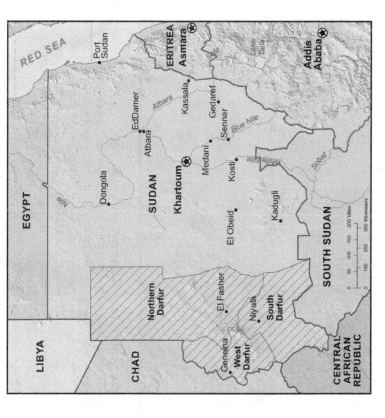

Map 56e

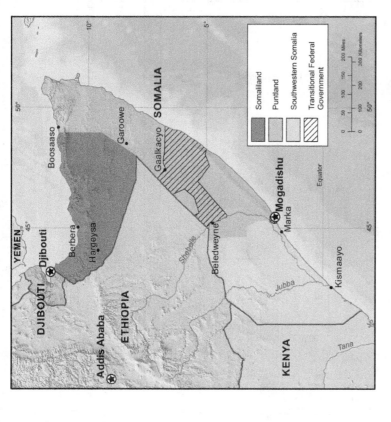

Sudan and the Darfur Region: Since Sudan achieved independence in 1956, military regimes favoring Islamic-oriented governments have dominated national politics. These regimes have embroiled the country in a civil war for nearly all of the past half-century. These wars have been rooted in the attempts of northern economic, political, and social interests dominated by Muslims to control territories occupied by non-Muslim, non-Arab southern Sudanese, such as the Dinka tribal groups. Since 1983, war and famine have resulted in more than 2 million deaths and over 4 million people displaced. The current regime is a mixture of military elite and an Islamist party that came to power in a 1989 coup. After more than five decades of conflict with the ruling north, South Sudan gained its independence in 2011. However, conflicts have continued to persist in the three Darfur provinces of western Sudan adjacent to the border with Chad and the Central African Republic, where government-backed Muslim militia have attacked and killed tens of thousands of non-Muslim tribal peoples. In 2005 and 2006, areas of conflict spilled over the borders of Sudan to involve both Chad and the Central African Republic. The Darfur region is relatively water-rich and forested in a country that is chiefly desert and is therefore desired by Muslim pastoral groups from the north for settlement purposes. Another cease-fire was agreed to in 2010, but it was short-lived; the Sudanese army launched raids and air strikes later in the year.

Somalia: With the ouster of the government led by Mohamed Said Barre in January 1991, turmoil, factional fighting, and anarchy have followed in Somalia, with several separate governments arising in different parts of the country. The northern clans declared an independent Republic of Somaliland. Although not recognized by any government, it has maintained a stable existence. Puntland, the central portion of Somalia, from the Horn of Africa to the coast of the Indian Ocean and the border with Ethiopia, has been a self-governing autonomous state since 1998. In 2004 a new UN-backed government, the Transitional Federal Government (TFG), was created for the entire country, but the government has not been able to gain effective control. In 2006 and 2007 a push by central government forces, backed up by units of the Ethiopian regular army, succeeded in driving Islamic extremist forces out of the Mogadishu region. However, Ethiopian troops pulled out in 2009, and there is still no unification of the country. In fact, the lack of effective governmental control has led to Somali pirates becoming a major threat to shipping in the Indian Ocean. By any definition, Somalia is a "disordered" or "failed" state, and to make matters worse, prolonged drought in eastern Africa resulted in catastrophic famine in southern Somalia in 2011. Tens of thousands of Somalis had already died by the time the famine was declared.

Map 56f

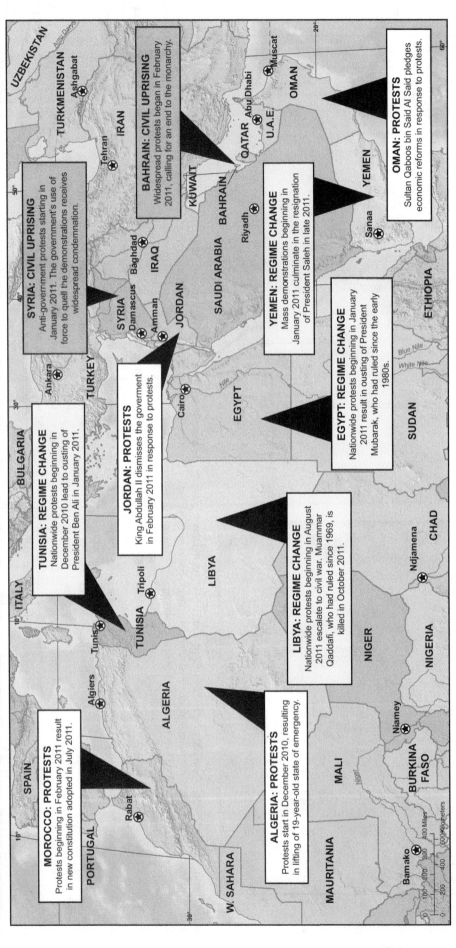

MOROCCO: PROTESTS

Protests beginning in February 2011 result in new constitution adopted in July 2011.

TUNISIA: REGIME CHANGE

Nationwide protests beginning in December 2010 lead to ousting of President Ben Ali in January 2011.

ALGERIA: PROTESTS

Protests start in December 2010, resulting in lifting of 19-year-old state of emergency.

LIBYA: REGIME CHANGE

Nationwide protests beginning in August 2011 escalate to civil war. Muammar Qaddafi, who had ruled since 1969, is killed in October 2011.

JORDAN: PROTESTS

King Abdullah II dismisses the government in February 2011 in response to protests.

SYRIA: CIVIL UPRISING

Anti-government protests starting in January 2011. The government's use of force to quell the demonstrations receives widespread condemnation.

BAHRAIN: CIVIL UPRISING

Widespread protests began in February 2011, calling for an end to the monarchy.

YEMEN: REGIME CHANGE

Mass demonstrations beginning in January 2011 culminate in the resignation of President Saleh in late 2011.

EGYPT: REGIME CHANGE

Nationwide protests beginning in January 2011 result in ousting of President Mubarak, who had ruled since the early 1980s.

OMAN: PROTESTS

Sultan Qaboos bin Said Al Said pledges economic reforms in response to protests.

Uprisings of North Africa and Southwest Asia: Late 2010 and early 2011 saw the beginning of an extraordinary wave of political change and potential change throughout North Africa and Southwest Asia. Referred to sometimes as the "Arab Spring," widespread demonstrations initiated changes in government policies in some countries, toppled regimes in others, and provoked civil war in Libya. The reasons for the uprisings varied to a certain degree by country, but pervasive poverty and dissatisfaction with government regimes—dictatorships in many cases—were largely behind the protests. Throughout the region, wealth and power have been held by a very small number of people. The event that triggered the wave of demonstrations occurred in Tunisia, where a street vendor, Muhammed Bouazizi, set himself on fire in protest of how he had been treated by a local official. Widespread demonstrations and riots followed in the country, ultimately leading to the ousting of long-time president Zine el Abidine Ben Ali. Empowered by the success of the Tunisian protests in ousting their leader, similar protests erupted throughout the region. In Egypt, social media helped facilitate the organization of demonstrations and to spread word beyond the country of the high level of frustration among its citizens. In February 2011, Egyptian president Hosni Mubarak resigned from his 30-year presidency. That same month, armed revolt in Libya sparked civil war. Widespread demonstrations in Syria, Bahrain, and Yemen gained traction later in the year, with protesters calling for the end of the existing governments. The Syrian demonstrations were met with harsh crackdowns by government forces, resulting in thousands of arrests and hundreds of deaths. In other countries, protests were met with quick government concessions. In Jordan, King Abdullah removed the prime minister and his cabinet. In Oman, Sultan Qaboos launched numerous policy changes to promote economic reform. In total, protests and demonstrations occurred in nearly 20 countries. The impacts of what began in late 2010 and early 2011 will be felt for many years to come.

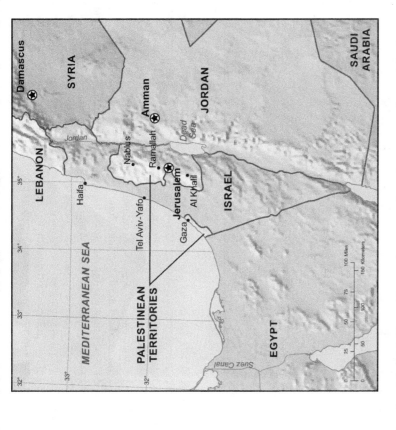

Côte d'Ivoire: Until relatively recently, its close ties to France following independence in 1960 and its development of cocoa production for export (along with significant foreign investment) made Côte d'Ivoire (Ivory Coast) one of the most prosperous of the tropical African states. Since 1999, however, political turmoil has disrupted economic development. In December 1999, a military coup in Côte d'Ivoire overthrew the elected government. In 2000, an election resulted in Laurent Gbagbo assuming the presidency. Another coup, this one a failure, was launched in 2002 with rebel forces claiming the northern half of the country. A unity government was established in 2003 with elections to be held in 2005. Gbagbo held to the presidency, however, and the elections were postponed until 2010. In this election, the country's electoral commission announced that Gbagbo had lost to former prime minister Alassane Ouattara, a result recognized internationally. The Ivorian constitutional council, however, ruled that Gbagbo was the winner. In the months that followed, the country has plunged into civil war. In 2011, Ouattara, with the support of UN and French forces, was able to finally oust Gbagbo from his stronghold in the country's largest city, Abidjan. UN forces will remain in the country until this most recent crisis is finally resolved.

Israel and Its Neighbors: The modern state of Israel was created out of the former British Protectorate of Palestine, inhabited primarily by Muslim Arabs, after World War II. Conflict between Arabs and Israeli Jews has been a constant ever since. Much of the present tension revolves around the West Bank area, not part of the original Israeli state but taken from Jordan, an Arab country, in the Six-Day War of 1967. Many Palestinians had settled this part of Jordan after the creation of Israel and remain as a majority population in the West Bank region today. Israel has established many agricultural settlements within the region since 1967, angering Palestinian Arabs. For Israel, the West Bank is the region of ancient Judea and this region, won in battle, will not be ceded back to Palestinian Arabs without protracted or severe military action. The West Bank, inhabited by nearly 400,000 Israeli settlers and 4 million Palestinians, is also the location of most of the suicide bombings carried out by Islamic militant groups from 2001 to 2009. By early 2008, the Gaza Strip had emerged as the most critical flashpoint in the area. The Israeli government and the Palestinian Authority had agreed to resume peace talks with the goal being a peace agreement by the end of the year. But in late 2008 and early 2009, Israeli troops responded to rocket attacks by Hamas, a leading Palestinian political party, by attacking Gaza in force. In late 2010, talks between Israel and the Palestinians had commenced, but were called off by the end of the year.

Map 56j

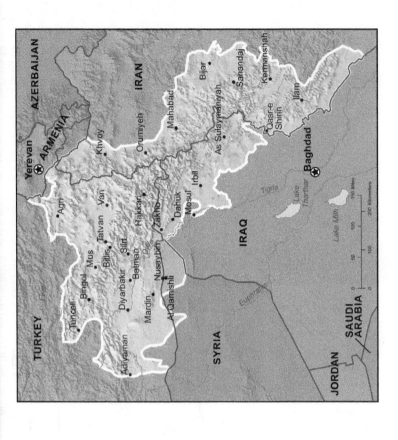

Map 56i

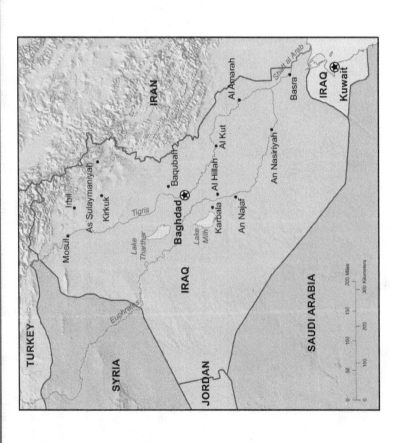

Iraq: Prior to the 1990-1991 invasion of Kuwait by Iraq and the subsequent United Nations coalition's military expulsion of Iraq from its neighbor, Iraq was one of the most prosperous countries in the Middle East and the only one with full capacity to feed itself, even without the vast oil revenues generated by the country's immense reserves. Despite the inefficiencies of the Baathist dictatorship of Saddam Hussein, the country had a solid agricultural base and burgeoning industry. The combination of military adventurism and conflict, in the form of a lengthy war with Iran and the ill-advised invasion of Kuwait, limited further economic development, however. Development was also problematic given the country's internal tensions between Arabic Sunni Muslims and Arabic Shiite Muslims, and between Arabs and Kurds and a few other minority populations in the northern parts of the country. Elections were held in 2009 and a new government was installed in 2010. In 2010, the U.S. ended combat operations with full withdrawal of troops at the end of 2011.

Kurdistan: Where Turkey, Iran, and Iraq meet in the high mountain region of the Tauros and Zagros mountains, a nation of 25 million people exists. This nation is "Kurdistan," but the Kurds, the occupants of this area for over 3,000 years, have no state, and receive much less attention than other stateless nations like the Palestinians. Following the 1991 Gulf War between Iraq and a U.S.-led coalition of European and Arabic states, the United Nations demarcated a Kurdish "Security Zone" in northern Iraq. From 1991 to 2003, the Security Zone was anything but secure as Iraqi militants from the south and Turks from the north infringed on Kurdish territory; and internal militant extremist groups, such as the Kurdish Workers' Party, staged periodic attacks on rival villages. During the 2003 U.S.-led invasion of Iraq that eliminated the Baathist regime of Saddam Hussein, the Kurds played an important role in securing the northern portions of Iraq for the American-British coalition and fought alongside American troops in expelling elements of the Iraqi army from cities like Mosul and Kirkuk. Rich in oil and history, Kurdistan will probably remain as a nation without a state, shared by Iraq, Turkey, and Iran--none of which is likely to give up substantial portions of territory for the establishment of a Kurdish state. In 2011, the portion of northern Iraq under Kurdish control was the most stable of that war-torn country.

Map 56l

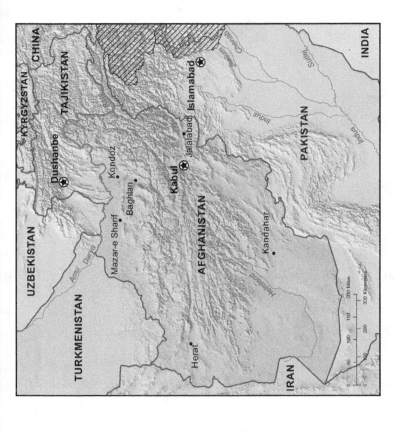

Afghanistan: In the aftermath of the tragic September 11, 2001, terrorist attacks, the United States (backed to varying degrees by its allies) declared a massive and global "war on terrorism," targeting terrorist groups and states that provide "safe harbor" to them. Front and center in this war was the Taliban regime of Islamic extremists that controlled about 95 percent of Afghanistan and harbored the al-Qaeda terrorist network. U.S. and British forces, aided by members of the Northern Alliance of Afghan rebels, expelled the Taliban government in 2002, and in 2003, Hamid Karzai became the first democratically elected president of the country. Despite the imposition of democracy, Afghanistan still is plagued by warlords in remote areas of the country who refuse to recognize the legally constituted government. In addition, significant pockets of resistance from remnants of the former Taliban regime and from al-Qaeda forces are engaged in ongoing military conflict with American and Pakistani troops along the Afghanistan-Pakistan border. Taliban resurgence, particularly based in Pakistan, grew throughout 2008 and into 2009, partly as the result of an ineffective and corrupt central government that, for all practical purposes, controls only the region of the capital city, Kabul. And that control is tenuous. In December 2009, U.S. President Barack Obama ordered an additional 30,000 U.S. military personnel into the country.

Map 56k

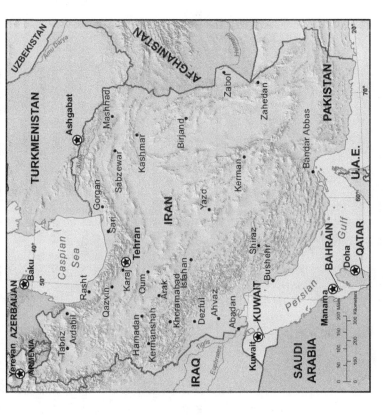

Iran: Iran has been at odds with the United States and Israel since the overthrow of the pro-Western government of the Shah and the installation of a fundamentalist Islamic republic in 1979. The Iranians took a large number of American hostages following the political revolution and held them for over a year. During an eight-year war between Iran and its nearest neighbor, Iraq, the United States provided military aid to Iraq, further straining the relations between Iran and the West. Iran's promise to continue development of nuclear facilities that could lead to the development of nuclear weapons has heightened distrust of Iran in the West. More likely, however, is that once Iran has developed facilities capable of producing weapons-grade plutonium, Israel will carry out the same type of preemptive strikes it has previously used on Iraq and Syria. Iran is a large and important country, poorly understood by the United States. In 2009, hard-line President Mahmoud Ahmadinejad won re-election in a highly contested and controversial vote. Millions of Iranians took to the street to protest, but Supreme Leader Ayatollah Khamenei endorsed Ahmadinejad as the winner and declared the protests illegal. Ahmadinejad has pushed for construction of an atomic power station, declaring production of nuclear fuel to be an "inalienable right." In response, the UN imposed sanctions on Iran in 2010. With an ancient imperial tradition, Iran is the historical core of Shiah Islam (nearly 90 percent of Iranians are Shiite Muslims), and it possesses enormous reserves of oil and natural gas.

Map 56n

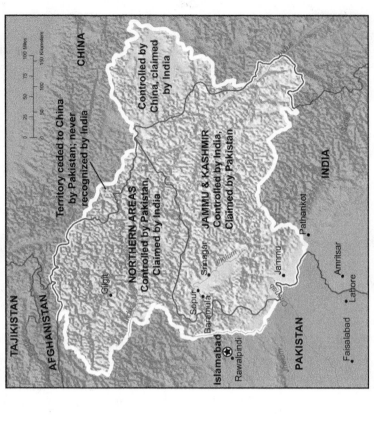

Kashmir Region: When the British withdrew from South Asia in 1947, the former states of British India were asked to decide whether they wanted to become part of a new Hindu India or a Muslim Pakistan. In the state of Jammu and Kashmir, the rulers were Hindu and the majority population was Muslim. The maharajah (prince) of Kashmir opted to join India, but an uprising of the Muslim majority precipitated a war between India and Pakistan over control of this high mountain region. In 1949 a cease-fire line was established by the UN, leaving most of the territory of Jammu and Kashmir in Indian hands. Since then, Pakistan and India have waged intermittent skirmishes over the disputed territory that holds the headwaters of the Indus River, a life-giving stream to desert Pakistan. While Jammu and Kashmir refers specifically to the state in northern India, "Kashmir" is used to describe the larger area of contention that includes Pakistan's northern areas and Azad Kashmir, as well as territory controlled by China. In 1999, extremist Muslim groups demanding independence escalated the periodic battles into a full-fledged, if small, war between two of Asia's major powers—both possessing nuclear weapons. The specter of nuclear exchange caused both Pakistan and India to back down, and while the area remains disputed, military activity has quieted somewhat. Given that there has been no resolution to the situation, Kashmir will continue to be at the leading edge of the simmering feud between Hindu and Muslim populations that has been part of South Asian politics since independence from Great Britain and the partition into separate states in 1947.

Map 56m

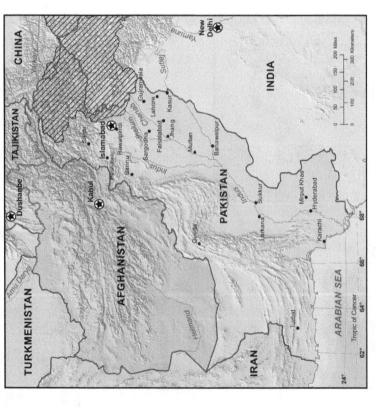

Pakistan: Pakistan's importance to the West and its potential as a flashpoint represent one of the most critical threats to world peace in the opening years of the twenty-first century. Pakistan is one of the ten most populous countries in the world; it possesses both nuclear weapons and a delivery system (as does its nearest neighbor and chief antagonist, India); and it teeters on the brink of being either a Western-style representative democracy or an Islamic fundamentalist state. Strategically, Pakistan lies at the western end of the core of the Muslim world (although large Muslim populations exist to the south and east in India, Malaysia, and Indonesia) and is immediately adjacent to U.S. military operations against the Taliban in Afghanistan. Physically, Pakistan is an incredibly rugged country, mixing a large river floodplain (the Indus) with high mountain country, with peaks in excess of 25,000 feet in elevation in the northwest. Culturally, the country is a mixture of different linguistic and ethnic groups. The government has tried to encourage the use of Urdu as the national language, but less than 10 percent of Pakistanis speak Urdu as their primary language. Pakistan's influence as a precarious U.S. ally in the war on terror has been tested recently. Terror attacks in Mumbai, India, in 2008 and 2011 have been linked to Islamic terror groups operating primarily in Pakistan and in 2011, al-Qaeda leader Osama bin Laden was shot and killed at a compound in the northern Pakistani city of Abbottabad.

-72-

Map 56o

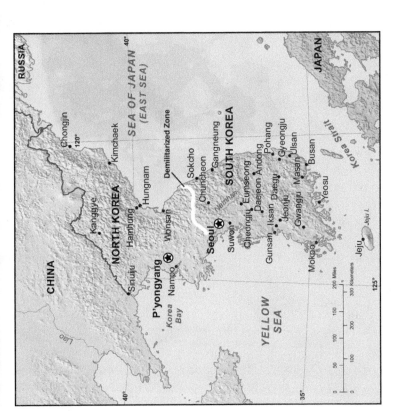

Map 56p

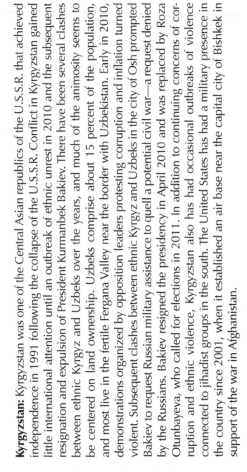

Kyrgyzstan: Kyrgyzstan was one of the Central Asian republics of the U.S.S.R. that achieved independence in 1991 following the collapse of the U.S.S.R. Conflict in Kyrgyzstan gained little international attention until an outbreak of ethnic unrest in 2010 and the subsequent resignation and expulsion of President Kurmanbek Bakiev. There have been several clashes between ethnic Kyrgyz and Uzbeks over the years, and much of the animosity seems to be centered on land ownership. Uzbeks comprise about 15 percent of the population, and most live in the fertile Fergana Valley near the border with Uzbekistan. Early in 2010, demonstrations organized by opposition leaders protesting corruption and inflation turned violent. Subsequent clashes between ethnic Kyrgyz and Uzbeks in the city of Osh prompted Bakiev to request Russian military assistance to quell a potential civil war—a request denied by the Russians. Bakiev resigned the presidency in April 2010 and was replaced by Roza Otunbayeva, who called for elections in 2011. In addition to continuing concerns of corruption and ethnic violence, Kyrgyzstan also has had occasional outbreaks of violence connected to jihadist groups in the south. The United States has had a military presence in the country since 2001, when it established an air base near the capital city of Bishkek in support of the war in Afghanistan.

Korean Peninsula: Although active military conflict has not existed since the 1950s, the Korean peninsula remains an important flashpoint. Since the end of the "Korean War," South Korea has flourished economically. North Korea, on the other hand, adopted a policy of diplomatic and economic self-reliance, becoming one of the world's most authoritarian and isolated states. Yet, North Korea so mismanaged and misallocated its resources that, by the mid-1990s, the country was unable to feed itself. An estimated 2 million North Koreans have died in the past decade as a result of severe food shortages. It continues to expend resources to maintain one of the world's largest armies. In 2006, North Korea announced the development of nuclear weapons and delivery systems designed to "protect" against American aggression. In 2009, North Korea conducted a nuclear test, which was followed by the test firing of several short-range missiles and a long-range rocket. Peninsular tensions reached another high in 2010 when the South Korean warship *Cheonan* exploded and sank. South Korea blamed North Korea, then ceased all cross-border trade. The world's attention refocused on the peninsula in December 2011 following the death of North Korean dictator Kim Jong-Il. His son, Kim Jong-Un, was named his successor, but there is much uncertainty about the future of the country and its relations with South Korea.

-73-

Unit III

Population, Health, and Human Development

Map 57   Population Growth Rates

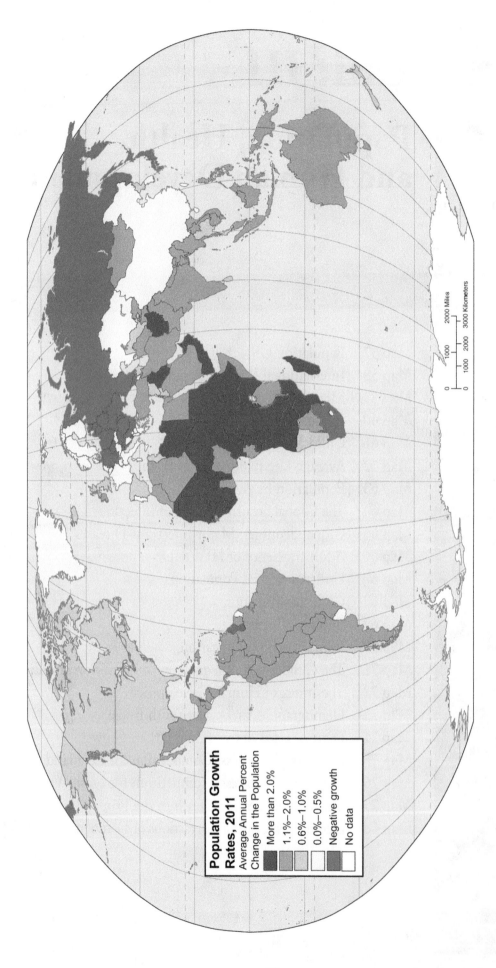

Population Growth Rates, 2011

Average Annual Percent Change in the Population

- More than 2.0%
- 1.1%–2.0%
- 0.6%–1.0%
- 0.0%–0.5%
- Negative growth
- No data

Of all the statistical measurements of human population, that of the rate of population growth is the most important. For a specific country, this figure will determine many things about the country's future ability to feed, house, educate, and provide medical services to its citizens. Some of the countries with the largest populations (such as India) also have high growth rates. Since these countries tend to be in developing regions, the combination of high population and high growth rates poses special problems for political stability and continuing economic development; the combination also carries heightened risks for environmental degradation. Many people believe that the rapidly expanding world population is a potential crisis that may cause environmental and human disaster by the middle of the twenty-first century.

Map 58   International Migrant Populations

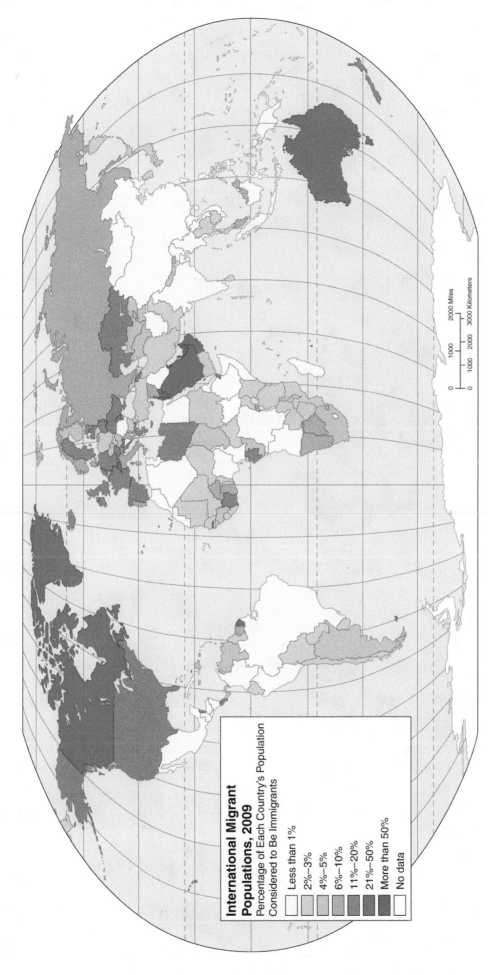

International Migrant Populations, 2009

Percentage of Each Country's Population Considered to Be Immigrants

- Less than 1%
- 2%–3%
- 4%–5%
- 6%–10%
- 11%–20%
- 21%–50%
- More than 50%
- No data

Migration—the movement from one place to another—takes a number of different forms. It may be a move within a country from an old job to a new one. It may also mean a migration, either forced or voluntary, from one country to another. The map here depicts international migration: migration between countries. Migration is distinguished from a refugee movement in that migrants are not defined as refugees granted a humanitarian and temporary protection status under international law. The Middle Americans who leave the Central American countries, Mexico, or the Caribbean for the United States plan to live in the United States permanently, although still retaining cultural and family ties to their native country. This map clearly shows that those countries viewed as having the most favorable opportunities for improvement in personal living conditions are those with the highest numbers of in-migrants; those countries that are overcrowded, with little economically upward mobility, or facing international conflict tend to be those with the greatest number of out-migrants.

Map 59 Migration Rates

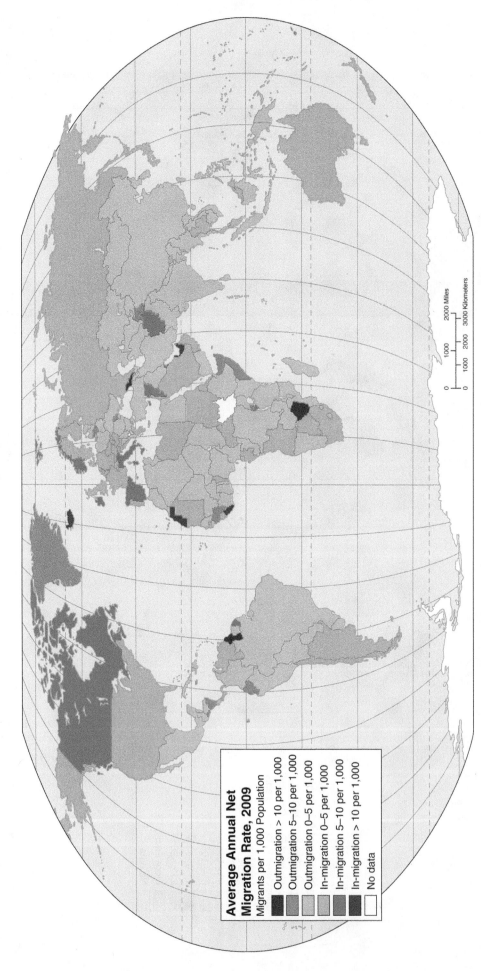

Average Annual Net Migration Rate, 2009
Migrants per 1,000 Population

- Outmigration > 10 per 1,000
- Outmigration 5–10 per 1,000
- Outmigration 0–5 per 1,000
- In-migration 0–5 per 1,000
- In-migration 5–10 per 1,000
- In-migration > 10 per 1,000
- No data

At the most fundamental level, international migration occurs because of two factors: *push* factors and *pull* factors. Push factors are those things that compel a person to leave his or her country. Push factors are many, varied, and are perceived in a negative light. Frequently cited push factors include political stresses (e.g., fear of persecution, war, or internal conflict), economic stresses (e.g., lack of employment opportunities), social stresses (e.g., lack of educational opportunities or adequate health care), and environmental stresses (e.g., natural disasters like a major earthquake or hurricane/typhoon,

desertification). Conversely, pull factors are those attributes of another country that a person finds attractive. As might be expected, they are the opposite of push factors. Thus, international migration is spurred by the perception that things are *bad* in one's own country and *better* in another. Both push and pull factors need be present. A person likely will not migrate to another country if it is perceived that conditions in that country are as bad or worse than in that person's home country.

Map 60 Infant Mortality Rates

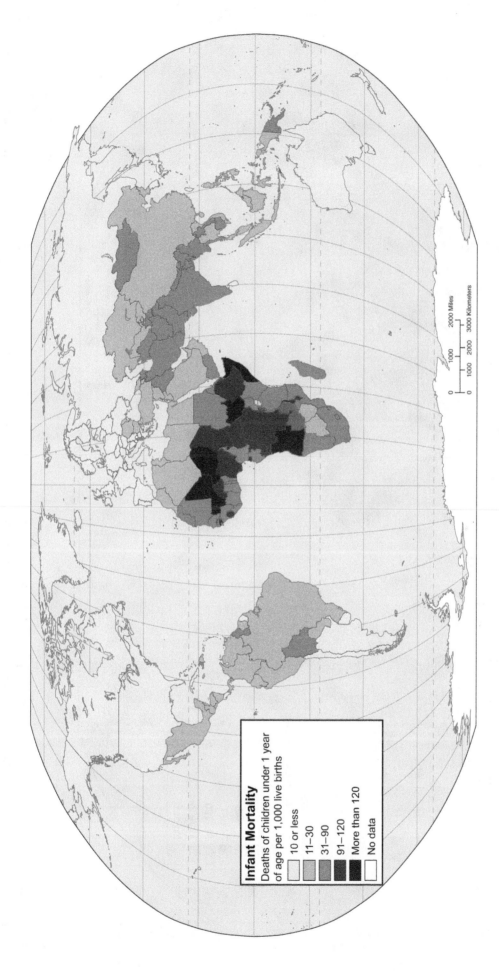

Infant Mortality

Deaths of children under 1 year
of age per 1,000 live births

- 10 or less
- 11–30
- 31–90
- 91–120
- More than 120
- No data

0 1000 2000 Miles
0 1000 2000 3000 Kilometers

Infant mortality rates are calculated by dividing the number of children born in a given year who die before their first birthday by the total number of children born that year and then multiplying by 1,000; this shows how many infants have died for every 1,000 births. Infant mortality rates are prime indicators of economic development. In highly developed economies, with advanced medical technologies, sufficient diets, and adequate public sanitation, infant mortality rates tend to be quite low. By contrast, in less developed countries, with the disadvantages of poor diet, limited access to medical technology, and the other problems of poverty, infant mortality rates tend to be high. Although worldwide infant mortality has decreased significantly during the last two decades, many regions of the world still experience infant mortality above the 10 percent level (100 deaths per 1,000 live births). Such infant mortality rates not only represent human tragedy at its most basic level, but also are powerful inhibiting factors for the future of human development. Comparing infant mortality rates in the midlatitudes and the tropics shows that children in most African countries are more than ten times as likely to die within a year of birth as children in European countries.

Map 61 Child Mortality Rates

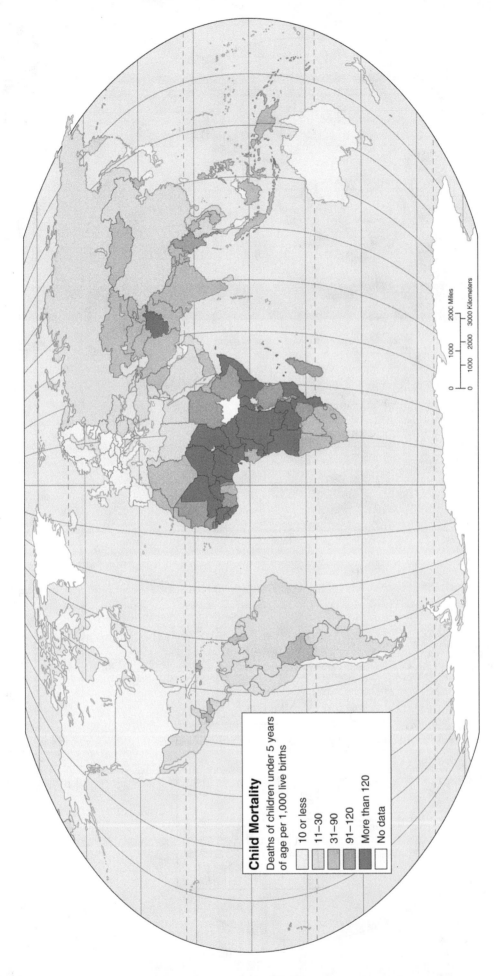

Child Mortality

Deaths of children under 5 years
of age per 1,000 live births

- 10 or less
- 11–30
- 31–90
- 91–120
- More than 120
- No data

0   1000   2000 Miles

0   1000   2000   3000 Kilometers

Child mortality rates are calculated by determining the probability that a child born in a specified year will die before reaching age 5, using current age-specific mortality rates for a population. The major sources of mortality rates are vital registration systems and estimates made from surveys and/or census reports. Along with infant mortality and average life expectancy rates, child mortality rates, according to the World Bank, "are probably the best general indicators of a community's current health status and are often cited as overall measures of a population's welfare or quality of life." Where infant mortality often reflects health care conditions, child mortality is usually a reflection of the inadequacy of nutrition, leading to early deaths from nutritionally related diseases. In some less developed countries in Africa and Asia, child mortality is also an indicator of the widespread presence of infectious diseases such as malaria, tuberculosis, and HIV/AIDS.

Map 62 Average Life Expectancy at Birth

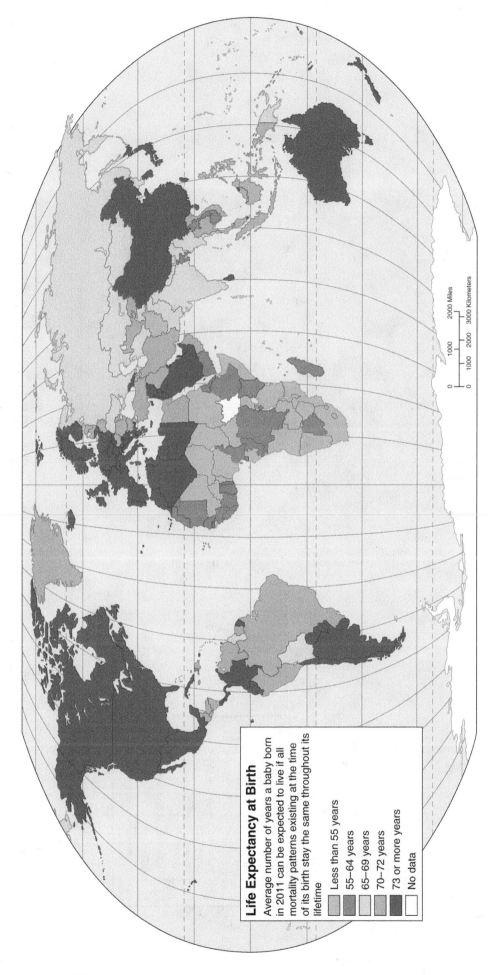

Life Expectancy at Birth

Average number of years a baby born in 2011 can be expected to live if all mortality patterns existing at the time of its birth stay the same throughout its lifetime

- Less than 55 years
- 55–64 years
- 65–69 years
- 70–72 years
- 73 or more years
- No data

0   1000   2000 Miles
0   1000   2000   3000 Kilometers

Average life expectancy at birth is a measure of the average longevity of the population of a country. Like all average measures, it is distorted by extremes. For example, a country with a high mortality rate among children will have a low average life expectancy. Thus, an average life expectancy of 45 years does not mean that everyone can be expected to die at the age of 45. More normally, what the figure means is that a substantial number of children die between birth and 5 years of age, thus reducing the average life expectancy for the entire population. In spite of the dangers inherent in misinterpreting the data, average life expectancy (along with infant mortality and several other measures) is a valid way of judging the relative health of a population. It reflects the nature of the health care system, public sanitation and disease control, nutrition, and a number of other key human need indicators. As such, it is a measure of well-being that is significant in indicating economic development and predicting political stability.

Map 63 Population by Age Group

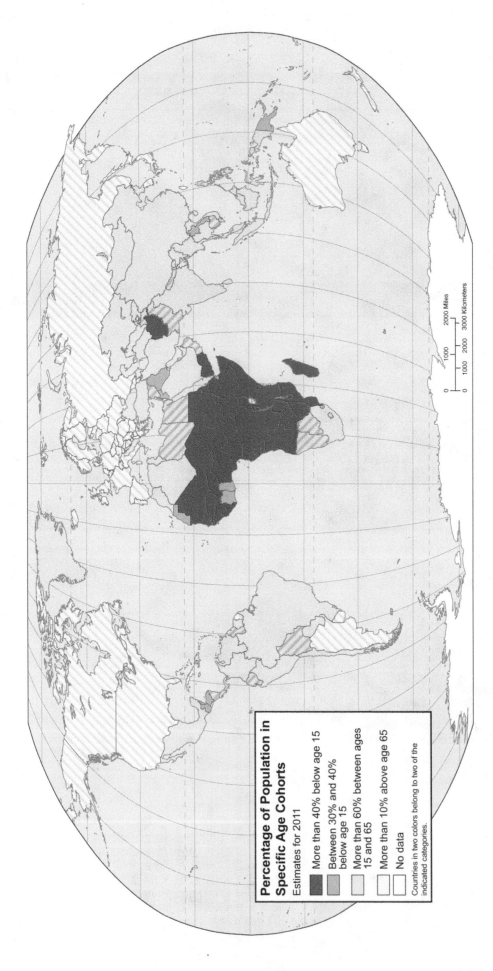

Percentage of Population in Specific Age Cohorts

Estimates for 2011

- More than 40% below age 15
- Between 30% and 40% below age 15
- More than 60% between ages 15 and 65
- More than 10% above age 65
- No data

Countries in two colors belong to two of the indicated categories.

0   1000   2000   3000 Kilometers
0   1000   2000 Miles

Of all the measurements that illustrate the dynamics of a population, age distribution may be the most significant, particularly when viewed in combination with average growth rates. The particular relevance of age distribution is that it tells us what to expect from a population in terms of growth over the next generation. If, for example, approximately 40–50 percent of a population is below the age of 15, that suggests that in the next generation about one-quarter of the total population will be women of childbearing age. When age distribution is combined with fertility rates (the average number of children born per woman in a population), an especially valid measurement

of future growth potential may be derived. A simple example: Nigeria, with a 2002 population of 130 million, has 43.6 percent of its population below the age of 15 and a fertility rate of 5.5; the United States, with a 2002 population of 280 million, has 21 percent of its population below the age of 15 and a fertility rate of 2.07. During the period in which those women presently under the age of 15 are in their childbearing years, Nigeria can be expected to add a total of approximately 155 million persons to its total population. Over the same period, the United States can be expected to add only 61 million.

Map 64 The Global Security Threat of Infectious Diseases

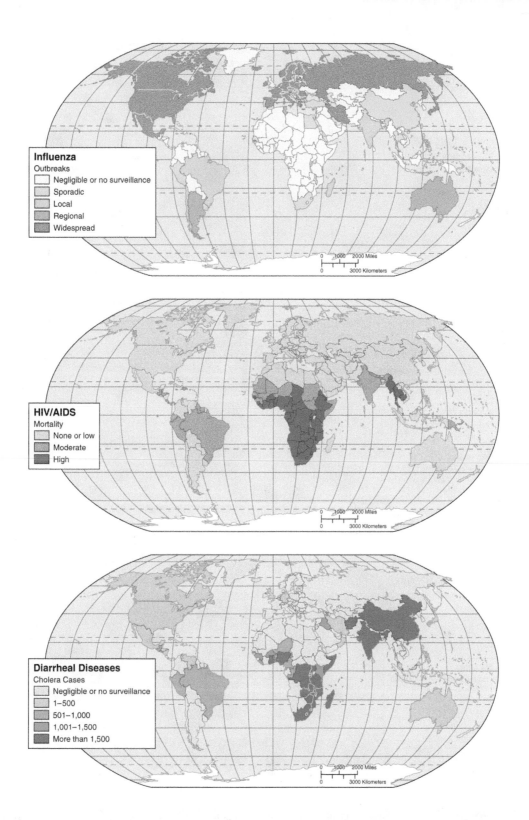

Influenza
Outbreaks
- Negligible or no surveillance
- Sporadic
- Local
- Regional
- Widespread

0 1000 2000 Miles
0 3000 Kilometers

HIV/AIDS
Mortality
- None or low
- Moderate
- High

0 1000 2000 Miles
0 3000 Kilometers

Diarrheal Diseases
Cholera Cases
- Negligible or no surveillance
- 1–500
- 501–1,000
- 1,001–1,500
- More than 1,500

0 1000 2000 Miles
0 3000 Kilometers

The infectious diseases shown in these maps account for more than nine out of every ten deaths worldwide from infectious disease. They are spread through various mechanisms, some (such as HIV/AIDS) requiring direct contact, while others (such as tuberculosis or influenza) may be contracted through airborne transmissions from an infected host. Still others, such as malaria and diarrheal diseases like cholera, require transmission by a vector or carrier. In malaria, the vector is the mosquito (most commonly *Aenopheles*), while the diarrheal diseases are transmitted by microscopic vectors (such as bacteria or viruses) that commonly live in the water that people drink. Infectious diseases such as these six do tend to have specific geographic distributions, sometimes as the result of climatic factors

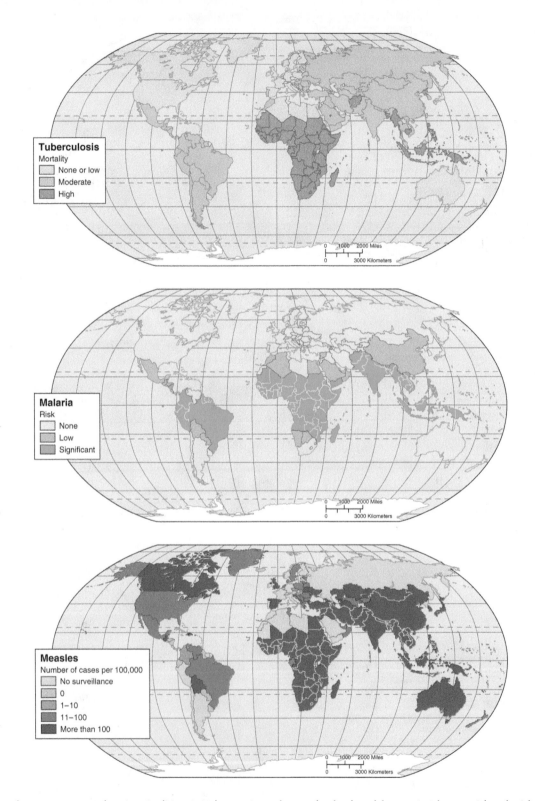

Tuberculosis
Mortality
- None or low
- Moderate
- High

Malaria
Risk
- None
- Low
- Significant

Measles
Number of cases per 100,000
- No surveillance
- 0
- 1–10
- 11–100
- More than 100

(malaria depends upon warm and moist conditions) and sometimes the result of cultural factors (such as rapid and widespread travel). It is the latter that helps to explain why influenza tends to have a greater impact in the developed world, even though the influenza viruses themselves often have their origins in less developed regions of Asia. One good way to avoid influenza is to never travel on a common carrier such as an airplane, train, or bus! None of these diseases has yet been controlled (to the extent that, say, poliomyelitis or smallpox have been controlled). But neither have they wrought the havoc caused by the bubonic plague in late medieval Europe. The sites where future concerns about the transmission of infectious diseases ought to be focused are the increasingly large urban concentrations in South America, Africa, and Asia.

Map 65 Global Scourges: Major Infectious Diseases

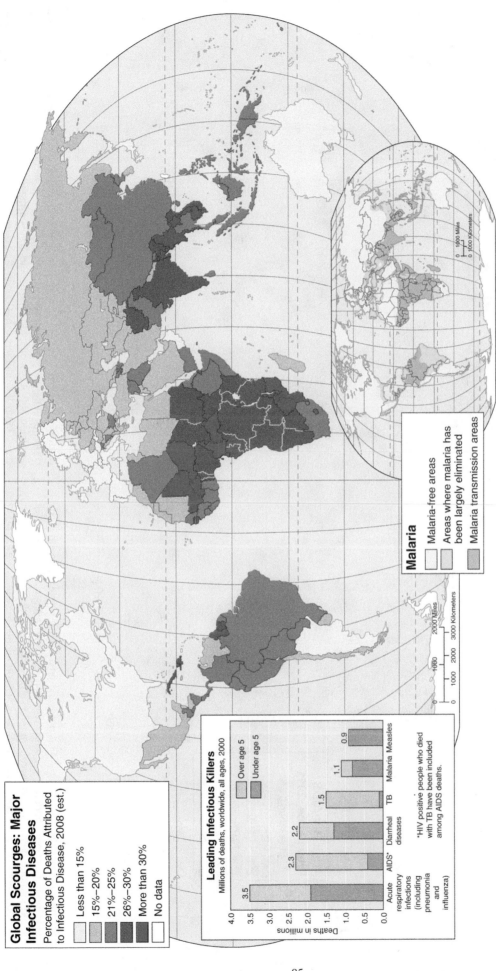

Global Scourges: Major Infectious Diseases

Percentage of Deaths Attributed to Infectious Disease, 2008 (est.)

- Less than 15%
- 15%–20%
- 21%–25%
- 26%–30%
- More than 30%
- No data

Leading Infectious Killers
Millions of deaths, worldwide, all ages, 2000

- Over age 5
- Under age 5

Disease	Deaths (millions)
Acute respiratory infections (including pneumonia and influenza)	3.5
AIDS*	2.3
Diarrheal diseases	2.2
TB	1.5
Malaria	1.1
Measles	0.9

*HIV positive people who died with TB have been included among AIDS deaths.

Deaths in millions (4.0, 3.5, 3.0, 2.5, 2.0, 1.5, 1.0, 0.5, 0.0)

Malaria

- Malaria-free areas
- Areas where malaria has been largely eliminated
- Malaria transmission areas

0 1000 2000 3000 Kilometers
0 1000 2000 Miles

0 1000 Miles
0 1000 Kilometers

Infectious diseases are the world's leading cause of premature death and at least half of the world's population is, at any time, at risk of contracting an infectious disease. Although we often think of infectious diseases as being restricted to the tropical world (malaria, dengue fever), many if not most of them have attained global proportions. A major case in point is HIV/AIDS, which quite probably originated in Africa but has, over the last two decades, spread throughout the entire world. Major diseases of the nineteenth century, such as cholera and tuberculosis, are making a major comeback in many parts of the world, in spite of being preventable or treatable. Part of the problem with infectious diseases is that they tend to be associated with poverty (poor nutrition, poor sanitation, substandard housing, and so on) and, therefore, are seen as a problem of undeveloped countries, with the consequent lack of funding for prevention and treatment. Infectious diseases are also tending to increase because life-saving drugs, such as antibiotics and others used in the fight against diseases, are losing their effectiveness as bacteria develop genetic resistance to them. The problem of global warming is also associated with a spread of infectious diseases as many disease vectors (certain species of mosquitoes, for example) are spreading into higher latitudes with increasingly warm temperatures and are spreading disease into areas where populations have no resistance to them. Infectious diseases have become something greater than simply a health issue of poor countries. They are now major social problems with potentially enormous consequences for the entire world.

-85-

Map 66   Adult Incidence of HIV/AIDS

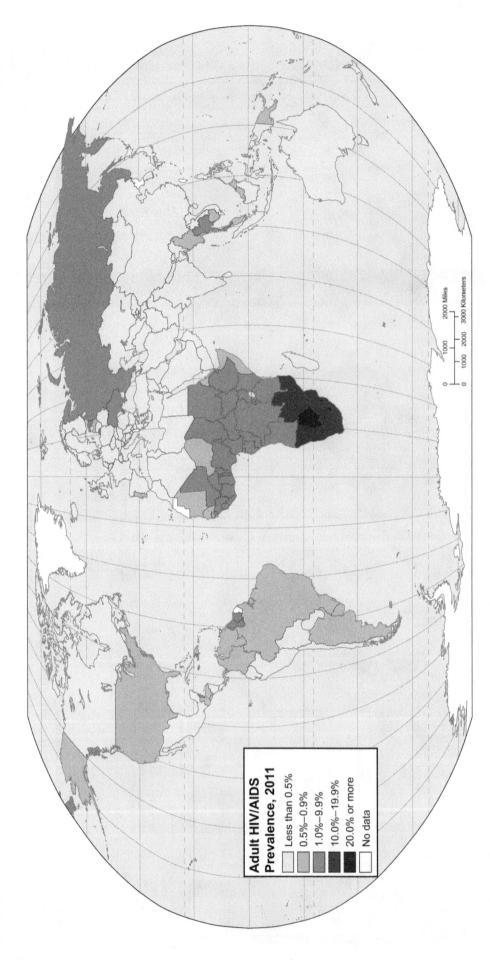

Adult HIV/AIDS Prevalence, 2011

- Less than 0.5%
- 0.5%–0.9%
- 1.0%–9.9%
- 10.0%–19.9%
- 20.0% or more
- No data

0   1000   2000 Miles

0   1000   2000   3000 Kilometers

Of all the infectious diseases, the one that poses the greatest risk to public health world-wide is the human immunodeficiency virus, which, if untreated, progresses to the deadly acquired immune deficiency syndrome, or AIDS. The highest incidence of AIDS among adult populations occurs in Sub-Saharan Africa, where public health systems are too poorly funded and undeveloped to treat HIV cases, and the medications needed to preserve health and reasonable longevity are too expensive. Since the rate of adult cases is high, large num-bers of children are also infected, having been born HIV-positive. Indeed, among all the world's children living with HIV, approximately 90 percent live in Sub-Saharan Africa. Other countries in the developing world also are high on the scale of HIV/AIDS incidence and the suspicion is that the official figures could go even higher if accurately reported. In recent years, HIV/AIDS incidence has declined slightly in those countries with the highest rates of infection, but rates remain alarmingly high, particularly in developing countries. World-wide, HIV/AIDS has a devastating impact on family structures (many children are orphaned by both parents dying of AIDS) and on the economic growth of developing countries.

Map 67 Undernourished Populations

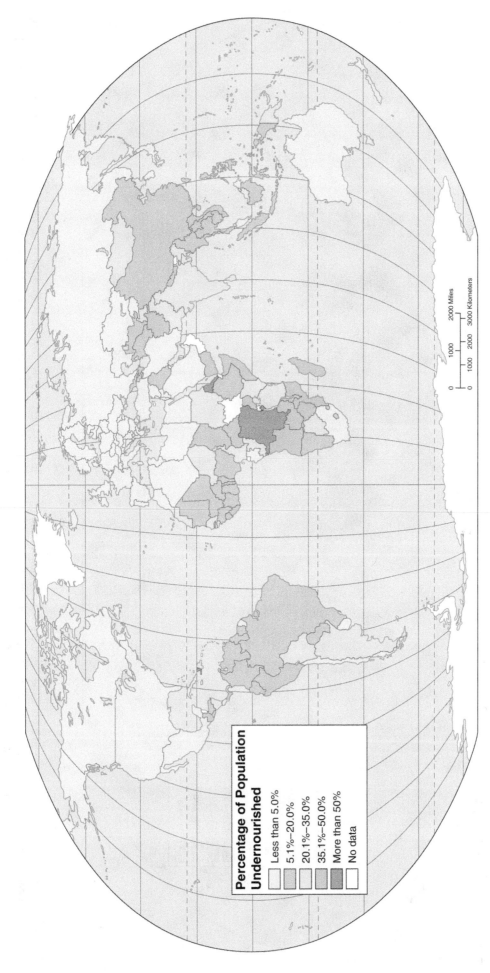

Percentage of Population Undernourished

- Less than 5.0%
- 5.1%—20.0%
- 20.1%—35.0%
- 35.1%—50.0%
- More than 50%
- No data

In order to maintain health and have sufficiently developed immune systems to fight off diseases, humans need to maintain a daily caloric intake of approximately 2,000 calories. Current estimates are that nearly 15 percent of the world's population have diets that do not constitute the minimum 2,000 calories for basic health maintenance. These countries are particularly susceptible to climate-induced famines, which may lower already minimal food intake, or to food emergencies produced by warfare, civil unrest, economic instability, and poor governance. It is little surprise, when looking at the map, that the countries at greatest risk are in Africa and Asia, where swelling populations have already approached (or, in some instances, exceeded) carrying capacity, or the ability of the environment to sustain a population at a given level. The causes of national malnutrition are as numerous as the countries that experience it but, again, the map is instructive. In Africa, where HIV/AIDS is prevalent among large segments of the working-age population, food production is limited simply by poor health (which, of course, begets low harvests, which contributes to poorer health). In South Asia, the problem tends to be magnified by huge populations that have outstripped the ability of the environment to support them. Bangladesh, for example, with an area about the size of West Virginia, is one of the world's ten most populous countries.

Map 68   Child Malnutrition

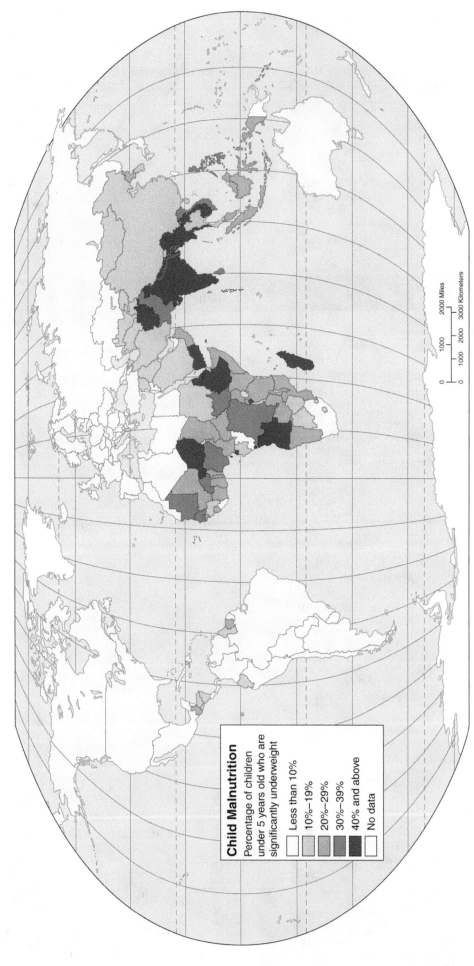

Child Malnutrition

Percentage of children
under 5 years old who are
significantly underweight

- Less than 10%
- 10%–19%
- 20%–29%
- 30%–39%
- 40% and above
- No data

0   1000   2000 Miles

0   1000   2000   3000 Kilometers

The weight of poverty is not evenly spread among the members of a population, falling disproportionately upon the weakest and most disadvantaged members of society. In most societies, these individuals are children, particularly female children. Children simply do not compete as successfully as adults for their (meager) share of the daily food supply. Where food shortages prevail, children tend to have the quality of their future lives severely compromised by poor nutrition, which, in a downward spiral, robs them of the energy necessary to compete more effectively for food. Children who are inadequately fed are less likely to do well in school, are more prone to debilitating disease, and will more often become a drain on scarce societal resources than well-fed children. Recently, health care officials in the more developed world have become concerned over the trend to "overnutrition," leading to obesity and related health problems in the world's economically developed countries. Nevertheless, child malnourishment remains one of the primary distinguishing factors between the "haves" and "have-nots."

Map **69** Illiteracy Rates

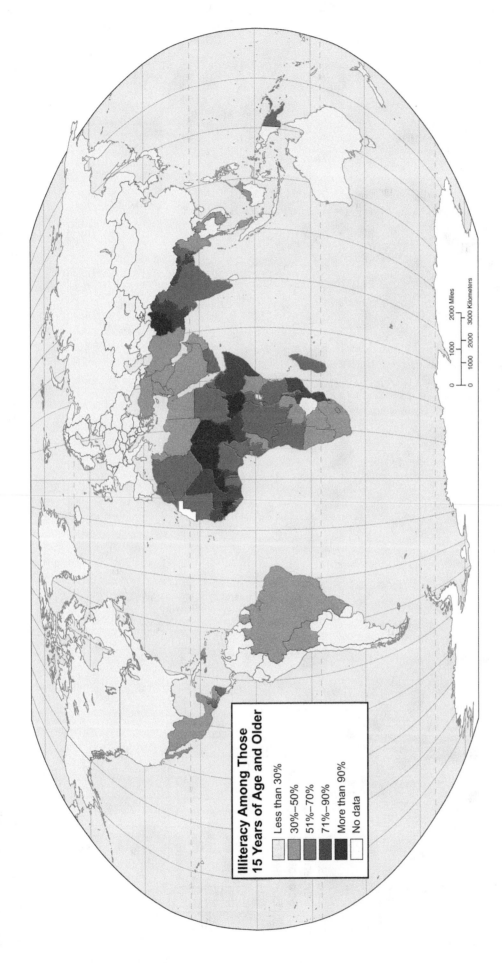

**Illiteracy Among Those
15 Years of Age and Older**

- Less than 30%
- 30%–50%
- 51%–70%
- 71%–90%
- More than 90%
- No data

0   1000   2000 Miles

0   1000   2000   3000 Kilometers

Illiteracy rates are based on the percentages of people age 15 or above (classed as adults in most countries) who are not able to write and read, with understanding, a brief, simple statement about everyday life written in their home or official language. As might be expected, illiteracy rates tend to be higher in the less-developed states, where educational systems are a low government priority. Rates of literacy or illiteracy also tend to be gender-differentiated, with women in many countries experiencing educational neglect or discrimination that makes it more likely they will be illiterate. In many developing countries, between five and ten times as many women will be illiterate as men, and the illiteracy rate for women may even exceed 90 percent. Both male and female illiteracy severely compromises economic development.

-89-

Map 70 Primary School Education

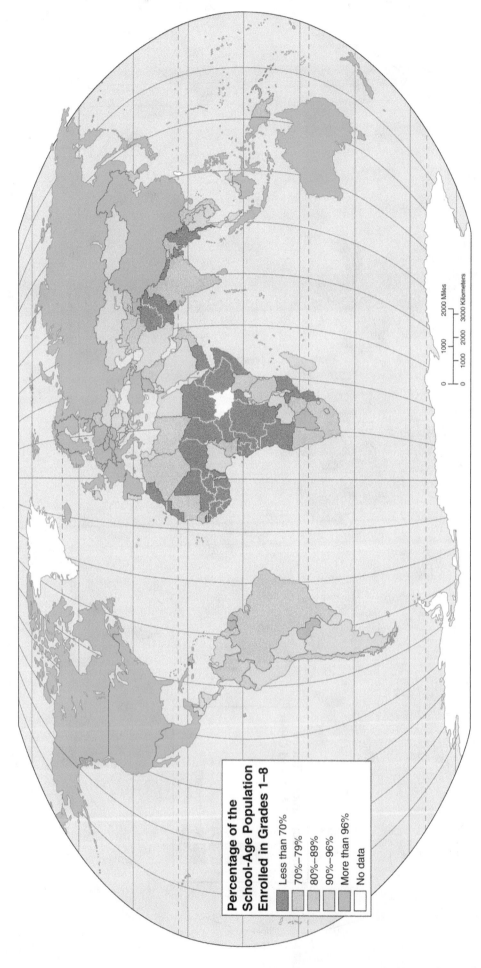

Percentage of the School-Age Population Enrolled in Grades 1–8

- Less than 70%
- 70%–79%
- 80%–89%
- 90%–96%
- More than 96%
- No data

0 1000 2000 2000 Miles
0 1000 2000 3000 Kilometers

Like many of the other measures illustrated in this atlas, primary school enrollment is a clear reflection of the division of the world into "have" and "have-not" countries. It is also a measure that has changed more rapidly over the last decade than demographic and other indicators of development, as countries of even very modest means have made concerted attempts to attain relatively high percentages of primary school enrollment. That they have been able to do so is good evidence of the fact that reasonably respectable levels of human development are feasible at even modest income levels. High primary school enrollment is also a reflection of the worldwide opinion that a major element in economic development is a well-educated, literate population. The links between human progress, as typified by higher levels of education, and economic growth are not automatic, however, and those countries without programs for maintaining the headway gained by improved education may be on the road to failure in terms of economic development.

Map 71

The Gender Gap: Inequalities in Education and Employment

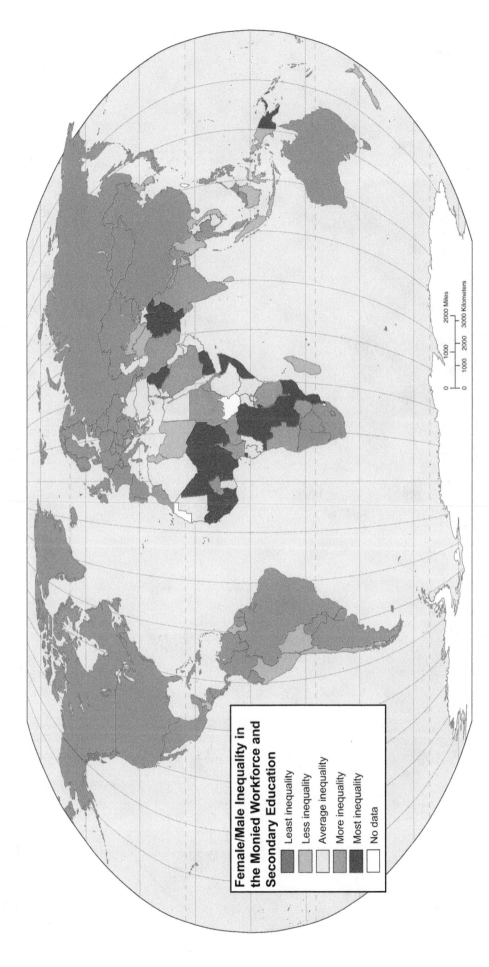

Female/Male Inequality in the Monied Workforce and Secondary Education

- Least inequality
- Less inequality
- Average inequality
- More inequality
- Most inequality
- No data

0   1000   2000 Miles
0   1000   2000   3000 Kilometers

Although women in developed countries, particularly in North America and Europe, have made significant advances in socioeconomic status in recent years, in most of the world females suffer from significant inequality when compared to their male counterparts. Women have received the right to vote in most of the world's countries, but in over 90 percent of these countries that right has only been granted in the last 50 years. In most regions, literacy rates for women still fall far short of those for men; in Africa and Asia, for example, only about half as many women as men are literate. Women marry considerably younger than men and attend school for shorter periods of time. Inequalities in education and employment are perhaps the most telling indicators of the unequal status of women in most of the world. Lack of secondary education in comparison with men prevents women from entering the workforce with equally high-paying jobs. Even where women are employed in positions similar to those held by men, they still tend to receive less compensation. The gap between rich and poor involves not only a clear geographic differentiation, but a clear gender differentiation as well.

Map 72 The Index of Human Development

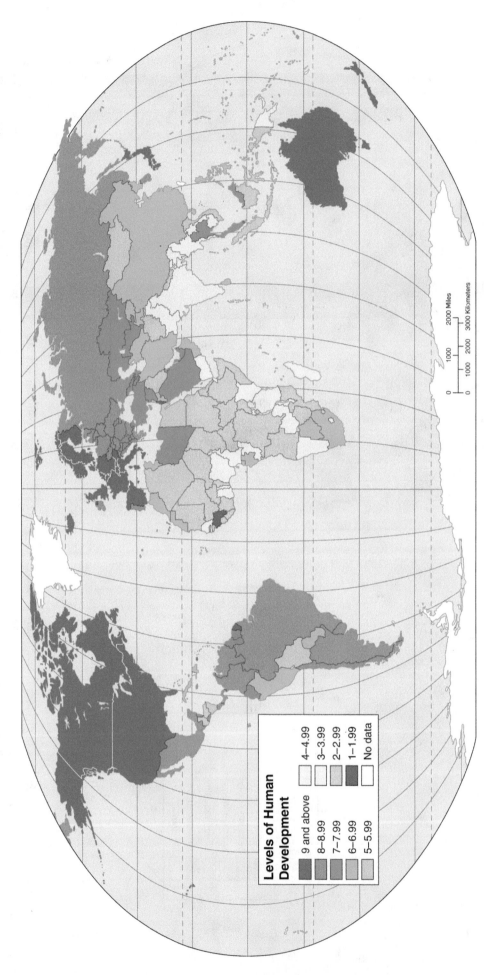

Levels of Human Development

■ 9 and above		□ 4–4.99	
■ 8–8.99		□ 3–3.99	
■ 7–7.99		■ 2–2.99	
■ 6–6.99		■ 1–1.99	
■ 5–5.99		□ No data	

0   1000   2000 Miles
0   1000   2000   3000 Kilometers

The development index on which this map is based takes into account a wide variety of demographic, health, and educational data, including population growth, per capita gross domestic income, longevity, literacy, and years of schooling. The map reveals significant improvement in the quality of life in Middle and South America, although it is questionable whether the gains made in those regions can be maintained in the face of the dramatic population increases expected over the next 30 years. More clearly than anything else, the map illustrates the near-desperate situation in Africa and South Asia. In those regions, the unparalleled growth in population threatens to overwhelm all efforts to improve the quality of life. In Africa, for example, the population is increasing by 20 million persons per year. With nearly 45 percent of the continent's population aged 15 years or younger, this growth rate will accelerate as the women reach childbearing age. Africa, along with South Asia, faces the very difficult challenge of providing basic access to health care, education, and jobs for a rapidly increasing population. The map also illustrates the striking difference in quality of life between those who inhabit the world's equatorial and tropical regions and those fortunate enough to live in the temperate zones, where the quality of life is significantly higher.

Map 73   Demographic Stress: The Youth Bulge

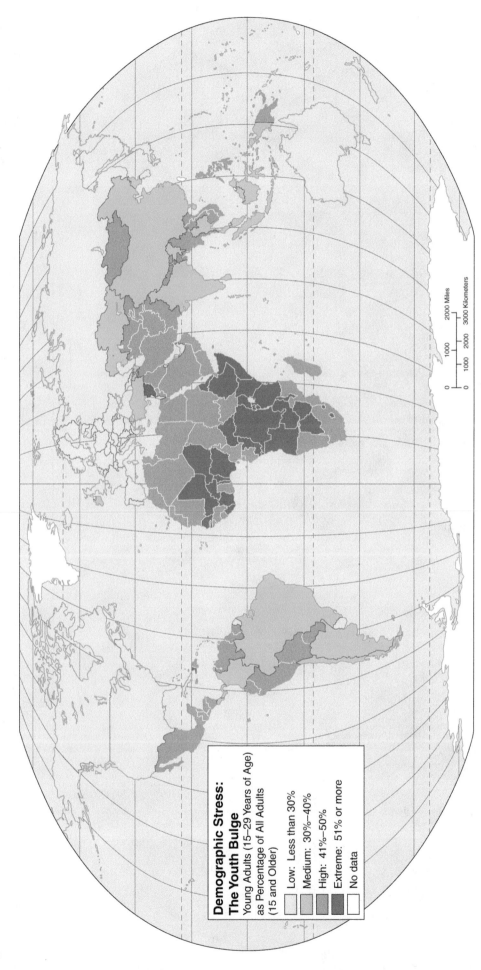

**Demographic Stress:
The Youth Bulge**
Young Adults (15–29 Years of Age)
as Percentage of All Adults
(15 and Older)

Low: Less than 30%
Medium: 30%–40%
High: 41%–50%
Extreme: 51% or more
No data

One of the greatest stresses of the demographic transition is when the death rate drops as the result of better public health and sanitation and the birth rate remains high for the same reasons it has always been high in traditional, agricultural societies: (1) the need for enough children to supply labor, which is one of the few ways to increase agricultural production in a non-mechanized agricultural system, and (2) the need for enough children to offset high infant and child mortality rates so that some children will survive to take care of parents in their old age. With declining death rates and steady birth rates, population growth skyrockets—particularly among the youngest cohorts of a

population (between the ages of birth and 15). While this is, on the one hand, a demographic benefit since it increases the size of the labor force in the next generation and thereby helps to accelerate economic growth, it also means more people of childbearing age in the next generation and, hence, greater numbers of births, which continue to swell the population in the youngest, most vulnerable, and most dependent portion of the population. The literature on population and conflict suggests that the larger the percentage of a population below the age of 25, the greater the chance for political violence and warfare.

Map 74   Demographic Stress: Rapid Urban Growth

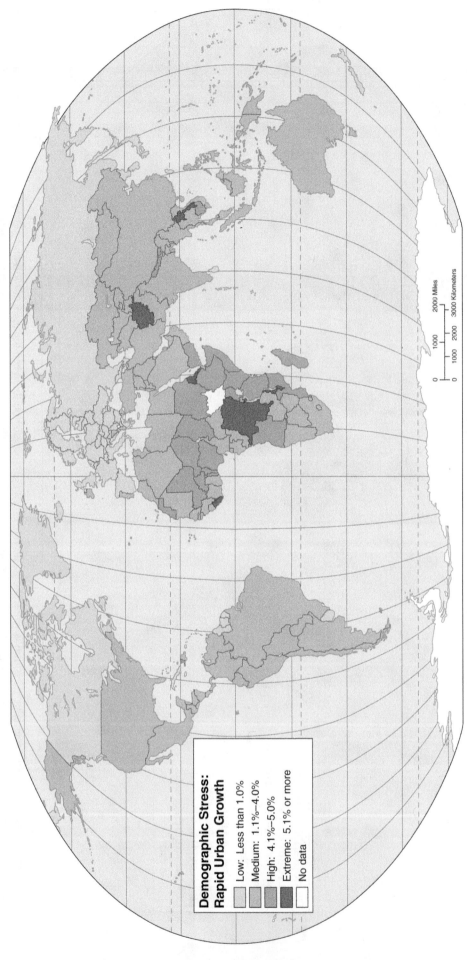

**Demographic Stress:
Rapid Urban Growth**

Low: Less than 1.0%
Medium: 1.1%—4.0%
High: 4.1%—5.0%
Extreme: 5.1% or more
No data

0   1000   2000 Miles
0   1000   2000   3000 Kilometers

The trend toward urbanization—an increasing percentage of a country's population living in a city—is normally a healthy, modern trend. But in many of the world's developing countries, increasing urbanization is the consequence of high physiologic population densities (too many people for the available agricultural land) and the flight of poorly educated, untrained rural poor to the cities, where they hope (often in vain) to find employment. High urbanization exists in many of the world's poorest countries, where the urban poor live in conditions that make the worst living conditions in the inner cities of developed countries look positively luxurious. In the urban slums of South America, Africa, and South Asia, millions of people live in temporary housing of cardboard and flattened aluminum cans, with no public services such as water, sewage, or electricity. In Africa, where only 40 percent of the population is urbanized (in comparison with more than 90 percent in North America and Europe), the population of urban poor is greater than the total urban population of the United States and the European Union. This represents an increasingly destabilizing element of modern urban societies.

Map 75   Demographic Stress: Competition for Cropland

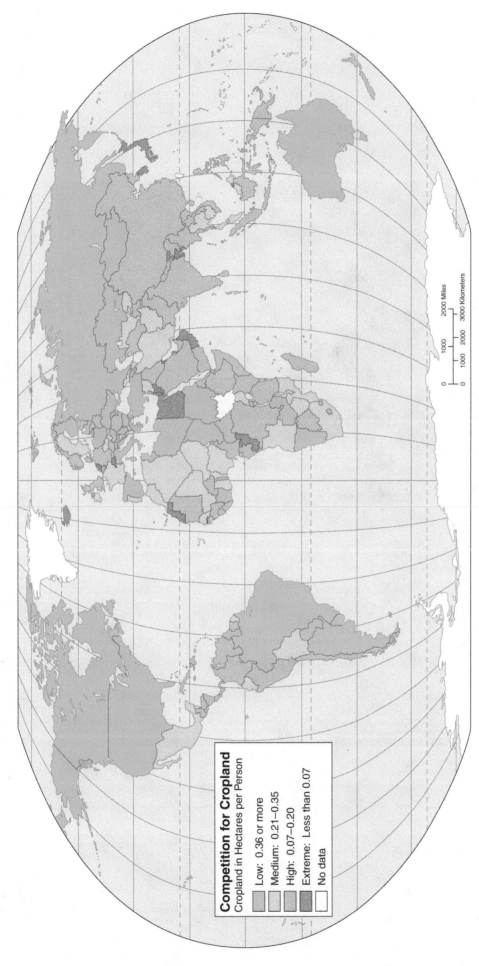

Competition for Cropland
Cropland in Hectares per Person

Low: 0.36 or more
Medium: 0.21–0.35
High: 0.07–0.20
Extreme: Less than 0.07
No data

0   1000   2000 Miles

0   1000   2000   3000 Kilometers

Many of the world's countries have reached the point where available acres or hectares of cropland are less than the numbers of people wishing to occupy them. For developed countries, which pay for agricultural imports with industrial exports, this is not an alarming trend and therefore countries like Germany or Italy (where the ratio between cropland and farmers is very low) have little to worry about. But in countries in South America, Africa, and South and East Asia, the trend toward more farmers and less available land *is* an alarming trend. In these developing regions, farmers depend on their crops for a relatively meager subsistence diet and—if they are lucky—a few

bushels of rice or corn to take to the local market to sell or exchange for the small surpluses of other farmers. Despite the broad global trends toward urbanization and more productive agriculture (and this generally means mechanized agriculture), farm occupation and subsistence cropping remain mainstays of the economy in Africa south of the Sahara, in much of western South America, and in much of South and East Asia. Here, the increasingly small margin between the numbers of farmers and the amount of available farmland can lead to conflict among tribal communities or even among members of a single family.

Map 76 · Demographic Stress: Competition for Fresh Water

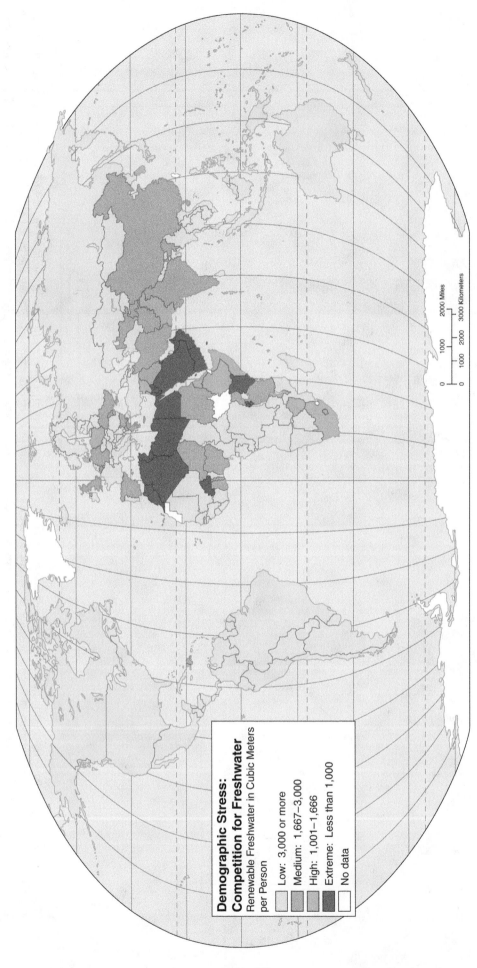

**Demographic Stress:
Competition for Freshwater**
Renewable Freshwater in Cubic Meters
per Person

- Low: 3,000 or more
- Medium: 1,667–3,000
- High: 1,001–1,666
- Extreme: Less than 1,000
- No data

As rates of urbanization have increased, the competition between city dwellers and farmers for water has also increased. And as the population of farmers relative to the available surface or groundwater supply has accelerated, so rural competition for access to fresh water for irrigation has increased. Predictably, this trend is most obvious in the world's drier regions. On this map, the greatest stress factors relating to water availability are in North and East Africa, the Middle East, and Central and East Asia. The current conflict between Israelis and Palestinians in the West Bank goes far beyond religion or politics: Some is the result of the more affluent Israeli farmers being able to drill wells to tap groundwater, which lowers the water table and causes previously accessible surface wells in Palestinian villages to go dry. And part of the reason behind the horrific Hutu-Tutsi civil war in Rwanda and the taking of European farmlands by the current government of Zimbabwe has more to do with the need for access to fresh water than with racial or ethnic differences. Given that fresh water is, for all practical purposes, a non-renewable resource, more conflicts over access to water are going to erupt in the future.

Map 77 Demographic Stress: Death in the Prime of Life

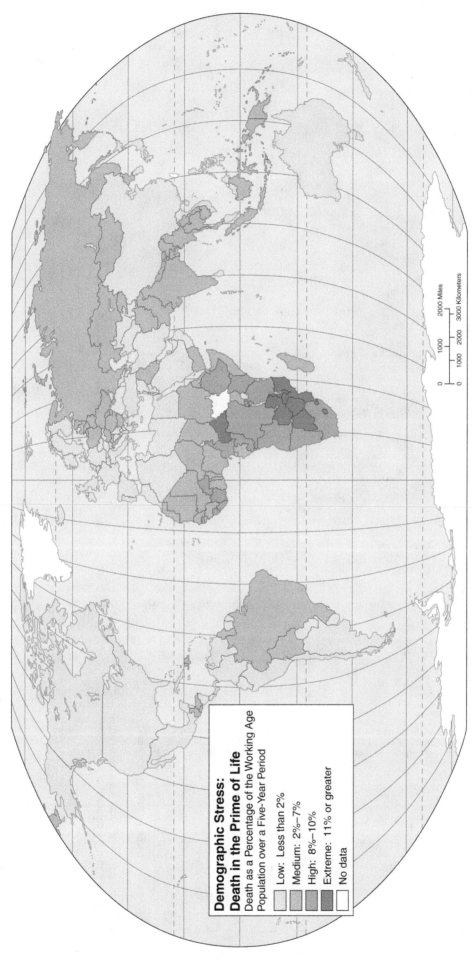

**Demographic Stress:
Death in the Prime of Life**

Death as a Percentage of the Working Age
Population over a Five-Year Period

Low: Less than 2%

Medium: 2%–7%

High: 8%–10%

Extreme: 11% or greater

No data

0   1000   2000   2000 Miles

0   1000   2000   3000 Kilometers

Most infectious diseases lay waste to the oldest and the youngest sectors of a population, leaving the healthier, working-age population able to reproduce itself and to continue to grow an economy. Modern infectious diseases—most particularly HIV/AIDS—impacts not the youngest or oldest but those in the prime of life, in their most productive and reproductive years. Indeed, medical data from the United Nations show that 90 percent of HIV/AIDS-related deaths occur in people of working age. Some of the most severely impacted countries in southern Africa lose between 10 percent and 20 percent of their working-age population every five years. Rates in the developed world are from 0.10

percent to 0.02 percent of this level. A prominent fact of life in much of the developing world—particularly in Sub-Saharan Africa—is long-distance labor migration. In this pattern, a man leaves his wife and family for extended periods of time (ten or more months of the year) to work in mines or on docks as sailors. These men are highly vulnerable to the acquisition of HIV, which is then transmitted to their wives when they return home on annual visits. Thus, both the male and the female portion of the working-age population are impacted by early mortality from AIDS. None of this bodes well for economic development in those affected areas of the world.

-97-

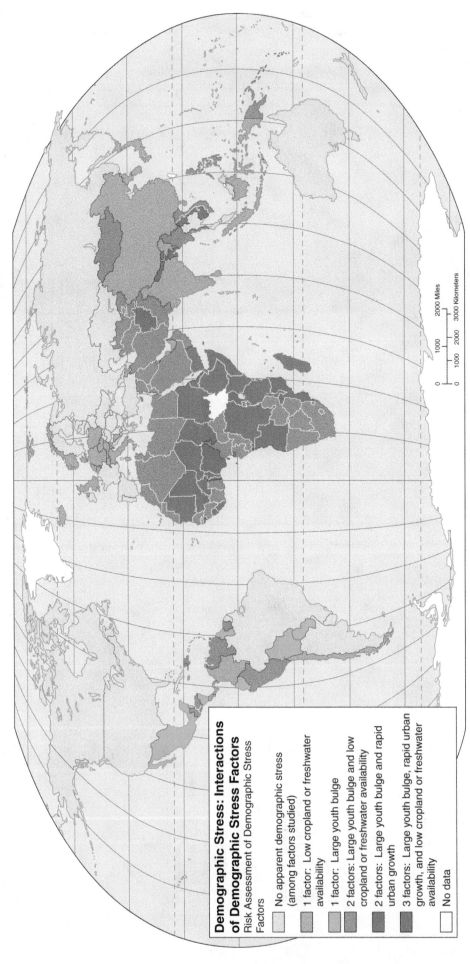

Demographic Stress: Interactions of Demographic Stress Factors
Risk Assessment of Demographic Stress Factors

No apparent demographic stress (among factors studied)

1 factor: Low cropland or freshwater availability

1 factor: Large youth bulge

2 factors: Large youth bulge and low cropland or freshwater availability

2 factors: Large youth bulge and rapid urban growth

3 factors: Large youth bulge, rapid urban growth, and low cropland or freshwater availability

No data

We have persisted in viewing internal and international conflicts as conflicts produced by religious differences, the acceptance or rejection of "freedom" or "democracy," or even, as argued by a prominent historian, a "Clash of Civilizations." While religious, political, and historical differences cannot be ignored in interpreting the causes of conflict, neither can simple demographic stresses produced by too many new urban dwellers without jobs or hopes of jobs, by too many farmers and too little farmland, and by too many deaths among people who should be in the most productive portions of their lives. A massive study by Population Action International, from which these last half-dozen or so maps have been drawn, shows quite clearly that countries suffering from multiple demographic risk factors are, were, and will be much more prone to civil conflict than countries with only one or two demographic risk factors. A look at this map provides a predictor of future civil unrest, violence, and even civil war.

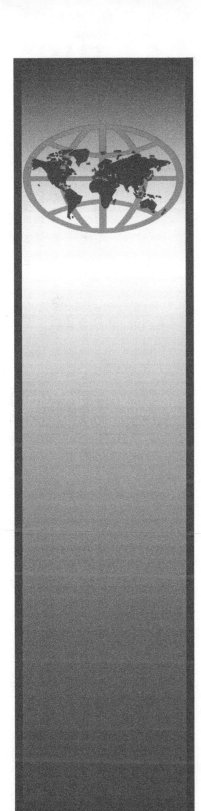

Unit IV

The Global Economy

Map 79   Membership in the World Trade Organization

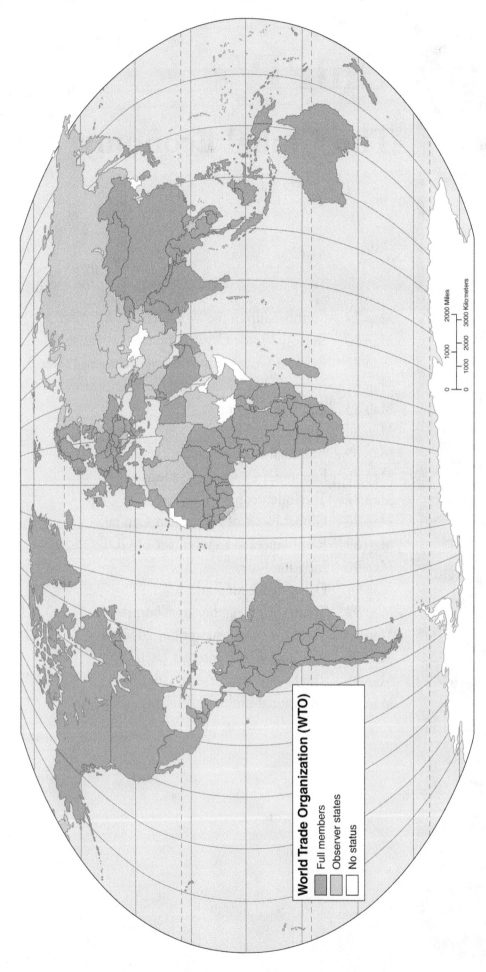

World Trade Organization (WTO)
- Full members
- Observer states
- No status

After World War II, the General Agreement on Tariffs and Trade (GATT) sponsored several rounds of negotiations, especially related to lower tariffs, but also issues such as dumping and other non-tariff questions. The last round of negotiations under GATT took place in Uruguay in 1986–1994 and set the stage for the World Trade Organization (WTO), which was formally established in 1995. Today the WTO has 153 members with more than 30 "observer" governments. With the exception of the Holy See (Vatican), observer governments are expected to begin negotiations for full membership within five years of becoming

observers. The objective of the WTO is to help international trade flow smoothly and fairly and to assure more stable and secure supplies of goods to consumers. To this end, it administers trade agreements, acts as a forum for trade negotiations, settles trade disputes, reviews national trade policies, assists developing countries through technical assistance and training programs, and cooperates with other international organizations. Increased globalization of the world's economy makes the administrative role of the WTO of increasing importance in the twenty-first century.

Map 80 Regional Trade Organizations

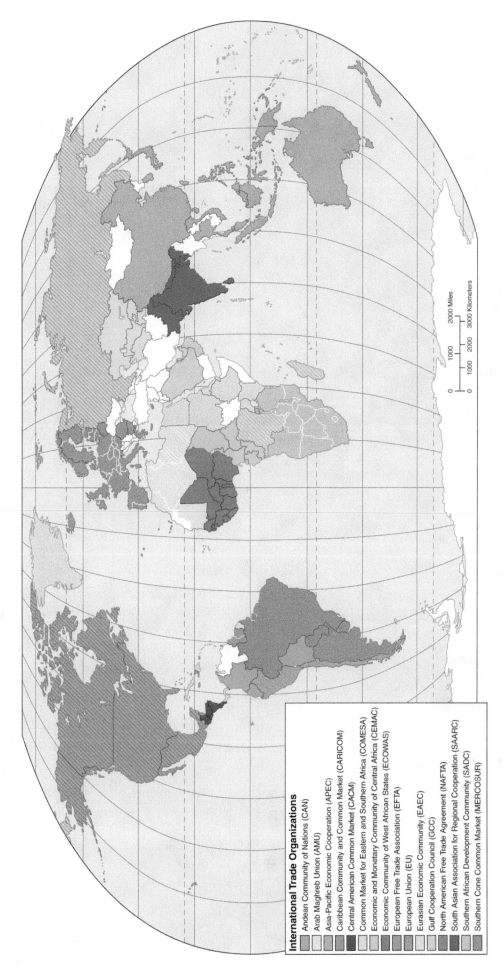

International Trade Organizations

Andean Community of Nations (CAN)
Arab Maghreb Union (AMU)
Asia-Pacific Economic Cooperation (APEC)
Caribbean Community and Common Market (CARICOM)
Central American Common Market (CACM)
Common Market for Eastern and Southern Africa (COMESA)
Economic and Monetary Community of Central Africa (CEMAC)
Economic Community of West African States (ECOWAS)
European Free Trade Association (EFTA)
European Union (EU)
Eurasian Economic Community (EAEC)
Gulf Cooperation Council (GCC)
North American Free Trade Agreement (NAFTA)
South Asian Association for Regional Cooperation (SAARC)
Southern African Development Community (SADC)
Southern Cone Common Market (MERCOSUR)

0   1000   2000 Miles
0 1000 2000 3000 Kilometers

One of the most pervasive influences in the global economy over the last half-century, particularly since the end of the Cold War, has been that of international trade organizations. Pioneered by the European Economic Community, founded in part to assist in rebuilding the European economy after World War II, these organizations have become major players in global movements of goods, services, and labor. Some have integrated to form financial and political unions, such as the European Community, which has grown into the European Union. Others, like the Asia-Pacific Economic Cooperation, and the Southern African Development Community, incorporate vastly different regions, states, and even economic systems, and are attempts to anticipate the direction of future economic growth. The role of international trade organizations is likely to grow greater in the next 50 years. In terms of purchasing power parity GDP, the North American Free Trade Agreement (NAFTA) is the largest trade bloc in the world and has restructured many segments of the Canadian, American, and Mexican economies (particularly in Mexico).

Map 81   Relative Wealth of Nations: Purchasing Power Parity

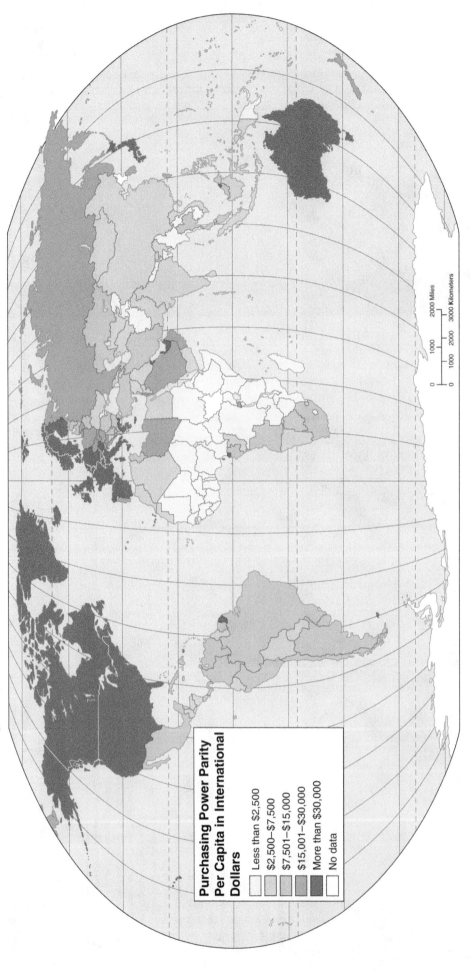

Purchasing Power Parity Per Capita in International Dollars

- Less than $2,500
- $2,500–$7,500
- $7,501–$15,000
- $15,001–$30,000
- More than $30,000
- No data

Of all the economic measures that separate the "haves" from the "have-nots," perhaps per capita purchasing power parity (PPP) is the most meaningful. While per capita figures can mask significant uneven distributions within a country, they are generally useful for demonstrating important differences between countries. Per capita GNP and GDP (Gross Domestic Product) figures, and even per capita income, have the limitation of seldom reflecting the true purchasing power of a country's currency at home. In order to get around this limitation, international economists seeking to compare national currencies developed the PPP measure, which shows the level of goods and services that holders of a country's money can acquire locally. By converting all currencies to the "international dollar," the World Bank and other organizations using PPP can now show more truly comparative values, since the new currency value shows the number of units of a country's currency required to buy the same quantity of goods and services in the local market as one U.S. dollar would buy in an average country. The use of PPP currency values can alter the perceptions about a country's true comparative position in the world economy. More than per capita income figures, PPP provides a valid measurement of the ability of a country's population to provide for itself the things that people in the developed world take for granted: adequate food, shelter, clothing, education, and access to medical care. A glance at the map shows a clear-cut demarcation between temperate and tropical zones, with most of the countries with a PPP above $7,500 in the midlatitude zones and most of those with lower PPPs in the tropical and equatorial regions. Where exceptions to this pattern occur, they usually stem from a tremendous maldistribution of wealth among a country's population.

Map 82   Inequality of Income and Consumption

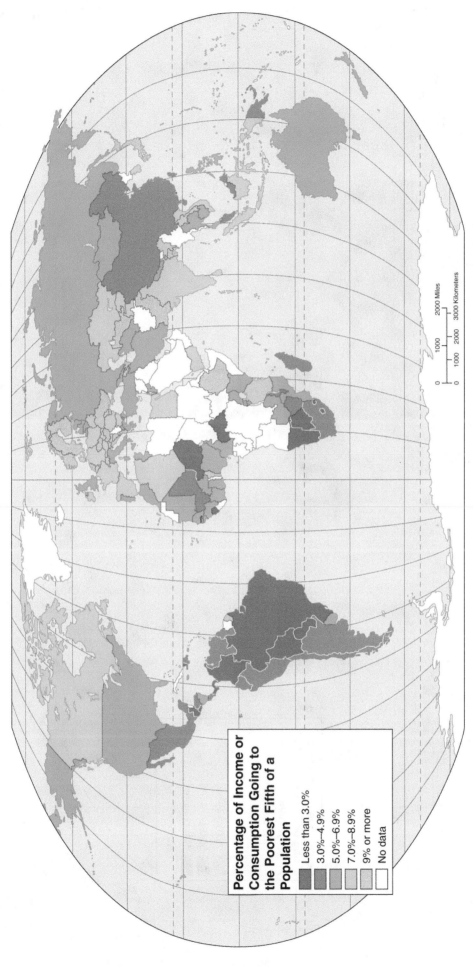

Percentage of Income or Consumption Going to the Poorest Fifth of a Population

Less than 3.0%
3.0%–4.9%
5.0%–6.9%
7.0%–8.9%
9% or more
No data

While it is more than arguably true that the poor get poorer and the rich get richer (and that, by the way, is just as true in some highly developed areas like the United States and the United Kingdom as it is in the lesser-developed regions), what is often ignored is the breadth of the inequality in distribution of incomes or in the levels of consumption of basic goods. In many of the world's developing countries—despite the rapid increases in economic growth of China and India over the last two decades—the poorest 20 percent of the population receives less than 7 percent of the income or consumption share. Although school participation rates have risen worldwide, in countries with the greatest inequalities of income, access to education remains low. If translated into ratios, the inequality ratio of many of the world's countries (including, as noted above, some in the highly developed world) is 8 or higher, meaning that the top 20 percent of the population spends and consumes at least eight times as much per person as the bottom 20 percent of the population.

Map 83 The World's Poorest

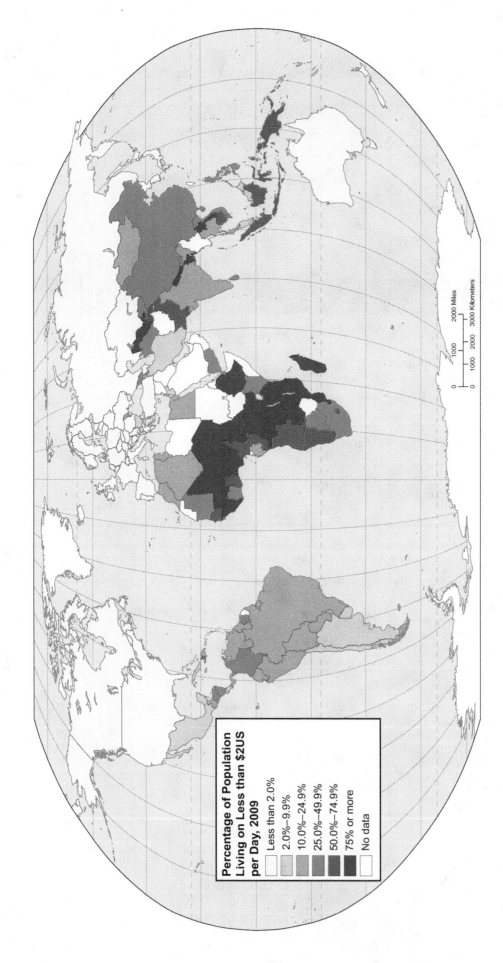

Percentage of Population Living on Less than $2US per Day, 2009

- Less than 2.0%
- 2.0%–9.9%
- 10.0%–24.9%
- 25.0%–49.9%
- 50.0%–74.9%
- 75% or more
- No data

Extreme poverty, represented by annual per capita incomes of approximately $300US, is found in rural areas (particularly those of subsistence rather than commercial agriculture) and in the urban slums of the developing world, where rural poor have fled the countryside for the city and the hope for jobs and a better life. The greatest number of countries with high percentages of extremely poor people is in Sub-Saharan Africa; the greatest populations of the extremely poor are in South Asia, where nearly half a billion people live under conditions of the most severe poverty. Few developing countries are on track to halve poverty by the UN and World Bank target date of 2015. Poverty begets poverty as the poor have the lowest levels of access to education, transportation, job training, health facilities, and other "amenities" of the more well-off. As a consequence, the children of the poorest are more than likely to end up in the same classification as their parents.

Map 84   Total Labor Force

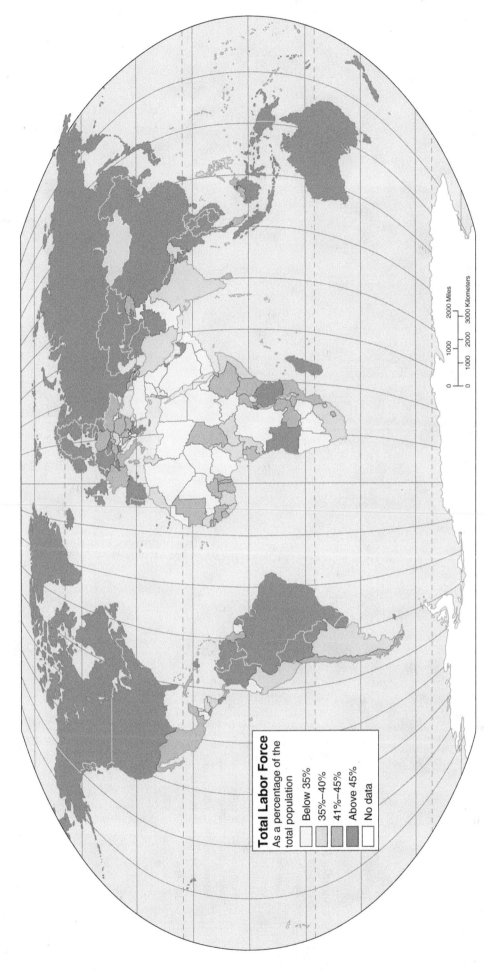

Total Labor Force
As a percentage of the total population

- Below 35%
- 35%–40%
- 41%–45%
- Above 45%
- No data

0   1000   2000 Miles
0   1000   2000   3000 Kilometers

The term *labor force* refers to the economically active portion of a population, that is, all people who work or are without work but are available for and are seeking work to produce economic goods and services. The total labor force thus includes both the employed and the unemployed (as long as they are actively seeking employment). Labor force is considered a better indicator of economic potential than employment/unemployment figures, since unemployment figures will include experienced workers with considerable potential who are temporarily out of work. Unemployment figures will also incorporate persons seeking employment for the first time (many recent college

graduates, for example). Generally, countries with higher percentages of total population within the labor force will be countries with higher levels of economic development. This is partly a function of levels of education and training and partly a function of the age distribution of populations. In developing countries, substantial percentages of the total population are too young to be part of the labor force. Also in developing countries, a significant percentage of the population consists of women engaged in household activities or subsistence cultivation. These people seldom appear on lists of either employed or unemployed seeking employment and are the world's forgotten workers.

Map 85   Employment by Economic Activity

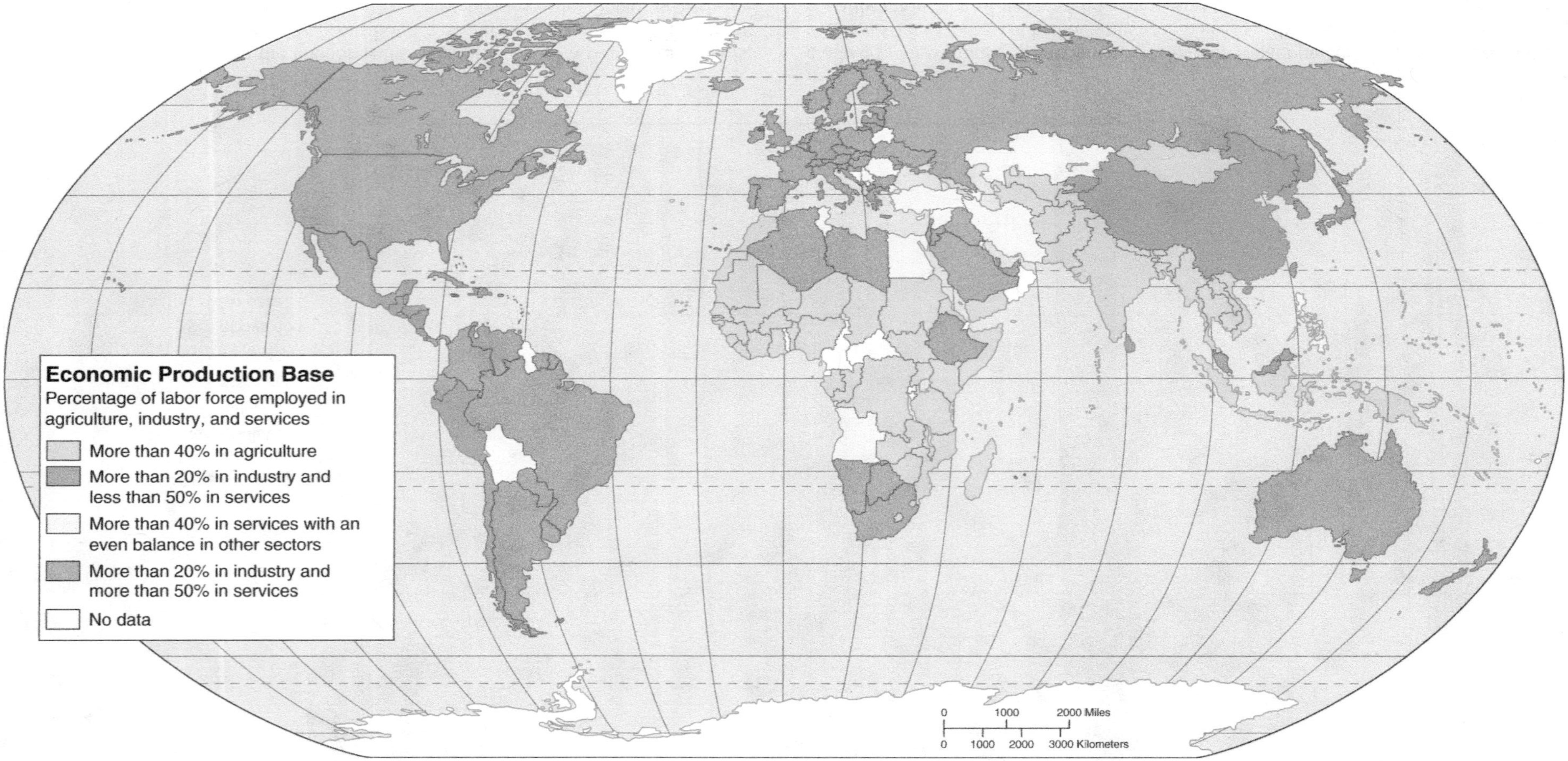

Economic Production Base
Percentage of labor force employed in agriculture, industry, and services

- More than 40% in agriculture
- More than 20% in industry and less than 50% in services
- More than 40% in services with an even balance in other sectors
- More than 20% in industry and more than 50% in services
- No data

0   1000   2000 Miles
0   1000   2000   3000 Kilometers

The employment structure of a country's population is one of the best indicators of the country's position on the scale of economic development. At one end of the scale are those countries with more than 40 percent of their labor force employed in agriculture. These are almost invariably the least developed, with high population growth rates, poor human services, significant environmental problems, and so on. In the middle of the scale are two types of countries: those with more than 20 percent of their labor force employed in industry and those with a fairly even balance among agricultural, industrial, and service employment but with at least 40 percent of their labor force employed in service activities. Generally, these countries have undergone the industrial revolution fairly recently and are

still developing an industrial base while building up their service activities. This category also includes countries with a disproportionate share of their economies in service activities primarily related to resource extraction. On the other end of the scale from the agricultural economies are countries with more than 20 percent of their labor force employed in industry and more than 50 percent in service activities. These countries are, for the most part, those with a highly automated industrial base and a highly mechanized agricultural system (the "postindustrial," developed countries). They also include, particularly in Middle and South America and Africa, industrializing countries that are also heavily engaged in resource extraction as a service activity.

Map 86 Economic Output by Sector

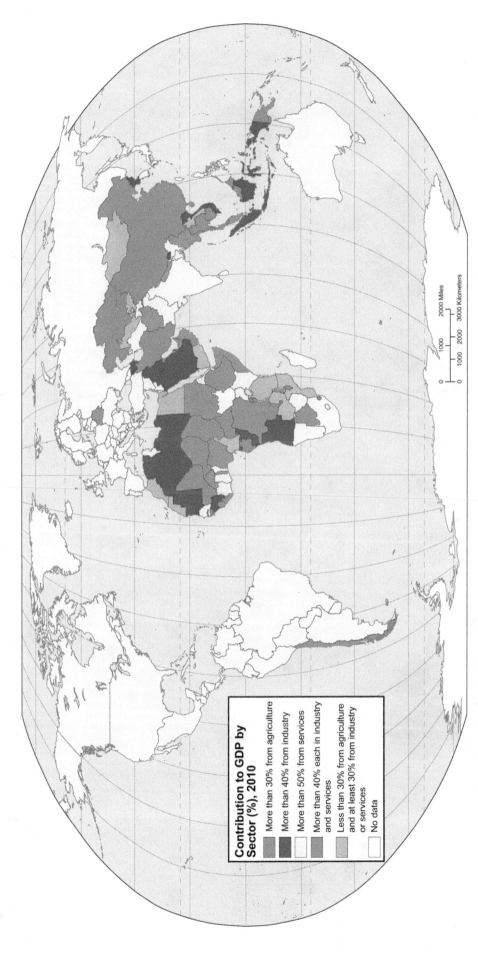

Contribution to GDP by Sector (%), 2010

- More than 30% from agriculture
- More than 40% from industry
- More than 50% from services
- More than 40% each in industry and services
- Less than 30% from agriculture and at least 30% from industry or services
- No data

The percentage of the gross domestic product (the final output of goods and services produced by the domestic economy, including net exports of goods and nonfactor, nonlabor, noncapital—services) that is devoted to agricultural, industrial, and service activities is considered a good measure of the level of economic development. In general, countries with more than 40 percent of their GDP derived from agriculture are still in a *colonial dependency* economy—that is, raising agricultural goods primarily for the export market and dependent upon that market (usually the richer countries). Similarly, countries with more than 40 percent of GDP devoted to both agriculture and services often emphasize resource extractive (primarily mining and forestry) activities. These also tend to be colonial dependency countries, providing raw materials for foreign markets. Countries with more than 40 percent of their GDP obtained from industry are normally well along the path to economic development. Countries with more than half of their GDP based on service activities fall into two ends of the development spectrum. On the one hand are countries heavily dependent on extractive activities, tourism, and other low-level service functions. On the other hand are countries that can properly be termed *postindustrial*: they have already passed through the industrial stage of their economic development and now rely less on the manufacture of products than on finance, research, communications, education, and other service-oriented activities.

Map 87   The Indebtedness of States

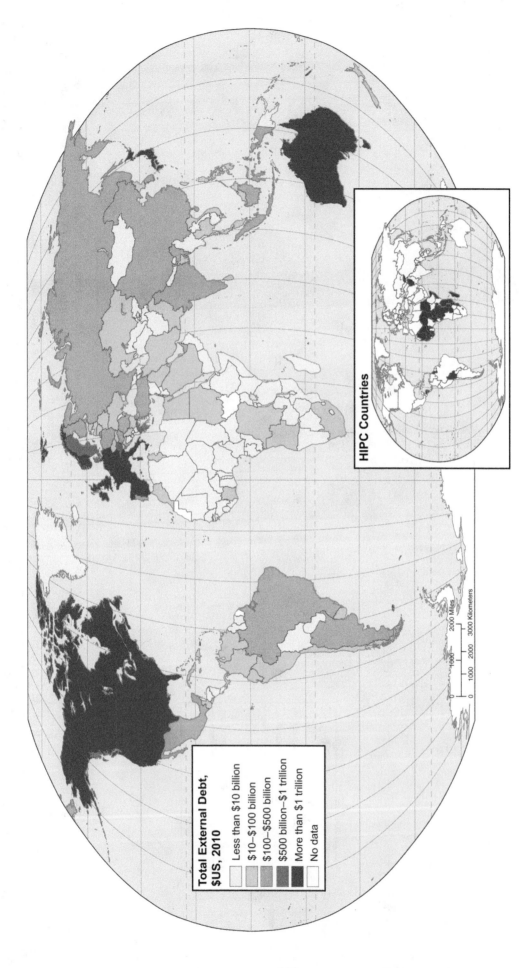

Total External Debt, $US, 2010
- Less than $10 billion
- $10–$100 billion
- $100–$500 billion
- $500 billion–$1 trillion
- More than $1 trillion
- No data

HIPC Countries

0   1000   2000   2000 Miles
0   1000   2000   3000 Kilometers

External debt is money or credit owed to foreign lenders. It generally is comprised of bonds and treasury bills (in the case of the United States) that are sold to foreign lenders and money owed to banks, governments, and international financial institutions. External debt is highly fluid and many countries of the world have "sustainable debt"—where a country can meet its debt service obligations. Other countries, particularly those in the developing world, have levels of debt (typically to international financial institutions such as the IMF and World Bank) that are beyond the government's ability to repay. These countries typically are in a constant "catch-up" situation in which they fall increasingly further into debt and cannot meet their obligations without receiving partial or total forgiveness of debt. The IMF and World Bank have jointly put together debt reduction packages for countries identified as Heavily Indebted Poor Countries (HIPC). As of 2010 approximately one-third of the U.S. national debt is that owed to foreign countries, with China and Japan accounting for over 44 percent of those holdings. Given the level of debt held by foreign countries, it is in the best interest of these countries to have the economy of the U.S. healthy.

Map 88 Global Flows of Investment Capital

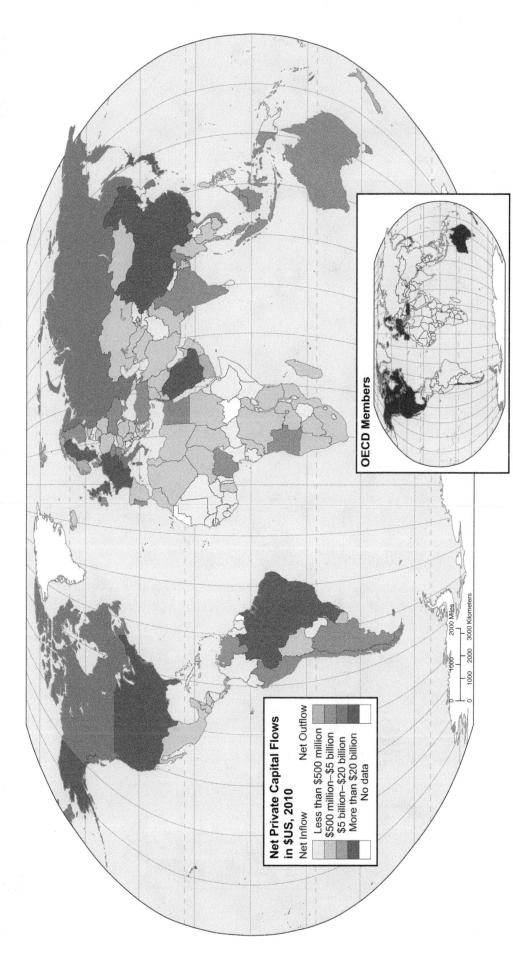

Net Private Capital Flows in $US, 2010

Net Inflow   Net Outflow

- Less than $500 million
- $500 million–$5 billion
- $5 billion–$20 billion
- More than $20 billion
- No data

OECD Members

0 1000 2000 3000 Kilometers
0 1000 2000 Miles

International capital flows include private debt and nondebt flows from one country to another, shown as flows into a country on the map. Nearly all of the capital comes from those countries that are members of the Organisation for Economic Co-operation and Development (OECD), shown on the inset map. Capital flows include commercial bank lending, other private credits, foreign direct investment, and portfolio investment. Most of these flows are indicators of the increasing influence developed countries exert over the developing economies. Foreign direct investment (FDI) for example, is a measure of the net inflow of investment monies used to acquire long-term management interest in businesses

located somewhere other than in the economy of the investor. Usually this means the acquisition of at least 10 percent of the stock of a company by a foreign investor and is, then, a measure of what might be termed "economic colonialism": control of a region's economy by foreign investors that could, in the world of the future, be as significant as colonial political control was in the past. International capital flows have increased greatly in the last decade as the result of the increasing liberalization of developing countries, the strong economic growth exhibited by many developing countries, and the falling costs and increased efficiency of communication and transportation services.

Map 89   Remittances as a Percentage of GDP

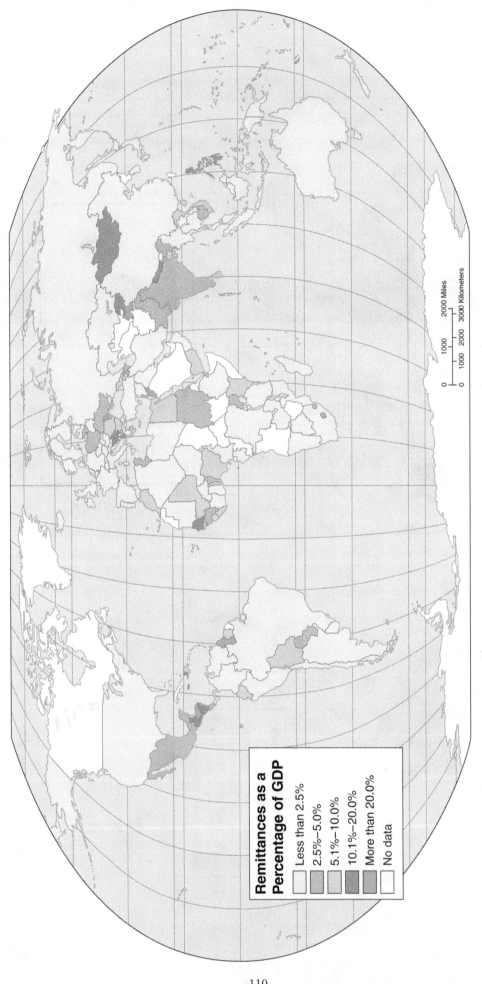

Remittances as a Percentage of GDP

- Less than 2.5%
- 2.5%–5.0%
- 5.1%–10.0%
- 10.1%–20.0%
- More than 20.0%
- No data

0   1000   2000 Miles

0   1000   2000   3000 Kilometers

As seen in Map 58, the wealthy countries of the world also have sizeable immigrant populations. In countries where economic pull factors are particularly strong, there may also be a large population of foreign workers who ultimately may return to their home country. Whether the move to a new country is temporary or permanent, the ties to the home country oftentimes remain strong. Economic ties can be particularly strong, as demonstrated by remittances. A remittance simply is the transfer of money from an individual to his or her home country. During the mid-2000s remittances exceeded $250 billion. In some smaller countries like Honduras and Tajikistan, remittances comprise more than a quarter of GDP. As would be expected, the bulk of this money is coming from workers employed in North America, Western Europe, and Japan.

Map 90   Inflation Rates

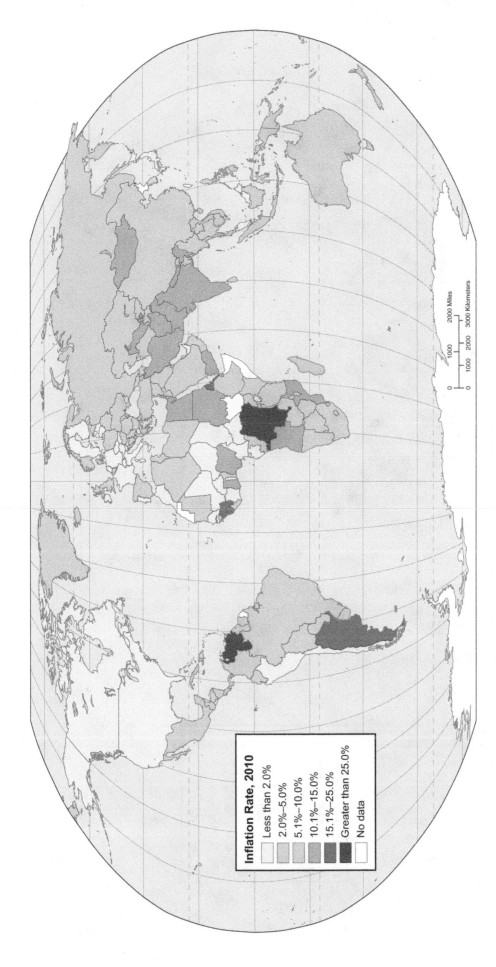

Inflation Rate, 2010

- Less than 2.0%
- 2.0%–5.0%
- 5.1%–10.0%
- 10.1%–15.0%
- 15.1%–25.0%
- Greater than 25.0%
- No data

The last half of the first decade of the twenty-first century saw economic decline on a global scale at levels not seen since the 1930s. In 2008, growth in GDP (gross domestic product —the market value of a country's goods and services produced during a year) began slowing. In many countries, the slowing growth of GDP has been accompanied by rising inflation rates. The inflation rate is a measure of the rise in the prices of goods and services. Inflation can influence economies both positively and negatively, but hyperinflation—extremely high

or out-of-control inflation—can seriously hinder a country's ability to produce goods and services. The most noteworthy example of recent hyperinflation is Zimbabwe. During the late-twentieth century Zimbabwe's inflation rate was relatively high—typically between 15 percent and 40 percent. During the early 2000s, hyperinflation set in, reaching as high as 11.2 million percent in 2008. In 2009 the country gained international notoriety when it issued a 100 trillion Zimbabwean dollar note.

Map **91**   Dependence on Trade

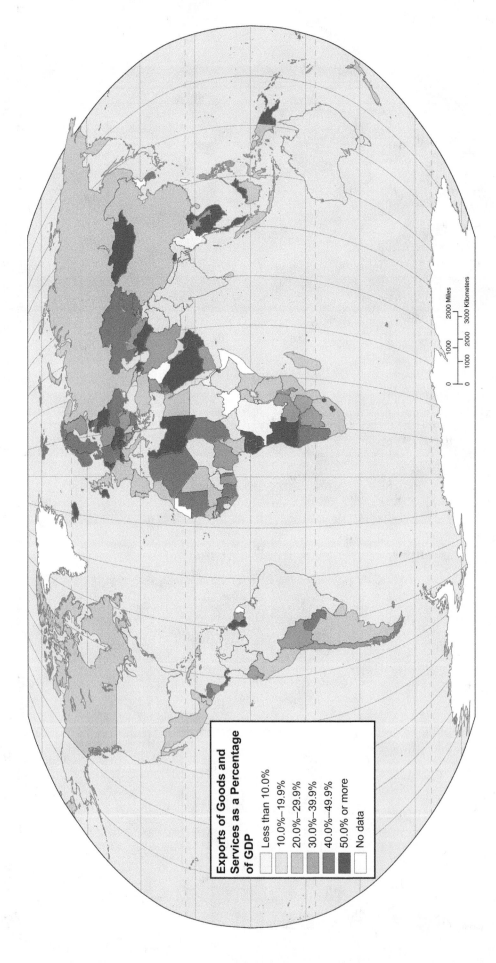

**Exports of Goods and
Services as a Percentage
of GDP**

- Less than 10.0%
- 10.0%–19.9%
- 20.0%–29.9%
- 30.0%–39.9%
- 40.0%–49.9%
- 50.0% or more
- No data

As the global economy becomes more and more a reality, the economic strength of virtually all countries is increasingly dependent upon trade. For many developing nations, with relatively abundant resources and limited industrial capacity, exports provide the primary base upon which their economies rest. Even countries like the United States, Japan, and Germany, with huge and diverse economies, depend on exports to generate a significant percentage of their employment and wealth. Without imports, many products that consumers want would be unavailable or more expensive; without exports, many jobs would be eliminated.

0   1000   2000 Miles

0   1000   2000   3000 Kilometers

Map 92   Trade with Neighboring Countries

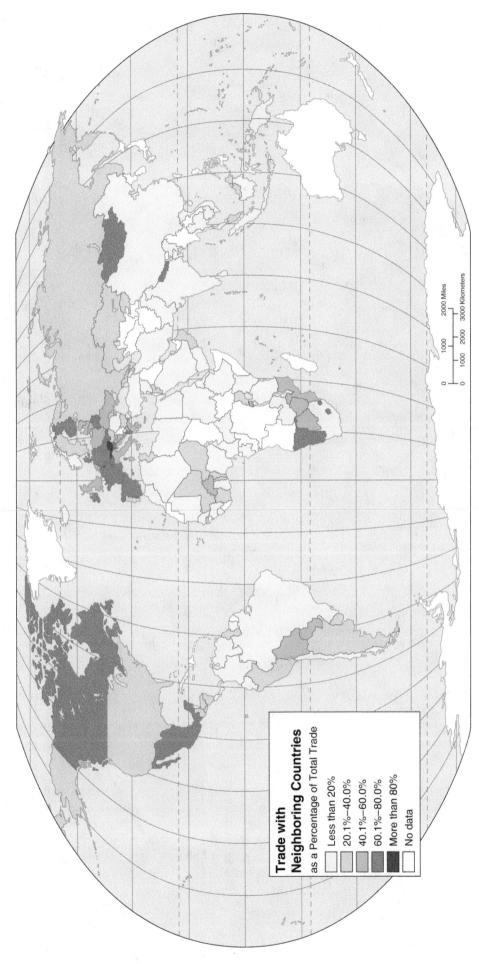

Trade with Neighboring Countries
as a Percentage of Total Trade

- Less than 20%
- 20.1%—40.0%
- 40.1%—60.0%
- 60.1%—80.0%
- More than 80%
- No data

Two important factors influencing international trade are proximity and relative wealth of trading partners. Proximity is important because transportation costs can be a large part of an economic activity. Relative wealth is an important influence on the goods and services a country may produce for export. Of course, the percentage of trade with neighboring countries isn't necessarily a strong indicator of a country's wealth or future growth, but the

patterns exhibited on this map are telling. The world's countries are increasingly interconnecting through regional trade agreements (see Map 80), and the influence of connectivity among EU and NAFTA states is evident here. Much of Africa, South Asia, and South America trades more with more distant countries such as the United States, Japan, and EU states. As regional trade blocs mature, look for the levels of cross-border trade to increase.

Map 93   The Cost of Consumption, 2010

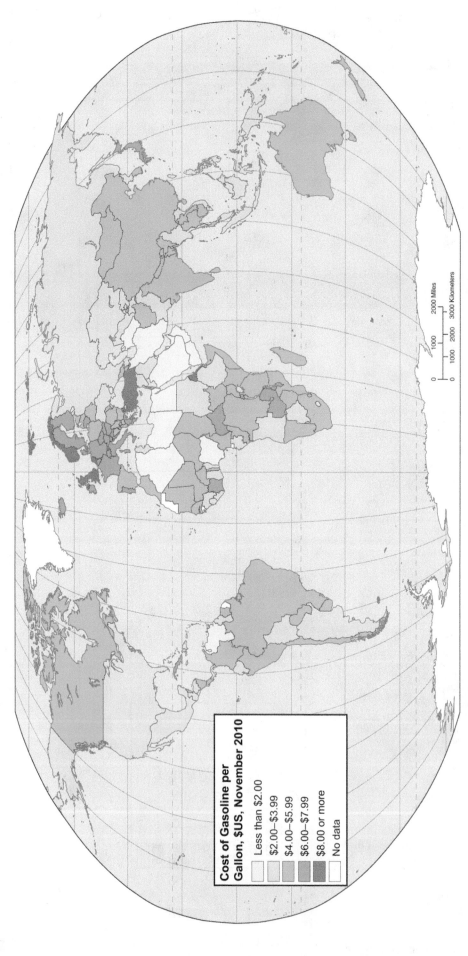

Cost of Gasoline per Gallon, $US, November 2010

- Less than $2.00
- $2.00–$3.99
- $4.00–$5.99
- $6.00–$7.99
- $8.00 or more
- No data

The year 2008 brought massive increases in the price of gasoline at the pump, creating considerable consternation among the American driving population, in particular. It is one thing to point out that gasoline prices are and historically have been considerably higher in Europe than in North America. But it is another to note that European spatial patterns of places of work and places of residence are significantly different than in North America. The North American metropolitan area evolved its spatial patterns in conjunction with the rise of privately owned automobiles; European cities, on the other hand, had spatial patterns well established centuries or even millennia before the automobile emerged as a common mode of transportation. As a consequence, such things as the journey to work are very different for many Europeans, who can walk from where they live to where they work, than it is for

Americans and Canadians, who often live considerable distances from their places of employment. A daily commute of 75 miles one way would not be considered unusual in America. In Europe it is virtually unheard of. There is also the component of the scale of organization of human activities: Because of the very large country in which Americans live, their spatial movements are customarily more extensive than those of Europeans, who live in countries the size of American states. So, yes, gasoline is much more expensive in Europe than in North America. But in North America, the increase in the cost of gasoline to and above $4.00 per gallon produces significantly more economic impact than proportionally similar increases in Europe. Similarly, the reduction in gasoline prices in late 2009 and throughout 2010 had a greater impact in North America—although its impact was overshadowed by larger forces.

Map 94 A Wired World: Internet Users

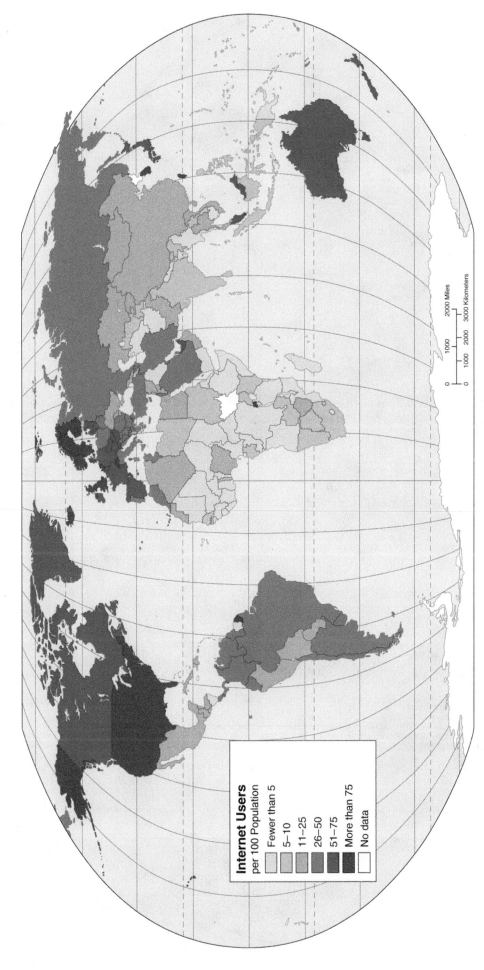

Internet Users
per 100 Population

- Fewer than 5
- 5–10
- 11–25
- 26–50
- 51–75
- More than 75
- No data

It is interesting to contemplate that a short quarter of a century ago, such a map could not have been created. The emergence of immediate, long-distance connectivity via the Internet has been one of the most important components of globalization. We now live, as author Thomas Friedman has noted, in a "flat world" where lines of connection are more important than distance and where virtually instantaneous connections have altered—perhaps forever—the way that we do business, exchange information, and transform our cultures. Some of the recent transformations we have seen, such as

the emergence of countries like China and India as major players in the international economy, are, in part, the consequence of access to the Internet. Originally conceived as a quick way for academics to exchange information, the Internet has become a cultural and social phenomenon that far exceeds its original purpose. Whether or not this will result in an eventual benefit to human well-being remains to be seen. Does the benefit of quick communication result in a cost to the complexity and richness of human cultures worldwide?

Map 95 The Rise of the Personal Computer

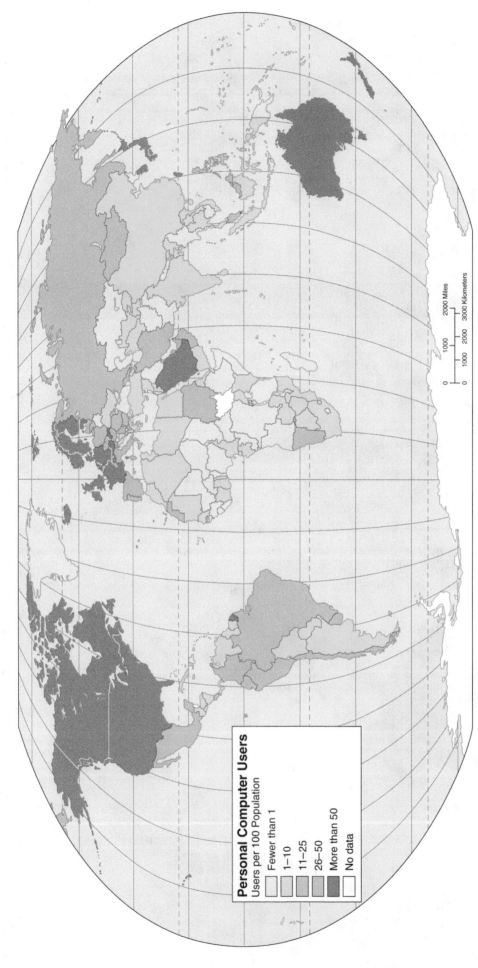

Personal Computer Users
Users per 100 Population

Fewer than 1
1–10
11–25
26–50
More than 50
No data

The Internet connections shown on the previous map would not be possible without personal computers—or at least not possible at their present scale. But personal computers do a great deal more than simply act as high-speed transmitters of information. They are incredibly powerful devices for the storage and analysis of data and are becoming, seemingly exponentially, even more powerful. When the use of mainframe computers became common on university campuses in the 1960s, they were used primarily for faculty and graduate student research. Now, an undergraduate can run on his or her laptop computer—in a matter of seconds—a program that would have required hours to run on an institutional computer from the 1960s, which occupied spaces similar to those required for medium-sized classrooms. Certainly computers have changed the way that businesses are run. But they have, perhaps, changed the daily lives of personal computer users even more.

Map 96 Traditional Links: The Telephone

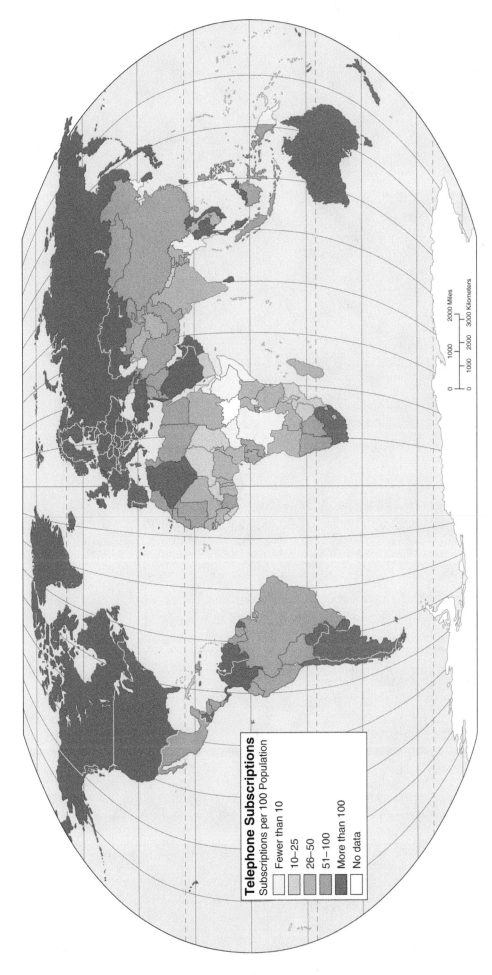

Telephone Subscriptions
Subscriptions per 100 Population

- Fewer than 10
- 10–25
- 26–50
- 51–100
- More than 100
- No data

0 1000 2000 Miles

0 1000 2000 3000 Kilometers

Not all of the world's communication takes place via computers and the Internet. A lot of person-to-person connection is still carried out via the telephone, and access to telephone connections is perhaps as good an indication of economic development (or, more important, the potential for economic development) as anything else. The map clearly shows the prevalence of telephone connectivity in the developed world. But it also shows an increasingly high degree of access to telephones in major countries in the developing world, such as India and China. If these countries are to continue to develop their economies at the pace of the last decade, then their degree of communication—including access to telephones—will also have to increase. The data shown on this map include users of both land lines and cellular phones. By the end of 2008, for the first time, the number of cellular phone users worldwide exceeded the number of those using the traditional land lines. As cellular phone complexity increases to include e-mail and other computer functions, the gap between cellular users and traditional phone users can be expected to widen.

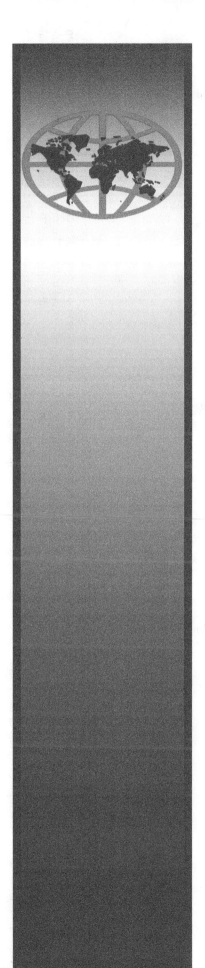

Unit V

Food and Energy

Map 97 The Value of Agriculture

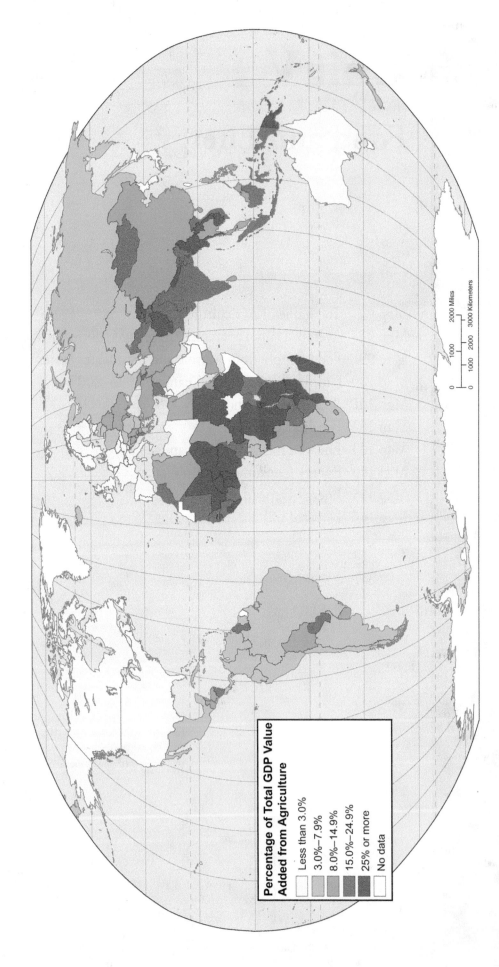

Percentage of Total GDP Value Added from Agriculture

- Less than 3.0%
- 3.0%–7.9%
- 8.0%–14.9%
- 15.0%–24.9%
- 25% or more
- No data

0   1000   2000 Miles

0   1000   2000   3000 Kilometers

When compared to the service and industrial sectors of the global economy, agriculture grew more slowly between 1990 and 2005. The highest rates of growth were recorded in the Sub-Saharan African region, where agriculture grew more than either service or industrial economies. It is clear from the Sub-Saharan African figures, as well as those from Middle and South America and Asia, that agriculture is still of vital economic importance to the developing regions of the world. Not only does agriculture contribute significantly to the gross domestic product of these countries, it represents the primary source of employment in nearly two-thirds of the world's countries. Even in the rapidly expanding service and industrial economies of India and China, agriculture still counts for nearly half of all employment. This contrasts with 4 percent of total agricultural employment in the United States and Germany, and only 1 percent in the United Kingdom.

Map 98 Average Daily Per Capita Supply of Calories (Kilocalories)

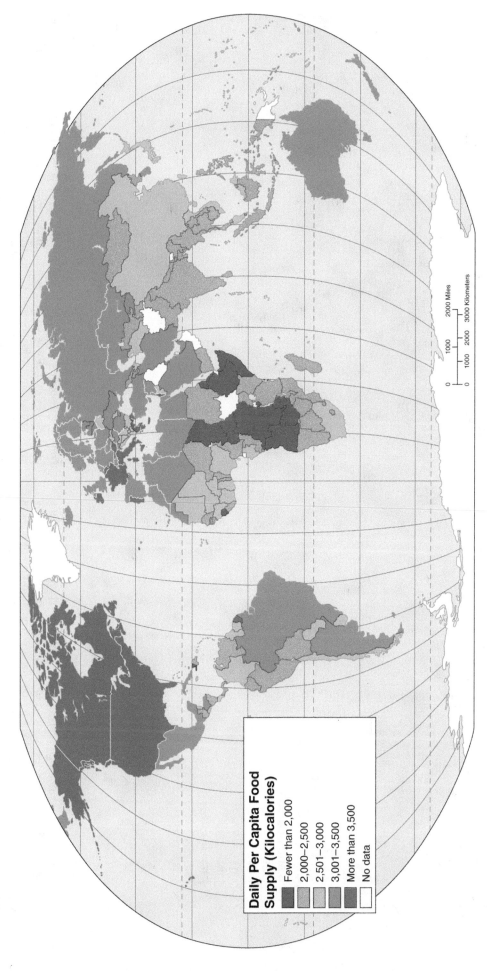

Daily Per Capita Food Supply (Kilocalories)
- Fewer than 2,000
- 2,000–2,500
- 2,501–3,000
- 3,001–3,500
- More than 3,500
- No data

0   1000   2000 Miles
0   1000   2000   3000 Kilometers

The data shown on this map, which indicate the presence or absence of critical food shortages, do not necessarily indicate the presence of starvation or famine. But they certainly do indicate potential problem areas for the next decade. The measurements are in calories from *all* food sources: domestic production, international trade, draw-down on stocks or food reserves, and direct foreign contributions or aid. The quantity of calories available is that amount, estimated by the UN's Food and Agriculture Organization (FAO), that reaches consumers. The calories actually consumed may be lower than the figures shown, depending on how much is lost in a variety of ways: in home storage (to pests such as rats and mice), in preparation and cooking, through consumption by pets and domestic animals, and as discarded foods, for example. The estimate of need is not a global uniform value, but is calculated for each country on the basis of the age and sex distribution of the population and the estimated level of activity of the population. Compare this map with Map 75 for a good measure of potential problem areas for food shortages within the next decade.

-121-

Map 99 Food Supply from Marine and Freshwater Systems

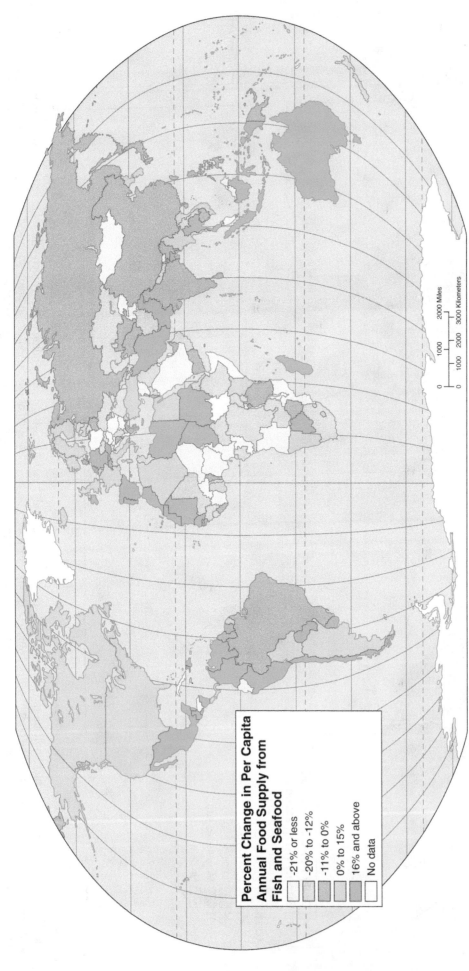

Percent Change in Per Capita Annual Food Supply from Fish and Seafood

- -21% or less
- -20% to -12%
- -11% to 0%
- 0% to 15%
- 16% and above
- No data

0 1000 2000 Miles
0 1000 2000 3000 Kilometers

Not that many years ago, food supply experts were confidently predicting that the "starving millions" of the world of the future could be fed from the unending bounty of the world's oceans. While the annual catch from the sea helped to keep hunger at bay for a time, by the late 1980s it had become apparent that without serious human intervention in the form of aquaculture, the supply of fish would not be sufficient to offset the population/food imbalance that was beginning to affect so many of the world's regions. The development of factory-fishing with advanced equipment to locate fish and process them before they went to market increased the supply of food from the ocean, but in that increase was sown the seeds of future problems. The factory-fishing system, efficient in terms of economics, was costly in terms of fish populations. In some well-fished areas, the stock of fish that was viewed as near infinite just a few decades ago has dwindled nearly to the point of disappearance. This map shows both increases and decreases in the amount of individual countries' food supplies from the ocean. The increases are often the result of more technologically advanced fishing operations. The decreases are usually the result of the same thing: Increased technology has brought increased harvests, which has reduced the supply of fish and shellfish and that, in turn, has increased prices. Most of the countries that have experienced sharp decreases in their supply of food from the world's oceans are simply no longer able to pay for an increasingly scarce commodity.

Map 100   Cropland Per Capita: Changes, 1996–2007

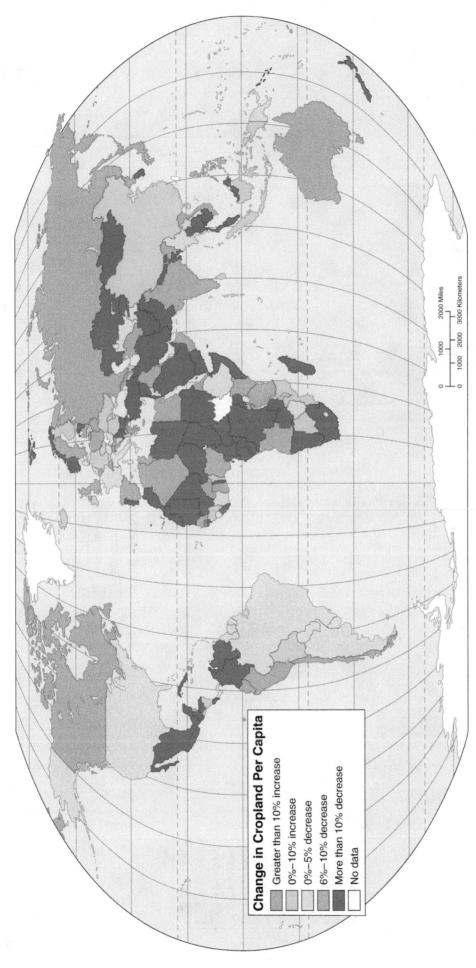

Change in Cropland Per Capita

- Greater than 10% increase
- 0%–10% increase
- 0%–5% decrease
- 6%–10% decrease
- More than 10% decrease
- No data

0   1000   2000 Miles
0   1000   2000   3000 Kilometers

As population has increased rapidly throughout the world, the area of cultivated land has increased at the same time; in fact, the amount of farmland per person has gone up slightly. Unfortunately, the figures that show this also tell us that since most of the best (or even good) agricultural land in 1985 was already under cultivation, most of the agricultural area added since the mid-1990s involves land that would have been viewed as marginal by the fathers and grandfathers of present farmers—marginal in that it was too dry, too wet, too steep to cultivate, too far from a market, and so on. The continued expansion of agricultural area is one reason that serious famine and starvation have struck only a few regions of the globe. But land, more than any other resource we deal with, is finite, and the expansion cannot continue indefinitely. Future gains in agricultural production are most probably going to come through more intensive use of existing cropland, heavier applications of fertilizers and other agricultural chemicals, and genetically engineered crops requiring heavier applications of energy and water, than from an increase in the amount of the world's cropland.

Map 101 World Pastureland, 2005

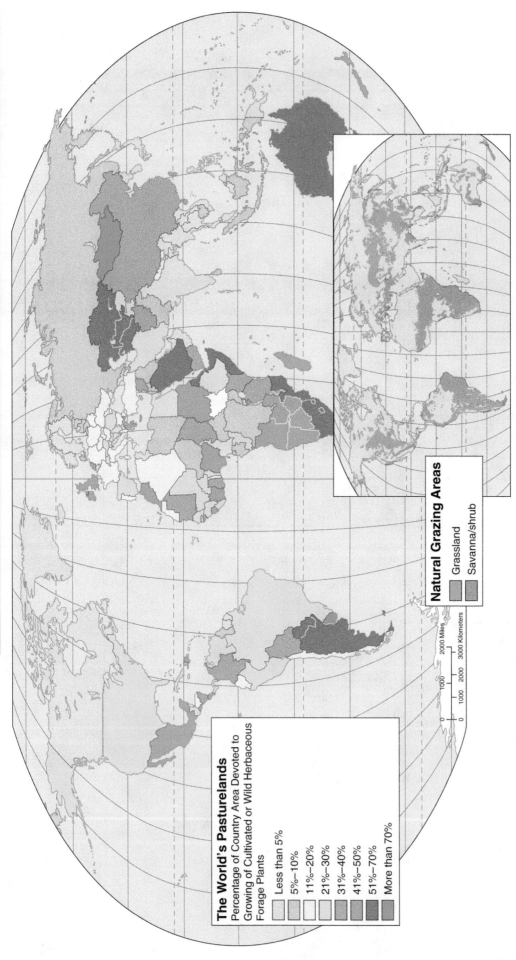

The World's Pasturelands
Percentage of Country Area Devoted to Growing of Cultivated or Wild Herbaceous Forage Plants

- Less than 5%
- 5%–10%
- 11%–20%
- 21%–30%
- 31%–40%
- 41%–50%
- 51%–70%
- More than 70%

Natural Grazing Areas

- Grassland
- Savanna/shrub

0   1000   2000 Miles
0   1000   2000   3000 Kilometers

More than 25 percent of the world's surface is considered pastureland—either native wild grasses or human-made pastures created by clearing forests and planting grass and other herbaceous forage plants for livestock feed. Two types of pasture predominate: the prairie and steppe grasses of the midlatitudes and the savanna grasses of the subtropics and tropics. These two primary grassland biomes are shown in the inset map. The larger map depicts pastureland as a proportion of land area of individual countries. You will note that many of the countries with high levels of pastureland (Argentina and Australia, for example) are among the world's leading exporters of livestock products. Other countries with high levels of pastureland (Saudi Arabia and the Central Asian states) consume the bulk of their products domestically. The significance of the distribution and use of pastureland is that—whether it is in the African Sahel, China, Brazil, or the United States—the world's pasturelands are deteriorating rapidly under increasing demands to produce more animal products than even a wealthier world can afford to pay for. Grassland degradation, particularly in areas where pastoral nomads use their animals as their chief source of food and income, creates woody scrublands where the carrying capacity for grazing animals is sharply diminished. In short, most of the world's pasturelands are overgrazed, and the world's supply of animal products is in jeopardy.

-124-

Map 102 Fertilizer Use, 2007

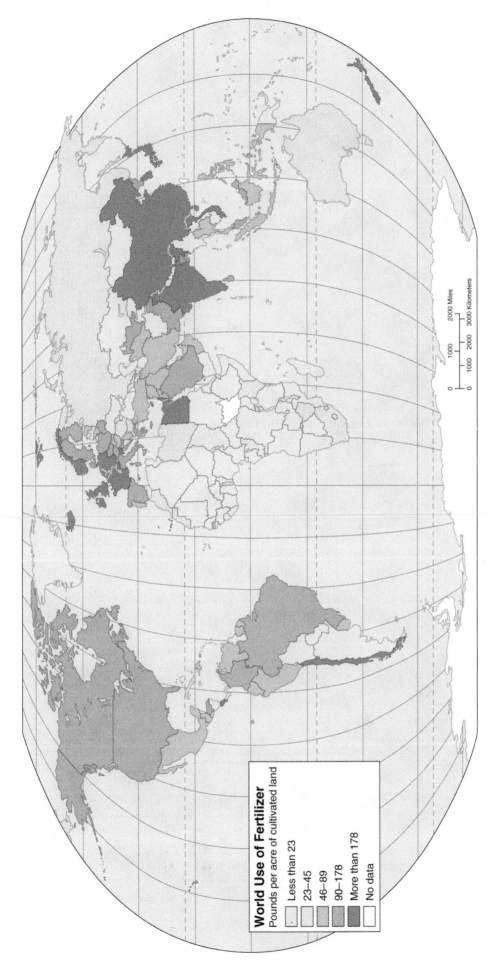

World Use of Fertilizer
Pounds per acre of cultivated land

- Less than 23
- 23–45
- 46–89
- 90–178
- More than 178
- No data

0 1000 2000 Miles
0 1000 2000 3000 Kilometers

The use of fertilizer to maintain the productivity of agricultural lands is a wonderful agricultural invention—as long as the fertilizers used are natural rather than artificial. In most of the world's developed countries, such as those in Europe and North America, the use of animal manure to fertilize fields has decreased dramatically over the past century, in favor of artificial fertilizers that are cheaper, easier to use, and—most important—increase crop yields more dramatically. The danger here is that artificial fertilizers normally have high concentrations of nitrates that tend to convert to nitrites in the soil, reducing the ability of soil bacteria to extract "free" nitrogen from the atmosphere. As more artificial fertilizer is used, natural soil fertility is decreased, creating the demand for more artificial fertilizers. In some areas, overuse of artificial fertilizers has actually created soils that are too "hot" chemically to produce crops. Countries with high fertilizer use in the developing world—northern South America, and Southwest, South, and East Asia—still tend to use more natural fertilizers. But as farmers in those areas gain more ability to buy and use artificial fertilizers, their soils will also begin to suffer from overfertilization. Global agriculture must come to grips with the need to maintain productivity, but to do so in a manner that is sustainable.

-125-

Map 103 Energy Production Per Capita

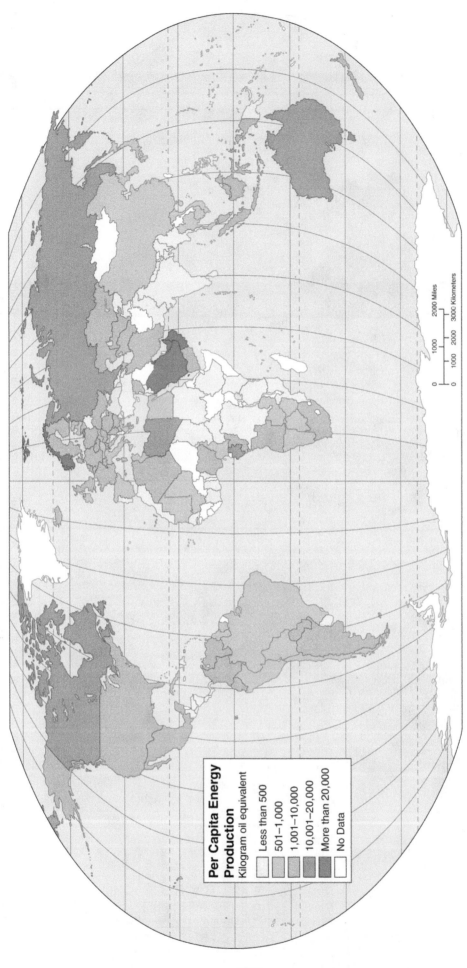

Per Capita Energy Production

Kilogram oil equivalent

- Less than 500
- 501–1,000
- 1,001–10,000
- 10,001–20,000
- More than 20,000
- No Data

Energy production per capita is a measure of the availability of mechanical energy to assist people in their work. This map shows the amount of all kinds of energy—solid fuel (primarily coal), liquid fuel (primarily petroleum), natural gas, geothermal, wind, solar, hydroelectric, nuclear, waste recycling, and indigenous heat pumps—produced per person in each country. With some exceptions, wealthier countries produce more energy per capita than poor ones. Countries such as Japan and many European states rank among the world's wealthiest, but are energy-poor and produce relatively little of their own energy.

They have the ability, however, to pay for imports. On the other hand, countries such as those of the Persian Gulf or the oil-producing states of Middle and South America may rank relatively low on the scale of economic development but rank high as producers of energy. In many poor countries, especially in Middle and South America, Africa, South Asia, and East Asia, large proportions of energy come from traditional fuels, such as firewood and animal dung. Indeed, for many in the developing world, the real energy crisis is a shortage of wood for cooking and heating.

Map 104 Energy Consumption Per Capita

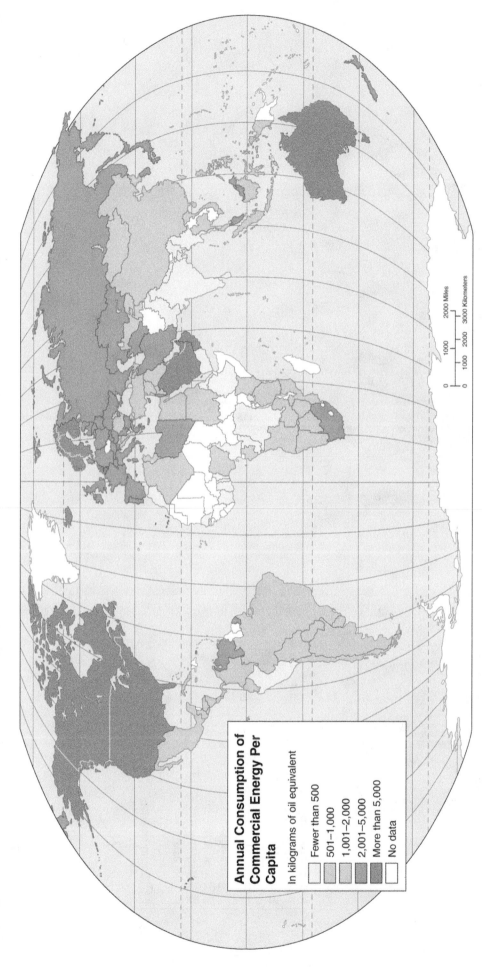

Annual Consumption of Commercial Energy Per Capita

In kilograms of oil equivalent

- Fewer than 500
- 501–1,000
- 1,001–2,000
- 2,001–5,000
- More than 5,000
- No data

Of all the quantitative measures of economic well-being, energy consumption per capita may be the most expressive. All of the countries defined by the World Bank as having high incomes consume at least 100 gigajoules of commercial energy (the equivalent of about 3.5 metric tons of coal) per person per year, with some, such as the United States and Canada, having consumption rates in the 300-gigajoule range (the equivalent of more than 10 metric tons of coal per person per year). With the exception of the oil-rich Persian Gulf states, where consumption figures include the costly "burning off" of excess energy in the form of natural gas flares at wellheads, most of the highest-consuming countries are in the Northern Hemisphere, concentrated in North America and Western Europe. At the other end of the scale are low-income countries, where consumption rates are often less than 1 percent of the United States and other high consumers. These figures do not, of course, include the consumption of noncommercial energy—the traditional fuels of firewood, animal dung, and other organic matter—widely used in the less developed parts of the world.

-127-

Map 105   Energy Dependency

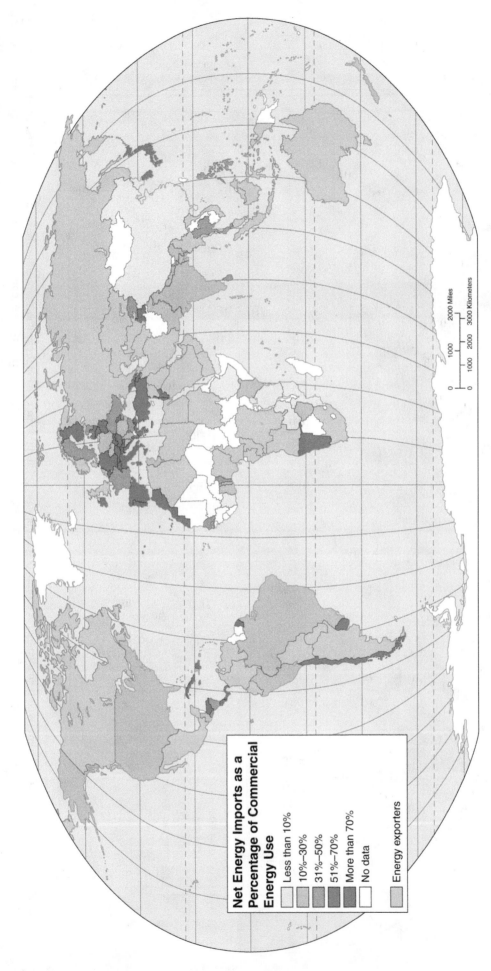

Net Energy Imports as a Percentage of Commercial Energy Use

- Less than 10%
- 10%–30%
- 31%–50%
- 51%–70%
- More than 70%
- No data

- Energy exporters

0   1000   2000 Miles
0   1000   2000   3000 Kilometers

The patterns on the map show dependence on commercial energy before transformation to other end-use fuels, such as electricity or refined petroleum products; energy from traditional sources, such as firewood or dried animal dung, is not included. Energy dependency is the difference between domestic consumption and domestic production of commercial energy and is most often expressed as a net energy import or export. The growth in global commercial energy use over the last decade indicates growth in the modern sectors of the economy (industry, transportation, and urbanization), particularly in the lesser-developed countries. Still, the primary consumers of energy—and those having the greatest dependence on foreign sources of energy—are the more highly-developed countries of Europe, North America, and Japan.

-128-

Map 106   Flows of Oil

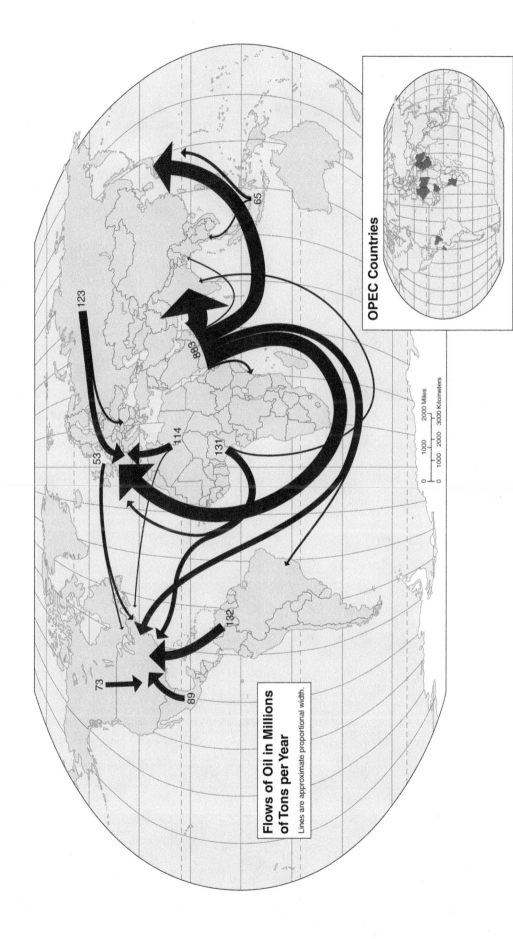

Flows of Oil in Millions of Tons per Year

Lines are approximate proportional width.

OPEC Countries

0   1000   2000 Miles

0   1000   2000   3000 Kilometers

The pattern of oil movements from producing region to consuming region is one of the dominant facts of contemporary international maritime trade. Supertankers carry a million tons of crude oil and charge rates in excess of $0.10 US per ton per mile, making the transportation of oil not only a necessity for the world's energy-hungry countries, but also an enormously profitable proposition. One of the major negatives of these massive oil flows is the damage done to the oceanic ecosystems—not just from the well-publicized and dramatic events like the wrecking of the *Exxon Valdez*, but

from the incalculable amounts of oil from leakage, scrubbings, purgings, and so on, which are a part of the oil transport technology. As seen above, much of the supply of the world's oil comes from countries belonging to the Organization of the Petroleum Exporting Countries (OPEC). In 1999, OPEC members controlled nearly two-thirds of the world's known oil reserves and more than one-third of the world's production. It is clear from the map that the primary recipients of these oil flows are the world's most highly-developed economies.

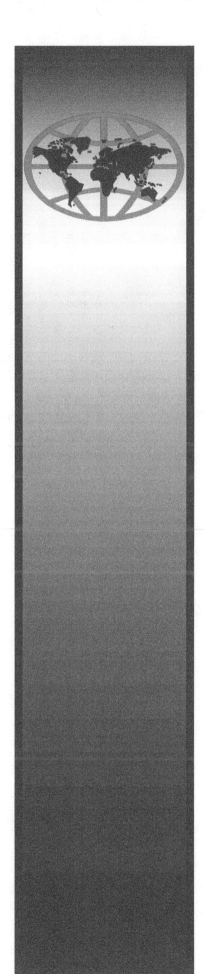

Unit VI

Environmental Conditions

Map 107 Deforestation and Desertification

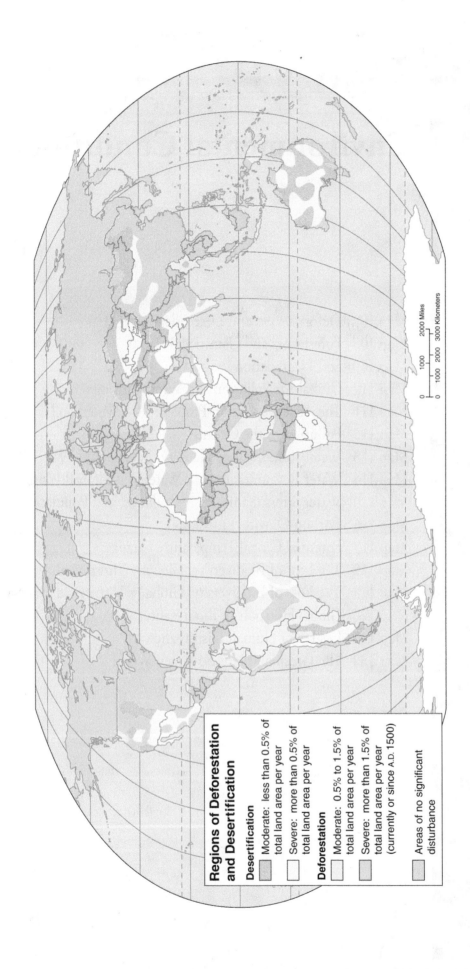

Regions of Deforestation and Desertification

Desertification

- Moderate: less than 0.5% of total land area per year
- Severe: more than 0.5% of total land area per year

Deforestation

- Moderate: 0.5% to 1.5% of total land area per year
- Severe: more than 1.5% of total land area per year (currently or since A.D. 1500)
- Areas of no significant disturbance

0   1000   2000 Miles
0   1000   2000   3000 Kilometers

While those of us in the developed countries of the world tend to think of environmental deterioration as the consequence of our heavily industrialized economies, in fact the worst examples of current environmental degradation are found within the world's less developed regions. There, high population growth rates and economies limited primarily to farming have forced the increasing use of more marginal (less suited to cultivation) land. In the world's grassland and arid environments, which occupy approximately 40 percent of the world's total land area, increasing cultivation pressures are turning vulnerable areas into deserts incapable of sustaining agricultural productivity. In the world's forested regions, particularly in the tropical forests of Middle and South America, Africa, and Asia, a similar process is occurring: Increasing pressure for more farmland is creating a process of deforestation, or forest clearing, that destroys the soil, reduces the biological diversity of the forest regions, and ultimately may have the capacity to alter the global climate by contributing to an increase in carbon dioxide in the atmosphere. This increases the heat trapped in the atmosphere and enhances the greenhouse effect.

Map 108 Forest Loss and Gain, 1990–2010

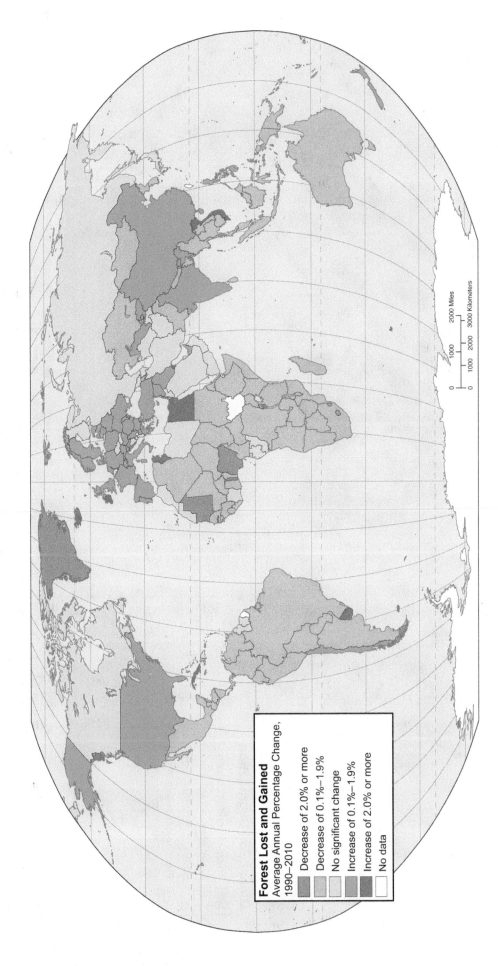

Forest Lost and Gained

Average Annual Percentage Change, 1990–2010

- Decrease of 2.0% or more
- Decrease of 0.1%–1.9%
- No significant change
- Increase of 0.1%–1.9%
- Increase of 2.0% or more
- No data

0   1000   2000 Miles
0 1000 2000 3000 Kilometers

During the 20 years included in this analysis, the world lost over 340 million acres of forest land. More than 50 percent of the world's total loss came in Sub-Saharan Africa—most of this loss represented land clearance for agricultural purposes. Approximately 40 percent of the world's total loss was in Brazil and, again, the majority of this loss resulted from land clearance for agriculture. At the global level, forest clearance seems to be slowing somewhat—but it still is an area of concern for a variety of reasons. Healthy forests act as a "carbon sink" and withdraw carbon dioxide from the atmosphere, aiding in the reduction of this important greenhouse gas and helping to reduce the impact of carbon dioxide on global warming. Equally important is the fact that forest clearance disturbs all other components of an ecosystem, from soil chemistry to water quality and quantity. There is a temptation to blame countries in Africa, Middle America, or South America for failing to protect these forests. But the agricultural products grown on cleared land, and the livestock pastured on areas cleared and replaced by grasslands, are generally consumed by the market of the more highly developed world.

-133-

Map 109 Soil Degradation

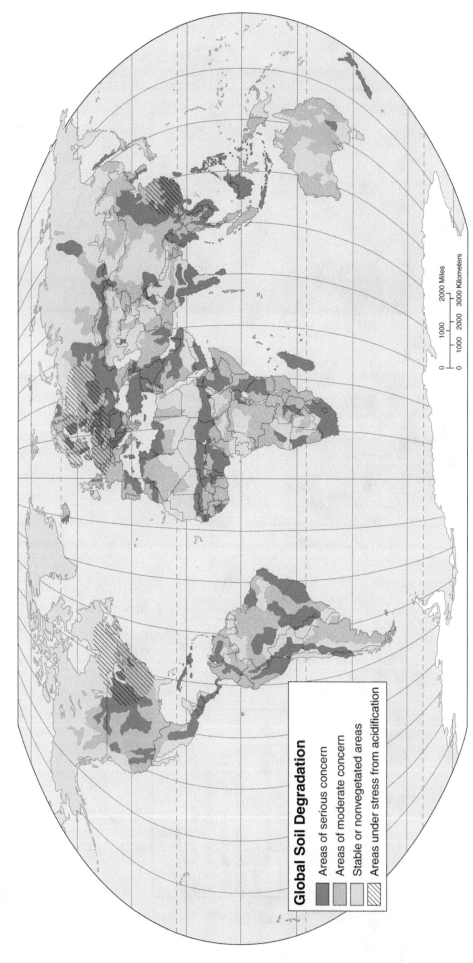

Global Soil Degradation

- Areas of serious concern
- Areas of moderate concern
- Stable or nonvegetated areas
- Areas under stress from acidification

0   1000   2000 Miles
0   1000   2000   3000 Kilometers

Recent research has shown that more than 3 billion acres of the world's surface suffer from serious soil degradation, with more than 22 million acres so severely eroded or poisoned with chemicals that they can no longer support productive crop agriculture. Most of this soil damage has been caused by poor farming practices, overgrazing of domestic livestock, and deforestation. These activities strip away the protective cover of natural vegetation—forests and grasslands—allowing wind and water erosion to remove the topsoil that contains the necessary nutrients and soil microbes for plant growth. But in some instances millions of acres of topsoil have been degraded by chemicals as well. In some instances

these chemicals are the result of overapplication of fertilizers, herbicides, pesticides, and other agricultural chemicals. In other instances, chemical deposition from industrial and urban wastes and from acid precipitation has poisoned millions of acres of soil. As the map shows, soil erosion and pollution are problems not just in developing countries with high population densities and increasing use of marginal lands, but in the more highly developed regions of mechanized, industrial agriculture as well. While many methods for preventing or reducing soil degradation exist, they are seldom used because of ignorance, cost, or perceived economic inefficiency.

Map 110 Global Air Pollution and Wind Currents

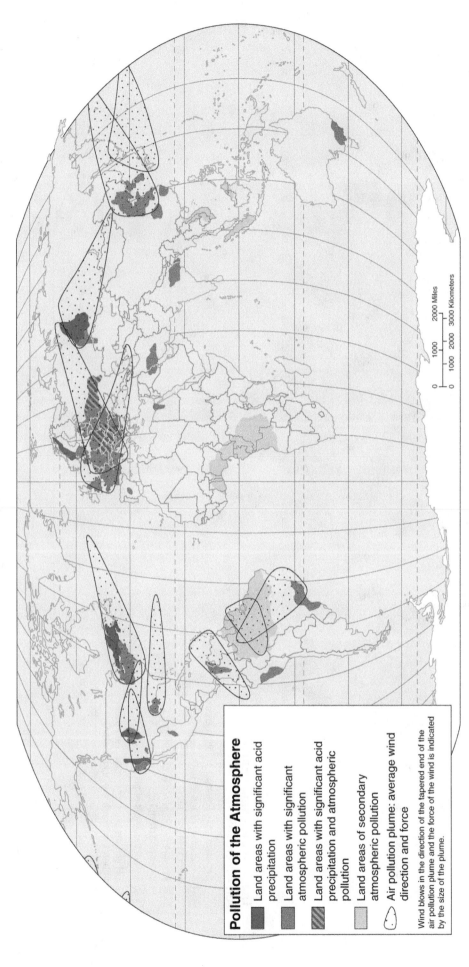

Pollution of the Atmosphere

- Land areas with significant acid precipitation
- Land areas with significant atmospheric pollution
- Land areas with significant acid precipitation and atmospheric pollution
- Land areas of secondary atmospheric pollution
- Air pollution plume: average wind direction and force

Wind blows in the direction of the tapered end of the air pollution plume and the force of the wind is indicated by the size of the plume.

0   1000   2000 Miles
0 1000 2000 3000 Kilometers

Almost all processes of physical geography begin and end with the flows of energy and matter among land, sea, and air. Because of the primacy of the atmosphere in this exchange system, air pollution is potentially one of the most dangerous human modifications in environmental systems. Pollutants (such as various oxides of nitrogen or sulfur) cause the development of acid precipitation, which damages soil, vegetation, wildlife, and fish. Air pollution in the form of smog is often dangerous for human health. And most atmospheric scientists believe that the efficiency of the atmosphere in retaining heat—the so-called greenhouse effect—is being enhanced by increased carbon dioxide, methane, and other gases produced by agricultural and industrial activities. The result, they fear, will be a period of global warming that will dramatically alter climates in all parts of the world.

Map 111　The Acid Deposition Problem: Air, Water, Soil

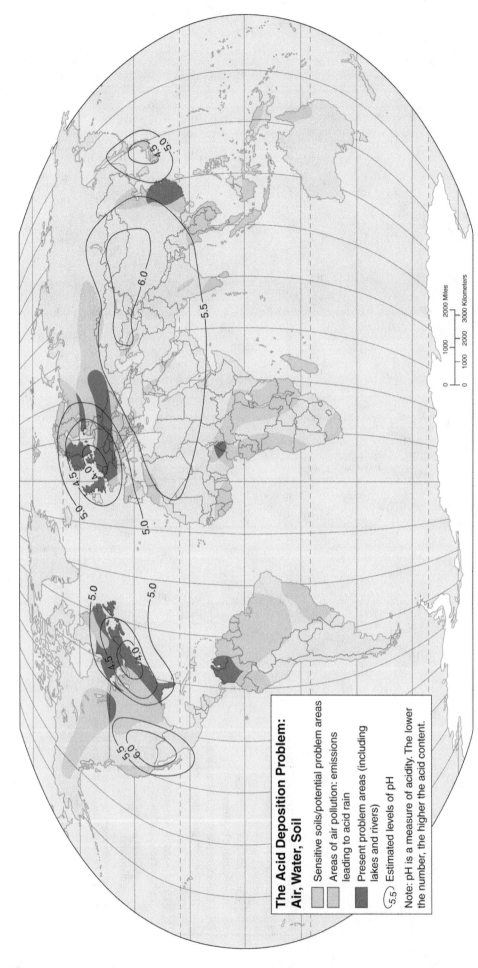

The Acid Deposition Problem: Air, Water, Soil

Sensitive soils/potential problem areas

Areas of air pollution: emissions leading to acid rain

Present problem areas (including lakes and rivers)

5.5 Estimated levels of pH

Note: pH is a measure of acidity. The lower the number, the higher the acid content.

0　1000　2000 Miles

0　1000　2000　3000 Kilometers

The term "acid precipitation" refers to increasing levels of acidity in snowfall and rainfall caused by atmospheric pollution. Oxides of nitrogen and sulfur resulting from incomplete combustion of fossil fuels (coal, oil, and natural gas) combine with water vapor in the atmosphere to produce weak acids that then "precipitate" or fall along with water or ice crystals. Some atmospheric acids formed by this process are known as "dry acid" precipitates and they too will fall to earth, although not necessarily along with rain or snow. In some areas of the world, the increased acidity of streams and lakes stemming from high

levels of acid precipitation or dry acid fallout has damaged or destroyed aquatic life. Acid precipitation and dry acid fallout also harm soil systems and vegetation, producing a characteristic "burned" appearance in forests that lends the same quality to landscapes that forest fires would. The region most dramatically impacted by acid precipitation is Central Europe, where decades of destructive environmental practices, including the burning of high-sulfur coal for commercial, industrial, and residential purposes, has destroyed hundreds of thousands of acres of woodlands.

Map 112 Pollution of the Oceans

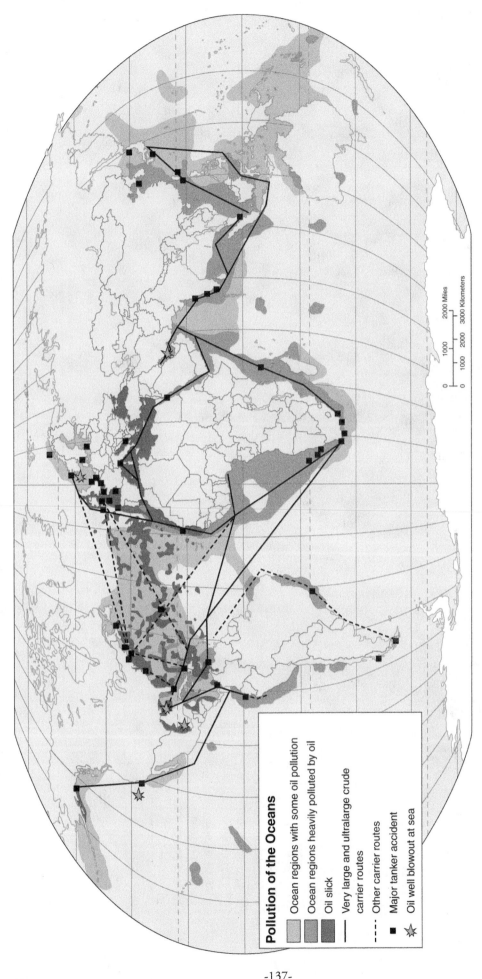

Pollution of the Oceans

- Ocean regions with some oil pollution
- Ocean regions heavily polluted by oil
- Oil slick
- Very large and ultralarge crude carrier routes
- Other carrier routes
- ■ Major tanker accident
- ☆ Oil well blowout at sea

The pollution of the world's oceans has long been a matter of concern to physical geographers, oceanographers, and other environmental scientists. The great circulation systems of the ocean are one of the controlling factors of the earth's natural environment, and modifications to those systems have unknown consequences. This map is based on what we can measure: (1) areas of oceans where oil pollution has been proven to have inflicted significant damage to ocean ecosystems and life forms (including phytoplankton, the oceans' primary food producers, equivalent to land-based vegetation) and (2) areas of oceans where unusually high concentrations of hydrocarbons from oil spills may have inflicted some damage to the oceans' biota. A glance at the map shows that there are few areas of the world's oceans where some form of pollution is not a part of the environmental system. What the map does not show in detail, because of the scale, are the dramatic consequences of large individual pollution events: the devastation produced by the 1991 Gulf War in the Persian Gulf, or the 2010 *Deepwater Horizon* oil spill in the Gulf of Mexico.

0 1000 2000 Miles
0 1000 2000 3000 Kilometers

Map 113 Water Resources: Availability of Renewable Water Per Capita

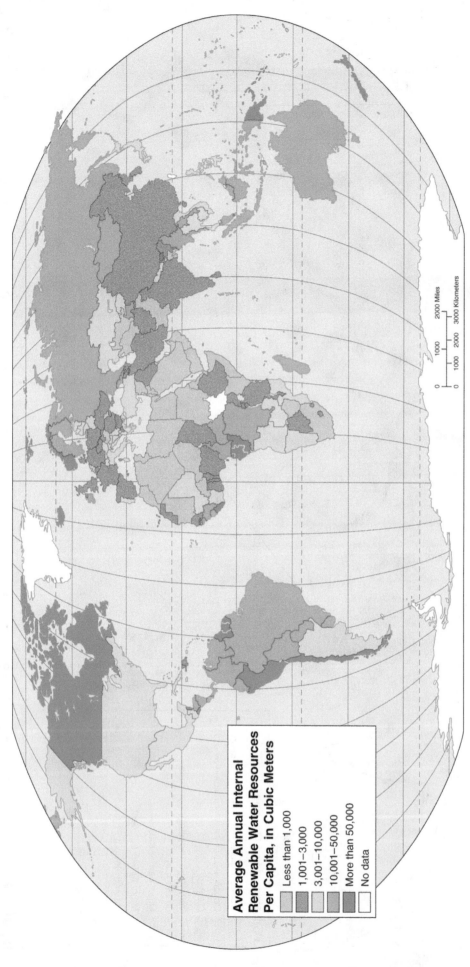

Average Annual Internal Renewable Water Resources Per Capita, in Cubic Meters

- Less than 1,000
- 1,001–3,000
- 3,001–10,000
- 10,001–50,000
- More than 50,000
- No data

2000 Miles

1000

0   1000   2000   3000 Kilometers

Renewable water resources are usually defined as the total water available from streams and rivers (including flows from other countries), ponds and lakes, and groundwater storage or aquifers. Not included in the total of renewable water would be water that comes from such nonrenewable sources as desalinization plants or melted icebergs. While the concept of renewable or flow resources is a traditional one in resource management, in fact, few resources, including water, are truly renewable when their use is excessive. The water resources shown here are indications of that principle. A country like the United States possesses truly enormous quantities of water. But the United States also uses enormous quantities of water. The result is that, largely because of excessive use, the availability of renewable water is much less than in many other parts of the world where the total supply of water is significantly less.

Map 114 Water Resources: Annual Water Withdrawal Per Capita

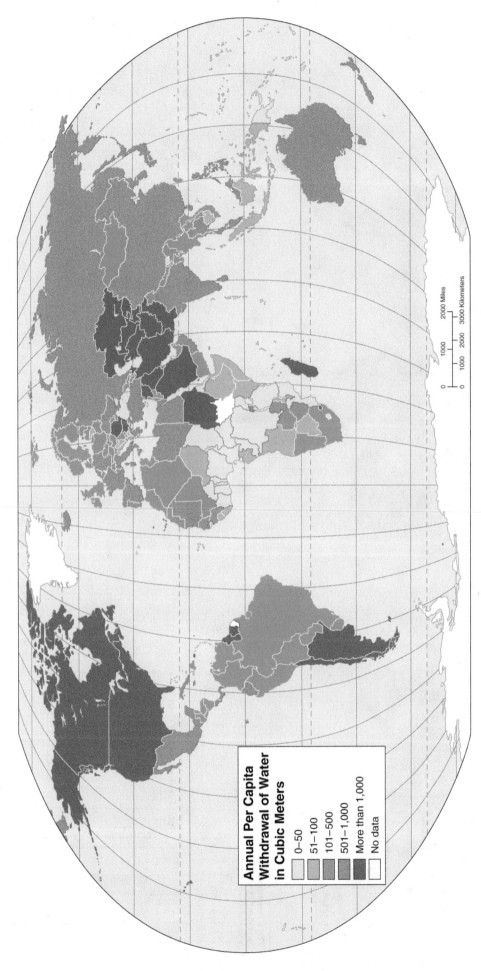

Annual Per Capita Withdrawal of Water in Cubic Meters

- 0–50
- 51–100
- 101–500
- 501–1,000
- More than 1,000
- No data

Water resources must be viewed like a bank account in which deposits and withdrawals are made. As long as the deposits are greater than the withdrawals, a positive balance remains. But when the withdrawals begin to exceed the deposits, sooner or later (depending on the relative sizes of the deposits and withdrawals) the account becomes overdrawn. For many of the world's countries, annual availability of water is insufficient to cover the demand. In these countries, reserves stored in groundwater are being tapped, resulting in depletion of the water supply (think of this as shifting money from a savings account to a checking account). The water supply can maintain its status as a renewable resource only if deposits continue to be greater than withdrawals, and that seldom happens. In general, countries with high levels of economic development and countries that rely on irrigation agriculture are the most spendthrift when it comes to their water supplies.

Map 115 Water Stress: Shortage, Abundance, and Population Density

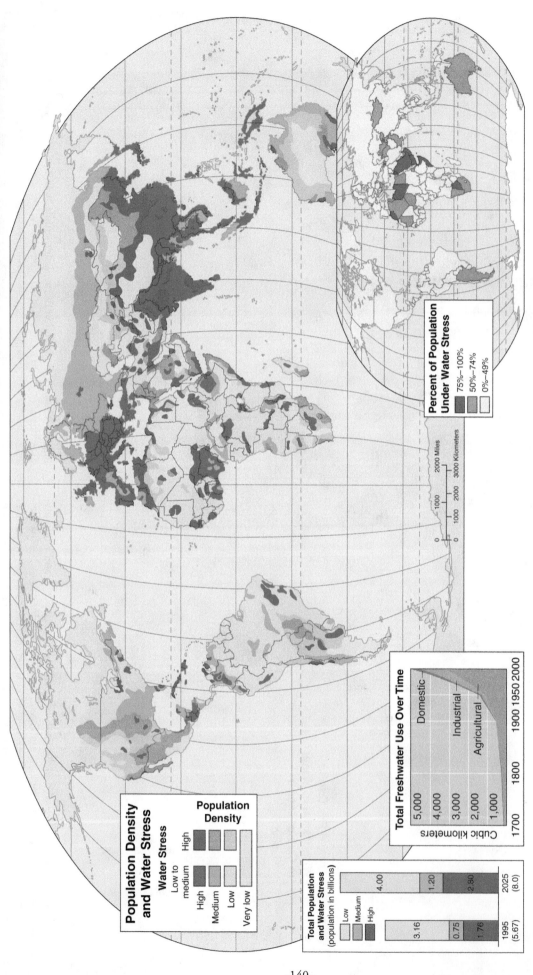

Population Density and Water Stress

Water Stress

Low to medium → High

Population Density

High	High
Medium	Medium
Low	Low
	Very low

Total Population and Water Stress (population in billions)

	1995 (5.67)	2025 (8.0)
Low	3.16	4.00
Medium	0.75	1.20
High	1.76	2.80

Total Freshwater Use Over Time

Cubic kilometers

5,000 / 4,000 / 3,000 / 2,000 / 1,000

1700 1800 1900 1950 2000

Domestic

Industrial

Agricultural

Percent of Population Under Water Stress

	75%–100%
	50%–74%
	0%–49%

0   1000   2000 Miles
0   1000   2000   3000 Kilometers

Maps such as the previous two, based on national-level data for water consumption and availability, should be used only to obtain national-level understanding. Information on water withdrawal and availability are regionally and locally based geographic phenomena and are linked not just with water supplies but with the density of human populations. Even areas (such as New England in the United States) in which water availability is high and withdrawal rates are relatively low show areas of stress in regions of high population density (cities such as Boston). This map, originally produced by scientists at the University of New Hampshire, attempts to show those areas of the world where populations will tend to be at high, medium, and low risk of stress because of water availability. It is important to note that many of the world's prime agricultural regions, such as the Great Plains of the United States or the Argentine Pampas, show the potential for high risk of water stress in the immediate future. Why is this important? Because the greatest single use of water on the planet is for irrigation (nearly 70 percent of the world's water use), and it is the continued expansion of irrigation systems that allows the increase in agricultural production that feeds the earth's more than six billion persons.

-140-

Map 116 Carbon Dioxide Emissions

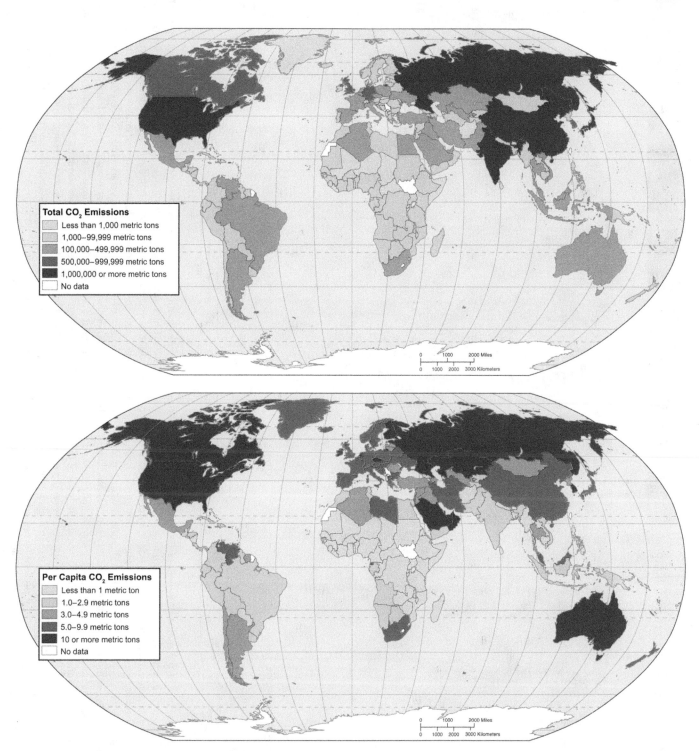

Carbon dioxide emissions are a major indicator of economic development, since they are generated largely by burning of fossil fuels for electrical power generation, for industrial processes, for domestic and commercial heating, and for the internal combustion engines of automobiles, trucks, buses, planes, and trains. Scientists have long known that carbon dioxide in the atmosphere increases the ability of the atmosphere to retain heat, a phenomenon known as the greenhouse effect. While the greenhouse effect is a natural process (and life on earth as we know it would not be possible without it), many scientists are concerned that an increase

in carbon dioxide in the atmosphere is augmenting this process, creating a global warming trend and a potential worldwide change of climate patterns. These climatological changes threaten disaster for many regions and their peoples in both the developed and less developed areas of the world. You will note from the maps that China and the United States are the leading producers of carbon dioxide emissions—both emit carbon dioxide at levels nearly four times that of Russia, the third-leading emitter. When examined on a per capita basis, note that the countries of the midlatitudes generate extremely high levels of carbon dioxide.

Map 117   Potential Global Temperature Change

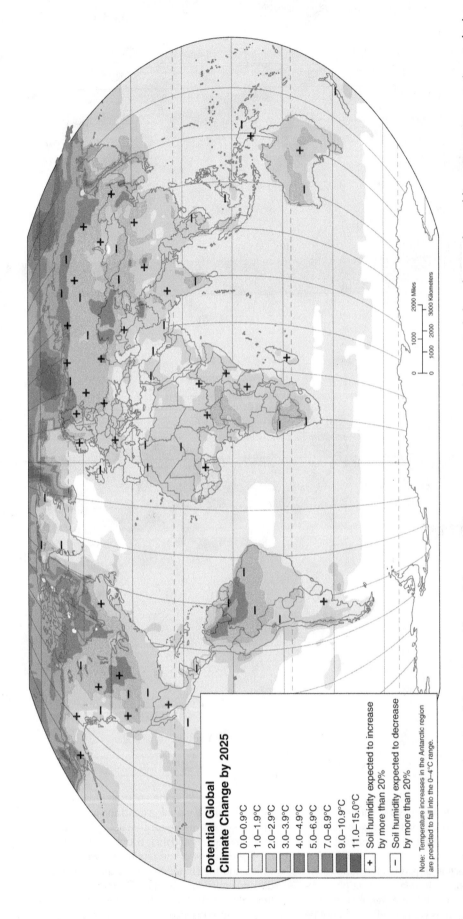

Potential Global Climate Change by 2025

- 0.0–0.9°C
- 1.0–1.9°C
- 2.0–2.9°C
- 3.0–3.9°C
- 4.0–4.9°C
- 5.0–6.9°C
- 7.0–8.9°C
- 9.0–10.9°C
- 11.0–15.0°C
- + Soil humidity expected to increase by more than 20%
- – Soil humidity expected to decrease by more than 20%

Note: Temperature increases in the Antarctic region are predicted to fall into the 0–4°C range.

According to atmospheric scientists, one of the major problems of the twenty-first century will be "global warming," produced as the atmosphere's natural ability to trap and retain heat is enhanced by increased percentages of carbon dioxide, methane, chlorinated fluorocarbons or "CFCs," and other "greenhouse gases" in the earth's atmosphere. Computer models based on atmospheric percentages of carbon dioxide resulting from present use of fossil fuels show that warming is not just a possibility but a probability. Increased temperatures would cause precipitation patterns to alter significantly as well and would produce a number of other harmful effects, including a rise in the level of the world's oceans that could flood most coastal cities. International conferences on the topic of the enhanced greenhouse effect have resulted in several international agreements to reduce the emission of carbon dioxide or to maintain it at present levels. Unfortunately, the solution is not that simple since reduction of carbon dioxide emissions is, in the short run, expensive—particularly as long as the world's energy systems continue to be based on fossil fuels. Chief among the countries that could be hit by serious international mandates to reduce emissions are those highest on the development scale who use the highest levels of fossil fuels and, therefore, produce the highest emissions, and those on the lowest end of the development scale, whose efforts to industrialize could be severely impeded by the more expensive energy systems that would replace fossil fuels. In April 2007, the Intergovernmental Panel on Climate Change—an international body of diplomats and scientists—issued the most dire warning yet about the virtual certainty of human-induced global warming and the impacts it would have on water supplies, species extinction, and sea levels. The report represented the best scientific conclusions possible but was criticized by many scientists as not going far enough. As severe as the language of the IPCC report was, it was toned down by the threat of refusal to sign by China and the United States.

Map 118 The Loss of Biodiversity: Globally Threatened Animal Species

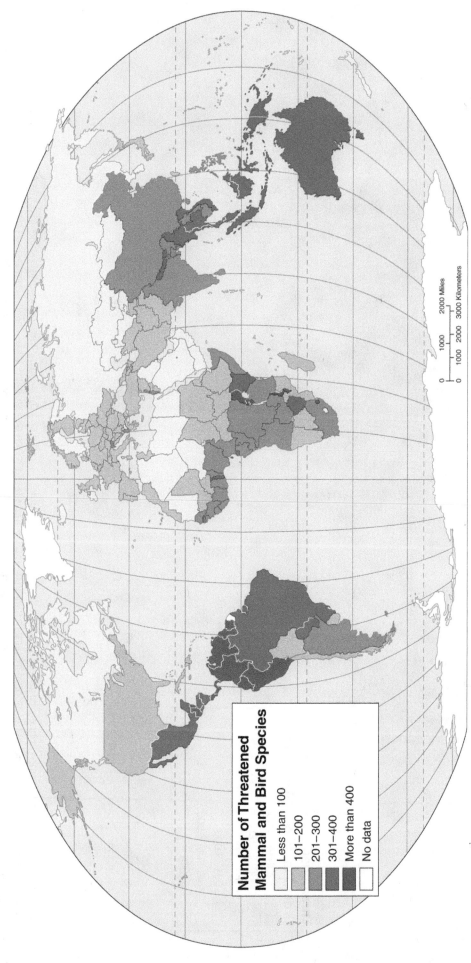

Number of Threatened Mammal and Bird Species

- Less than 100
- 101–200
- 201–300
- 301–400
- More than 400
- No data

0 1000 2000 Miles
0 1000 2000 3000 Kilometers

Threatened species are those in grave danger of going extinct. Their populations are becoming restricted in range, and the size of the populations required for sustained breeding is nearing a critical minimum. *Endangered species* are in immediate danger of becoming extinct. Their range is already so reduced that the animals may no longer be able to move freely within an ecozone, and their populations are at the level where the species may no longer be able to sustain breeding. Most species become threatened first and then endangered as their range and numbers continue to decrease. When people think of animal extinction, they think of large herbivorous species like the rhinoceros or fierce

carnivores like lions, tigers, or grizzly bears. Certainly these animals make almost any list of endangered or threatened species. But there are literally hundreds of less conspicuous animals that are equally threatened. Extinction is normally nature's way of informing a species that it is inefficient. But conditions in the early twenty-first century are controlled more by human activities than by natural evolutionary processes. Species that are endangered or threatened fall into those categories because, somehow, they are competing with us or with our domesticated livestock for space and food. And in that competition, the endangered animals are always going to lose.

Map 119   The Loss of Biodiversity: Globally Threatened Plant Species

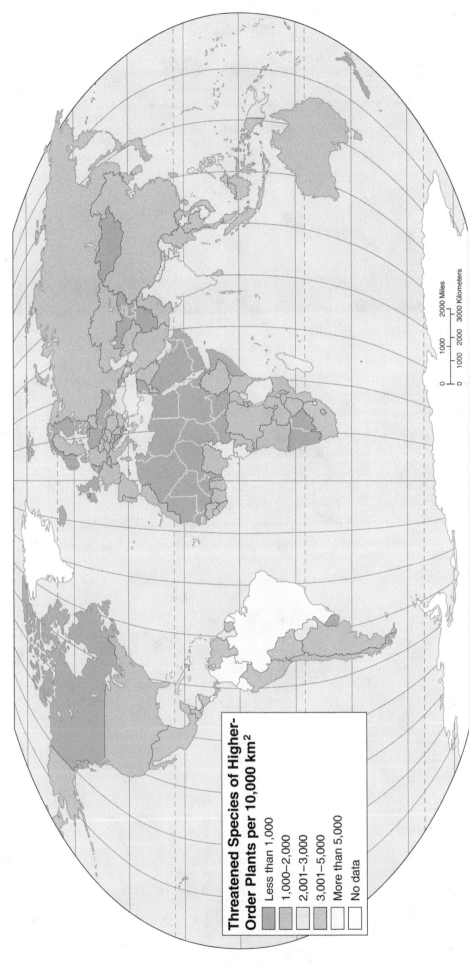

Threatened Species of Higher-Order Plants per 10,000 km²

- Less than 1,000
- 1,000–2,000
- 2,001–3,000
- 3,001–5,000
- More than 5,000
- No data

1000   2000 Miles

0   1000   2000   3000 Kilometers

While most people tend to be more concerned about the animals on threatened and endangered species lists, the fact is that many more plants are in jeopardy, and the loss of plant life is, in all ecological regions, a more critical occurrence than the loss of animal populations. Plants are the primary producers in the ecosystem; that is, plants produce the food upon which all other species in the food web, including human beings, depend for sustenance. It is plants from which many of our critical medicines come, and it is plants that maintain the delicate balance between soil and water in most of the world's regions. When environmental scientists speak of a loss of biodiversity, what they are most often describing is a loss of the richness and complexity of plant life that lends stability to ecosystems. Systems with more plant life tend to be more stable than those with less. For these and other reasons, the scientific concern over extinction is greater when applied to plants than to animals. It is difficult for people to become as emotional over a teak tree as they would over an elephant. But as great a tragedy as the loss of the elephant would be, the loss of the teak would be greater.

Map 120   Global Hotspots of Biodiversity

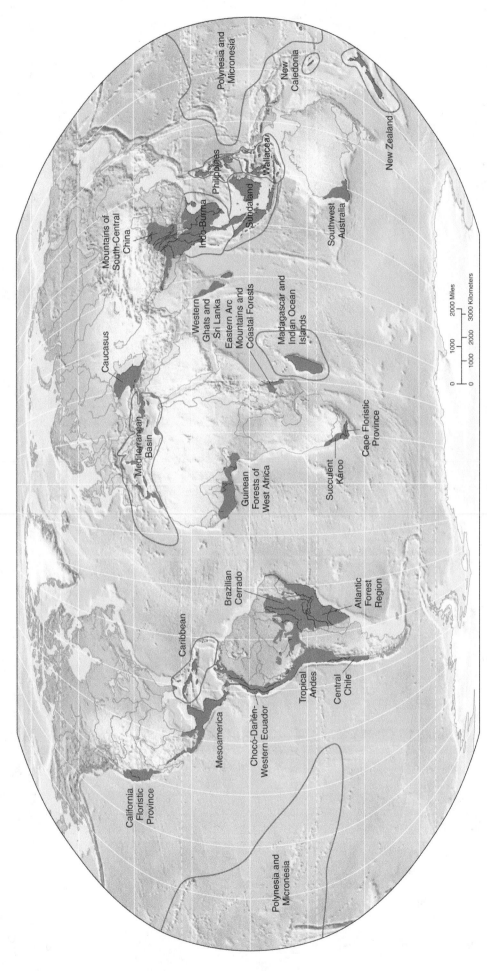

Where we have normally thought of tropical forest basins such as Amazonia as the world's most biologically diverse ecosystems, recent research has discovered the surprising fact that a number of hotspots of biological diversity exist outside the major tropical forest regions. These hotspot regions contain slightly less than 2 percent of the world's total land area but may contain up to 60 percent of the total world's terrestrial species of plants and animals. Geographically, the hotspot areas are characterized by vertical zonation (that is, they tend to

be hilly to mountainous regions), long known to be a factor in biological complexity. They are also in coastal locations or near large bodies of water, locations that stimulate climatic variability and, hence, biological complexity. Although some of the hotspots are sparsely populated, others, such as "Sundaland," are among the world's most densely populated areas. Protection of the rich biodiversity of these hotspots is, most biologists feel, of crucial importance to the preservation of the world's biological heritage.

Map 121   Degree of Human Disturbance

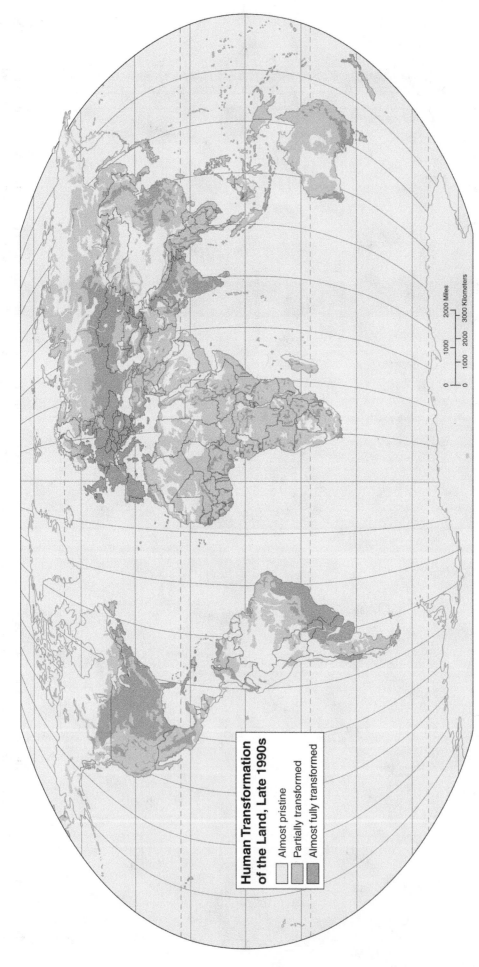

**Human Transformation
of the Land, Late 1990s**

Almost pristine
Partially transformed
Almost fully transformed

0   1000   2000 Miles
0   1000   2000   3000 Kilometers

The data on human disturbance have been gathered from a wide variety of sources, some of them conflicting and not all of them reliable. Nevertheless, at a global scale, this map fairly depicts the state of the world in terms of the degree to which humans have modified its surface. The almost pristine areas, covered with natural vegetation, generally have population densities under ten persons per square mile. These areas are, for the most part, in the most inhospitable parts of the world: too high, too dry, or too cold for permanent human habitation in large numbers. The partially transformed areas are normally agricultural areas, either subsistence (such as shifting cultivation) or extensive (such as livestock grazing). They often contain areas of secondary vegetation, regrown after removal of original vegetation by humans. They are also often marked by a density of livestock in excess of carrying capacity, leading to overgrazing, which further alters the condition of the vegetation. The almost fully transformed areas are those of permanent and intensive agriculture and urban settlement. The primary vegetation of these regions has been removed, with no evidence of regrowth or with current vegetation that is quite different from natural (potential) vegetation. Soils are in a state of depletion and degradation, and, in drier lands, desertification is a factor of human occupation. The disturbed areas match closely those areas of the world with the densest human populations.

Map 122 The Green and Not-So-Green World

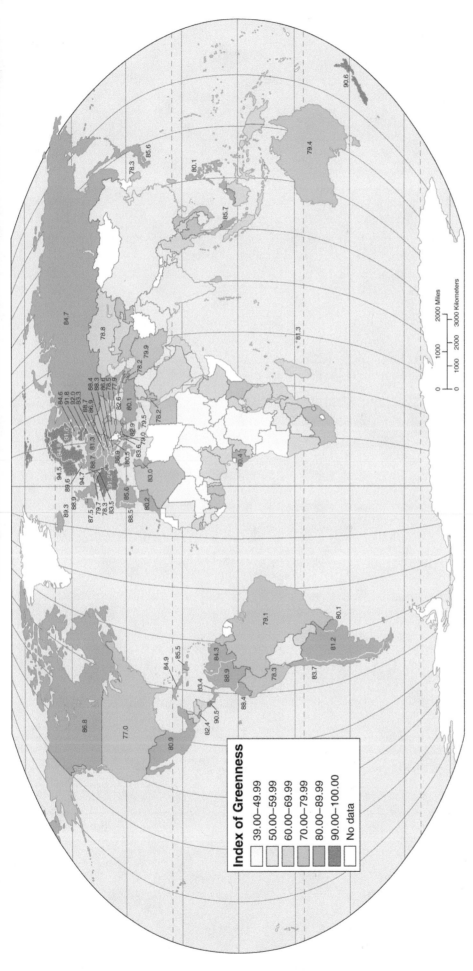

Index of Greenness

- 39.00–49.99
- 50.00–59.99
- 60.00–69.99
- 70.00–79.99
- 80.00–89.99
- 90.00–100.00
- No data

The index of "greenness" ranks countries according to their greenhouse gas emissions, the quality of their water resources, their protection of plant and animal habitats, and other factors. As might be expected, the "greenest" countries also tend to be relatively affluent and in cooler climates. There are obvious exceptions to this generalization (Mexico, for example), but, in general, we find countries like Sweden (no. 1), Switzerland, Norway, Finland, France, New Zealand, and Denmark ranking high on the index while poorer countries in warmer climates (much of South and East Asia, much of Sub-Saharan Africa) generally tend to rank lower on the index. There is a pretty clear correlation between affluence and "greenness"—that is, wealthy countries not only recognize the importance of "being green" but have the ability to pay for it. Still, some of the world's more affluent countries, like the United States and Australia, rank rather lower on the scale. The relatively low ranking (not quite in the top third of the countries

in the index) attained by the United States—despite its excellent record of controlling water and air pollution—results from its persistent reliance on fossil fuels and a correspondingly high release of greenhouse gas emissions. Sweden, whose per capita income is similar to that of the United States, uses renewable resources (particularly hydroelectric power) to keep its emissions low and its ranking on the scale of "greenness" high. Similarly, France (no. 7) maintains a high rank because of a reliance on nuclear power, which curbs greenhouse gas emissions. In Sub-Saharan Africa, the level of carbon dioxide emissions is low but water quality and sanitation are poor. Rapid industrialization in countries like Brazil, India, and China have impacted emissions levels, as well as water and sanitation levels. These countries appear rather lower on the index (China, for example, ranks 134th among 186 countries). The rankings shown on the map are based on 2008 data; it will be interesting to see how the patterns will change in 20 years.

-147-

Unit VII

Regions of the World

Map 123 North America: Physical Features

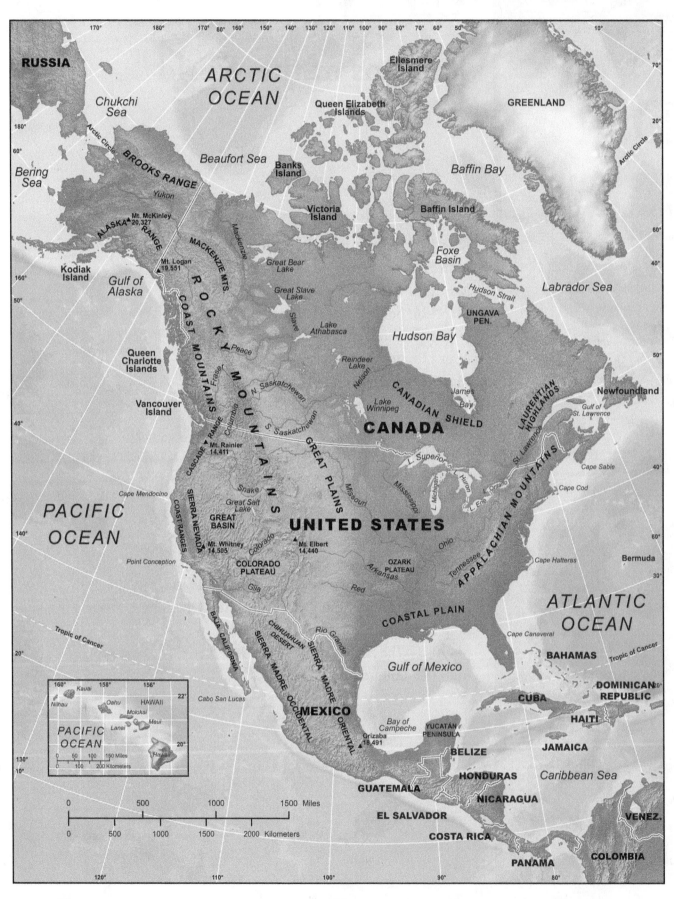

Map 124   North America: Political Divisions

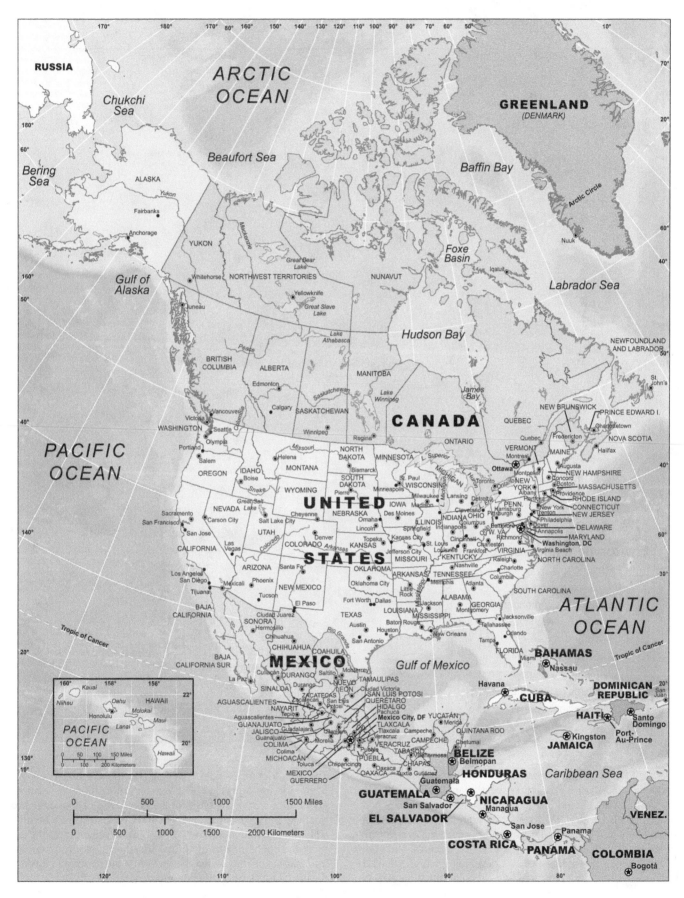

Map **125**   North America: Land Use

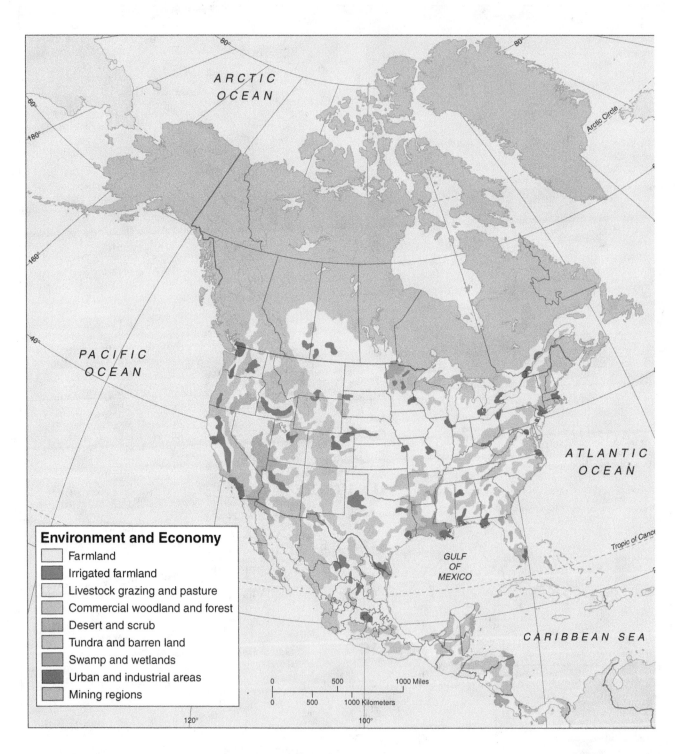

Environment and Economy
- Farmland
- Irrigated farmland
- Livestock grazing and pasture
- Commercial woodland and forest
- Desert and scrub
- Tundra and barren land
- Swamp and wetlands
- Urban and industrial areas
- Mining regions

The use of land in North America represents a balance between agriculture, resource extraction, and manufacturing that is unmatched. The United States, as the world's leading industrial power, is also the world's leader in commercial agricultural production. Canada, despite its small population, is a ranking producer of both agricultural and industrial products, and Mexico has begun to emerge from its developing nation status to become an important industrial and agricultural nation as well.

The countries of Middle America and the Caribbean are just beginning the transition from agriculture to modern industrial economies. Part of the basis for the high levels of economic productivity in North America is environmental: a superb blend of soil, climate, and raw materials. But just as important is the cultural and social mix of the plural societies of North America, a mix that historically aided the growth of the economic diversity necessary for developed economies.

Map **126** South America: Physical Features

Caribbean Sea

NICARAGUA

BARBADOS

GRENADA

COSTA
RICA

TRINIDAD &
TOBAGO

PANAMA

Lake
Maracaibo

Orinoco

GUYANA

ANDES

VENEZUELA

SURINAME

LLANOS

GUIANA
SHIELD

FRENCH
GUIANA
(FR.)

ATLANTIC
OCEAN

COLOMBIA

Galapagos
Islands

Equator

ECUADOR

▲Chimborazo
20,702

Negro

Amazon

Punta Negra

Amazon

AMAZON
BASIN

Madeira

BRAZIL

Cabo de
São Roque

PERU

Araguaia

São Francisco

ANDES

Lake
Titicaca

PLANALTO DO
MATO GROSSO

ALTIPLANO

BOLIVIA

Paraguay

Atacama Desert

Tropic of Capricorn

PACIFIC
OCEAN

ANDES

PARAGUAY

Paraná

BRAZILIAN
HIGHLANDS

Tropic of Capricorn

GRAN CHACO

Iguazu Falls

Aconcagua
22,831

CHILE

▲ ARGENTINA

URUGUAY

Paraná

ATLANTIC
OCEAN

PAMPAS

Punta Lavapié

Negro

PATAGONIA

0   250   500   750   1000 Miles

0   500   1000   1500 Kilometers

Falkland
Islands

Tierra del Fuego

Scotia
Sea

South Georgia

Cape Horn

Drake Passage

Map 127   South America: Political Divisions

Map 128　South America: Land Use

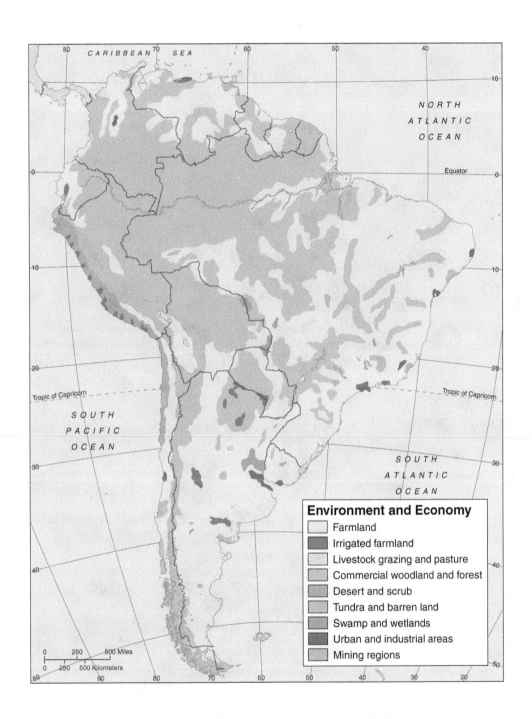

South America is a region just beginning to emerge from a colonial-dependency economy in which raw materials flowed from the continent to more highly developed economic regions. With the exception of Brazil, Argentina, Chile, and Uruguay, most of the continent's countries still operate under the traditional mode of exporting raw materials in exchange for capital that tends to accumulate in the pockets of a small percentage of the population. The land-use patterns of the continent are, therefore, still dominated by resource extraction and agriculture. A problem posed by these patterns is that little of the continent's land area is actually suitable for either commercial forestry or commercial crop agriculture without extremely high environmental costs. Much of the agriculture, then, is based on high-value tropical crops that can be grown in small areas profitably, or on extensive livestock grazing. Even within the forested areas of the Amazon Basin where forest clearance is taking place at unprecedented rates, much of the land use that replaces forest is grazing.

Map 129   Europe: Physical Features

Greenland

ARCTIC OCEAN

BARENTS
SEA

GREENLAND
SEA

Pechora

ICELAND

Arctic Circle

NORWEGIAN
SEA

Vychegda

Svernaya Dvina

Lake
Onega

Sukhona

ATLANTIC
OCEAN

Faroe Is.

Shetland Is.

SWEDEN

Gulf of Bothnia

FINLAND

Lake
Ladoga

Rybinsk
Reservoir

Volga

NORWAY

ESTONIA

Volga

NORTH
SEA

Skagerrak

Kattegat

BALTIC SEA

LATVIA

RUSSIA

Dvina

DENMARK

LITHUANIA

RUSSIA

UNITED
IRELAND KINGDOM

BELARUS

NETHERLANDS

Elbe

Vistula

Thames

Dnieper

BELGIUM

GERMANY

POLAND

Rhine

Oder

UKRAINE

SEA OF
AZOV

LUXEMBOURG

Seine

CZECHIA

SLOVAKIA

CARPATHIANS

MOLDOVA

Meuse

Danube

Loire

AUSTRIA

HUNGARY

ROMANIA

BLACK
SEA

SWITZERLAND

ALPS

FRANCE

Bay of
Biscay

▲ Mont Blanc
15,771

SLOVENIA

Po

CROATIA

Danube

Rhone

BOSNIA &
HERZEGOVINA

SERBIA

BULGARIA

PYRENEES

MONACO

SAN
MARINO

APENNINES

MONTENEGRO

KOSOVO

PORTUGAL

ANDORRA

Ebro

Gulf of
Lion

Corsica

VATICAN
CITY

ADRIATIC SEA

MACEDONIA

TURKEY

40°

Tagus

ALBANIA

AEGEAN
SEA

SPAIN

Sardinia

TYRRHENIAN
SEA

ITALY

GREECE

Balearic Is.

CYPRUS

MEDITERRANEAN

Sicily

IONIAN
SEA

Crete

SEA

MALTA

TUNISIA

MOROCCO

ALGERIA

0	250	500	750 Miles
0	250	500	750	1000 Kilometers

LIBYA

EGYPT

Map **130**   Europe: Political Divisions

Map 131   Europe: Land Use

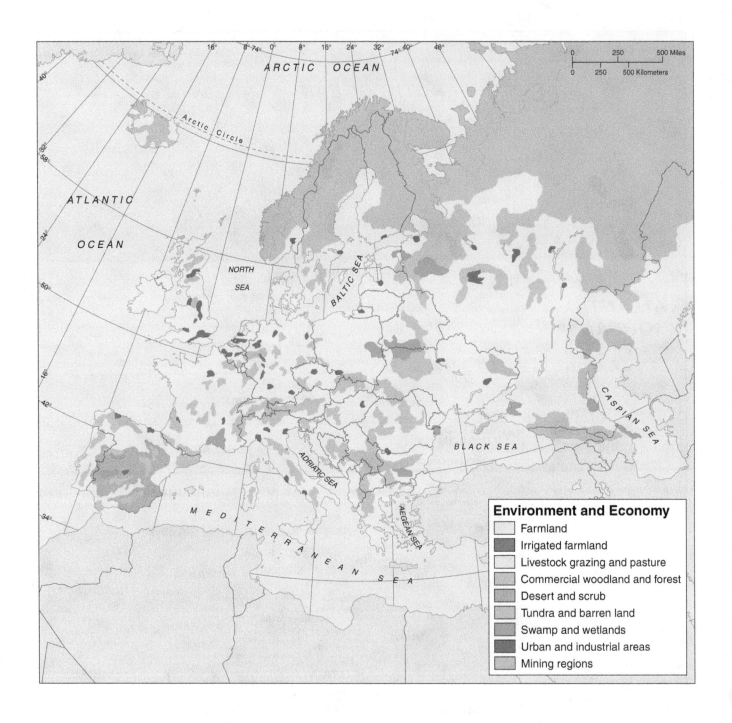

Environment and Economy

- Farmland
- Irrigated farmland
- Livestock grazing and pasture
- Commercial woodland and forest
- Desert and scrub
- Tundra and barren land
- Swamp and wetlands
- Urban and industrial areas
- Mining regions

More than any other continent, Europe bears the imprint of human activity—mining, forestry, agriculture, industry, and urbanization. Virtually all of Western and Central Europe's natural forest vegetation is gone, lost to clearing for agriculture beginning in prehistory, to lumbering that began in earnest during the Middle Ages, or, more recently, to disease and destruction brought about by acid precipitation. Only in the far north and the east do some natural stands remain. The region is the world's most heavily industrialized, and the industrial areas on the map represent only the largest and most significant. Not shown are the industries that are found in virtually every small town, village, and smaller city throughout the industrial countries of Europe. Europe also possesses abundant raw materials and a very productive agricultural base. The mineral resources have long been in a state of active exploitation and the mining regions shown on the map are, for the most part, old regions in upland areas that are somewhat less significant now than they may have been in the past. Agriculturally, the northern European plain is one of the world's great agricultural regions, but most of Europe contains decent land for agriculture.

Map 132 Asia: Physical Features

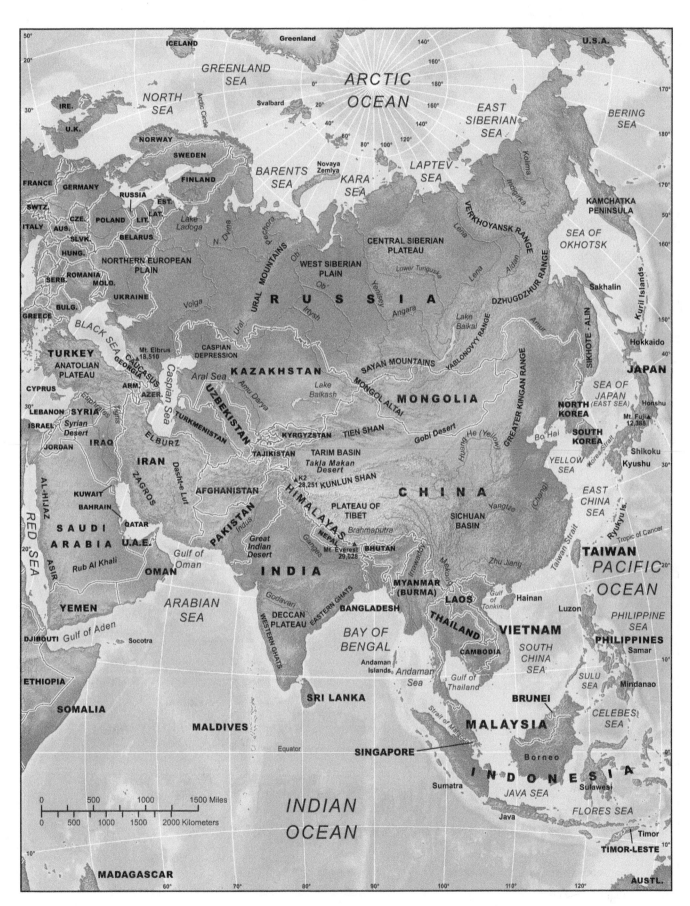

Map 133   Asia: Political Divisions

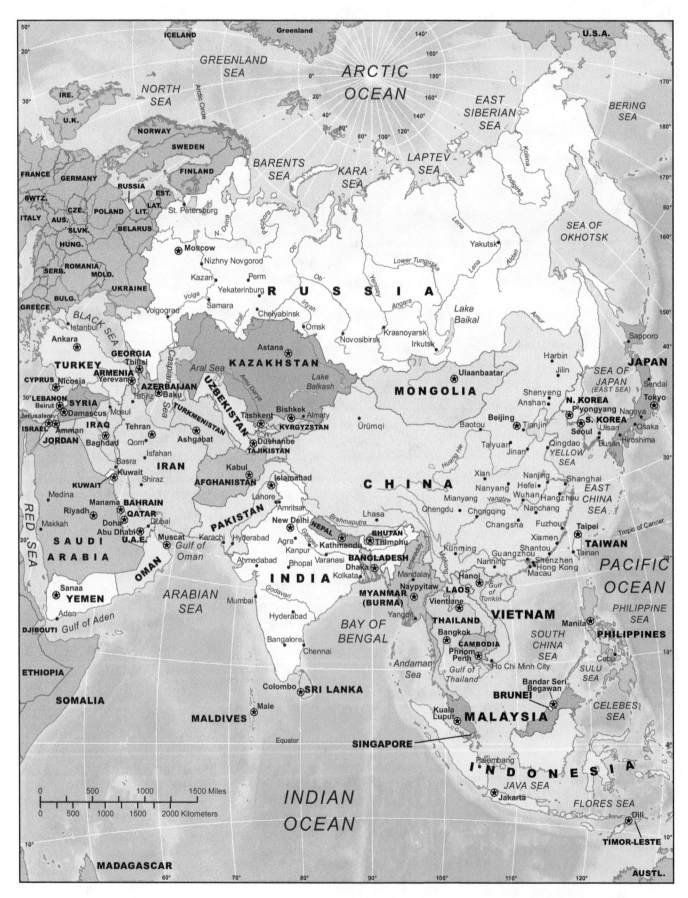

Map 134 Asia: Land Use

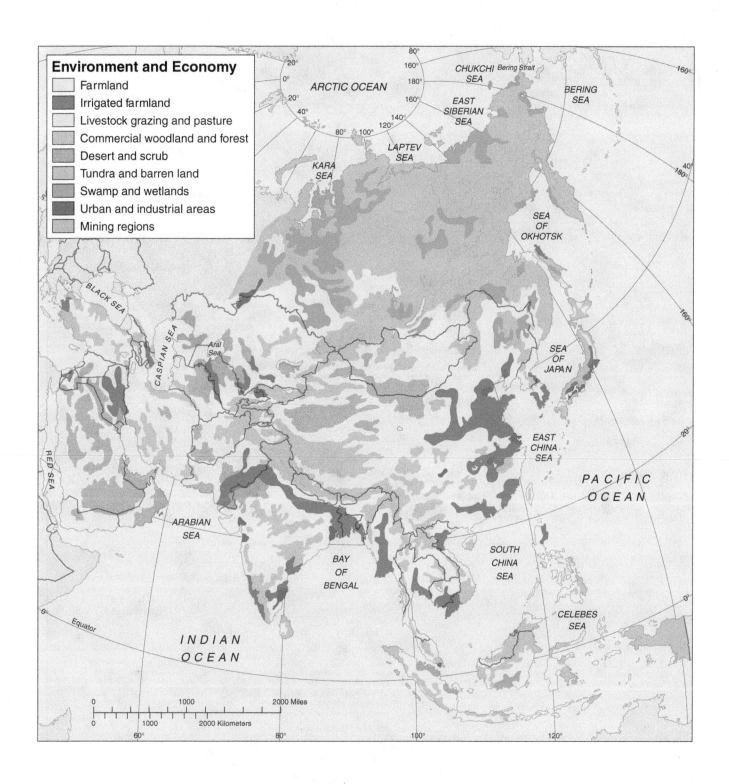

Environment and Economy
- Farmland
- Irrigated farmland
- Livestock grazing and pasture
- Commercial woodland and forest
- Desert and scrub
- Tundra and barren land
- Swamp and wetlands
- Urban and industrial areas
- Mining regions

Asia is a land of extremes of land use with some of the world's most heavily industrialized regions, barren and empty areas, and productive and densely populated farm regions. Asia is a region of rapid industrial growth. Yet Asia remains an agricultural region with three out of every four workers engaged in agriculture. Asian commercial agriculture and intensive subsistence agriculture is characterized by irrigation. Some of Asia's irrigated lands are desert, requiring additional water. But most of the Asian irrigated regions have sufficient precipitation for crop agriculture, and irrigation is a way of coping with seasonal drought—the wet-and-dry cycle of the monsoon—often gaining more than one crop per year on irrigated farms. Agricultural yields per unit area in many areas of Asia are among the world's highest. Because the Asian population is so large and the demands for agricultural land so great, Asia is undergoing rapid deforestation, and some areas of the continent have only small remnants of a once-abundant forest reserve.

Map 135   Africa: Physical Features

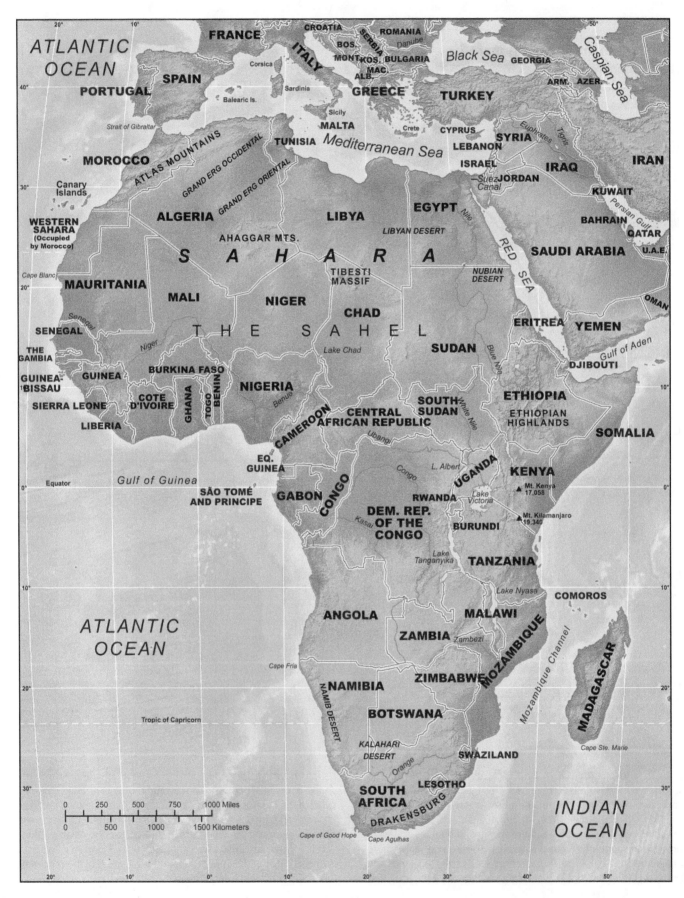

Map 136   Africa: Political Divisions

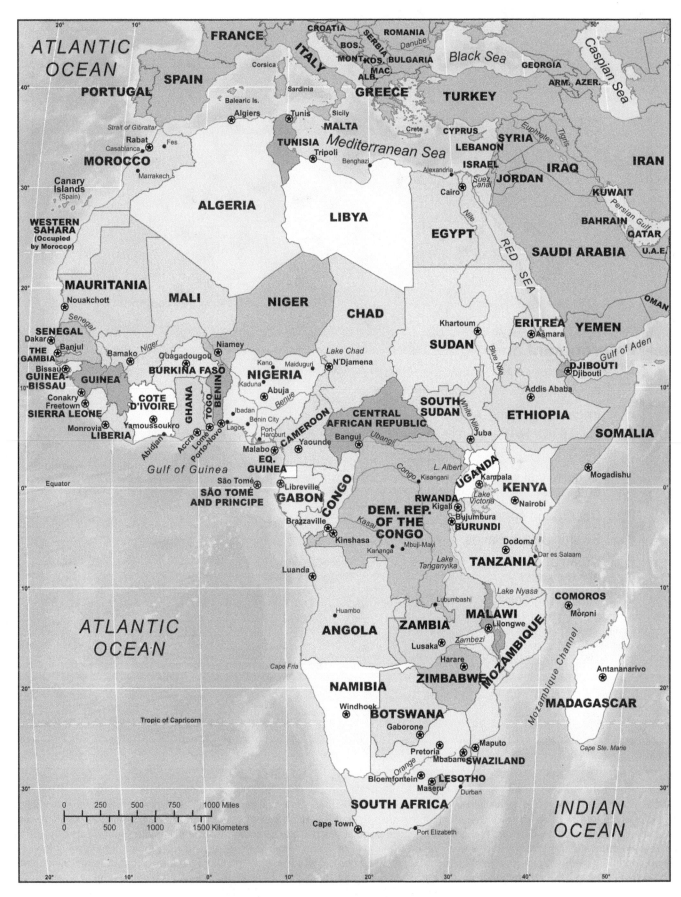

Map 137   Africa: Land Use

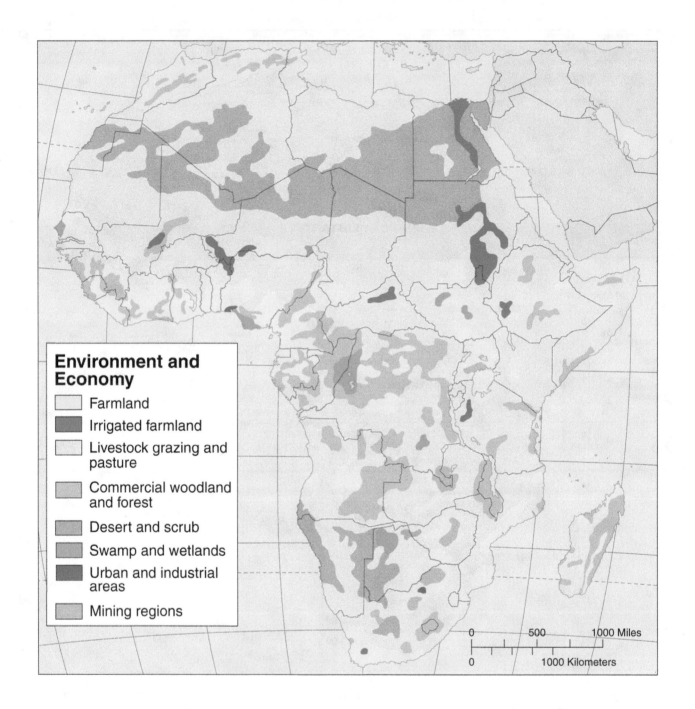

Environment and Economy

- Farmland
- Irrigated farmland
- Livestock grazing and pasture
- Commercial woodland and forest
- Desert and scrub
- Swamp and wetlands
- Urban and industrial areas
- Mining regions

0   500   1000 Miles

0   1000 Kilometers

Africa's economic landscape is dominated by subsistence or marginally commercial agricultural activities and raw material extraction, engaging three-fourths of Africa's workers. Much of this grazing land is very poor desert scrub and bunch grass that is easily impacted by cattle, sheep, and goats. Growing human and livestock populations place enormous stress on this fragile support capacity and the result is desertification: the conversion of even the most minimal of grazing environments or land suitable for crop farming to virtual desert conditions. Although the continent has approximately 20 percent of the world's total land area, the proportion of Africa's arable land is small. The agricultural environment is also uncertain; unpredictable precipitation and poor soils hamper crop agriculture.

Map **138**   Australia and Oceania: Physical Features

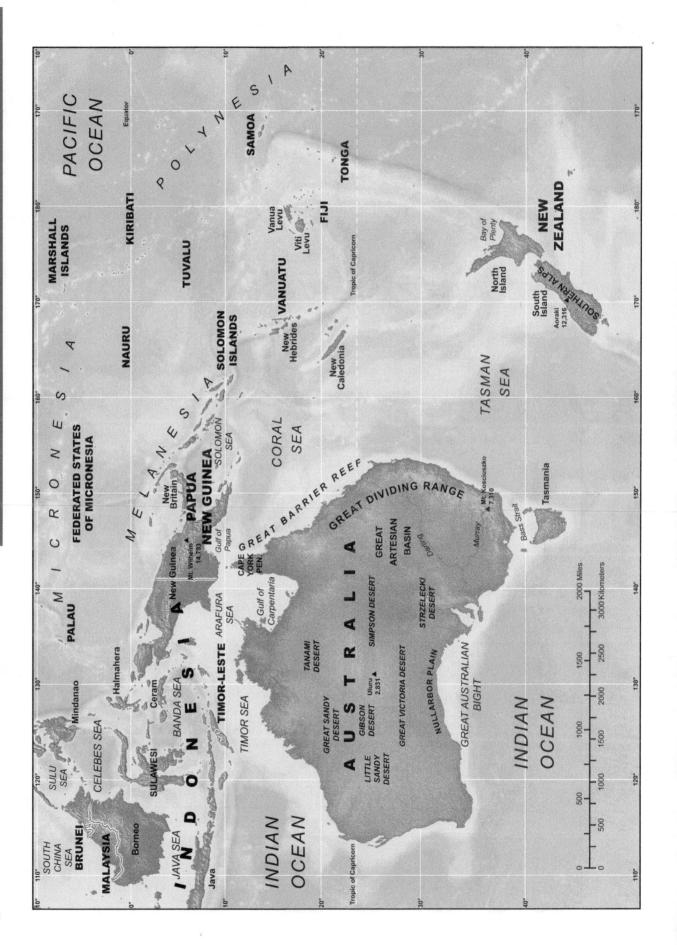

PACIFIC OCEAN

MICRONESIA

POLYNESIA

MELANESIA

MARSHALL ISLANDS

KIRIBATI

NAURU

TUVALU

SAMOA

TONGA

FIJI

VANUATU

SOLOMON ISLANDS

FEDERATED STATES OF MICRONESIA

PALAU

Vanua Levu

Viti Levu

New Hebrides

New Caledonia

CORAL SEA

SOLOMON SEA

New Britain

PAPUA NEW GUINEA

Mt. Wilhelm 14,793

New Guinea

Gulf of Papua

GREAT BARRIER REEF

GREAT DIVIDING RANGE

GREAT ARTESIAN BASIN

SIMPSON DESERT

STRZELECKI DESERT

Murray

Darling

Mt. Kosciuszko 7,310

Bass Strait

Tasmania

TASMAN SEA

Bay of Plenty

North Island

South Island

Aoraki 12,316

SOUTHERN ALPS

NEW ZEALAND

Tropic of Capricorn

CAPE YORK PEN.

Gulf of Carpentaria

ARAFURA SEA

TIMOR-LESTE

TIMOR SEA

BANDA SEA

Ceram

Halmahera

Mindanao

CELEBES SEA

SULU SEA

SULAWESI

INDONESIA

BRUNEI

MALAYSIA

Borneo

JAVA SEA

Java

SOUTH CHINA SEA

TANAMI DESERT

GREAT SANDY DESERT

GIBSON DESERT

Uluru 2,831

LITTLE SANDY DESERT

GREAT VICTORIA DESERT

NULLARBOR PLAIN

GREAT AUSTRALIAN BIGHT

AUSTRALIA

GREAT

DESERT

INDIAN OCEAN

INDIAN OCEAN

Equator

Tropic of Capricorn

Tropic of Capricorn

2000 Miles

3000 Kilometers

2500

2000

1500

1500

1000

1000

500

500

0

0

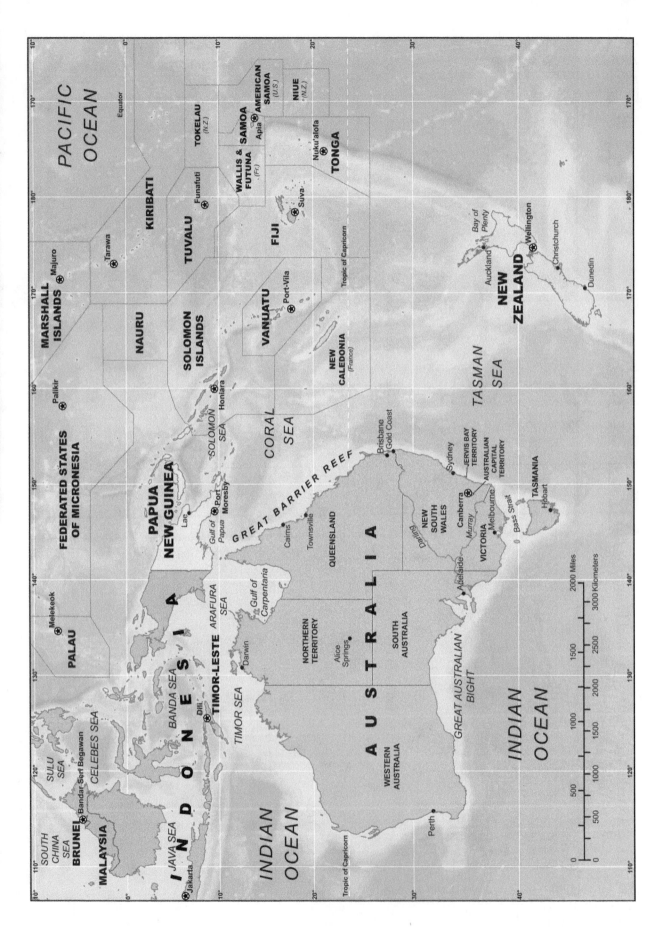

Map **139** Australia and Oceania: Political Divisions

Map 140 Australia and Oceania: Land Use

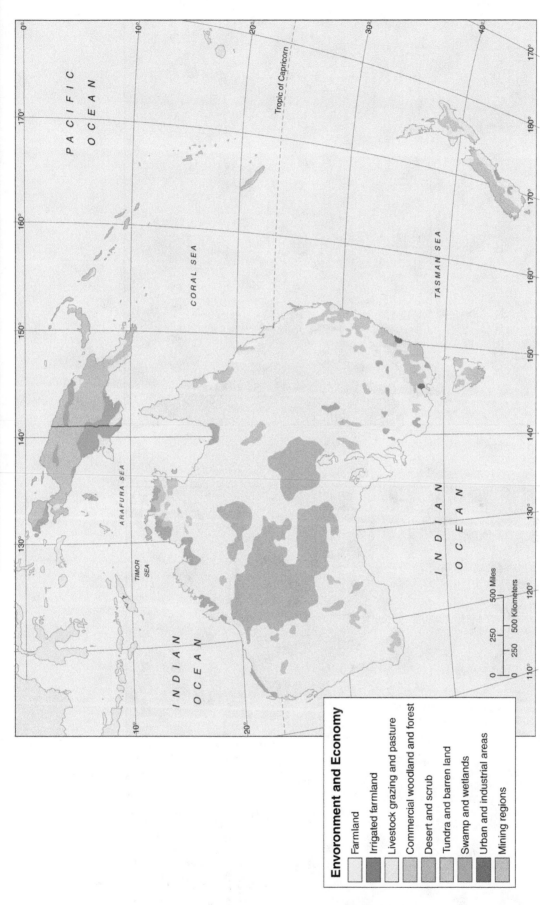

Envoroment and Economy

- Farmland
- Irrigated farmland
- Livestock grazing and pasture
- Commercial woodland and forest
- Desert and scrub
- Tundra and barren land
- Swamp and wetlands
- Urban and industrial areas
- Mining regions

Australasia is dominated by the world's smallest and most uniform continent. Flat, dry, and mostly hot, Australia has the simplest of land use patterns: Where rainfall exists, so does agricultural activity. Two agricultural patterns dominate the map: livestock grazing (primarily sheep) and wheat farming, although some sugar cane production exists in the north and some cotton is grown elsewhere. Only about 6 percent of the continent consists of arable land, so the areas of wheat farming, dominant as they may be in the context of Australian agriculture, are small.

Australia also supports a healthy mineral resource economy, with iron, copper, and precious metals making up the bulk of the extraction. Elsewhere in the region, tropical forests dominate Papua New Guinea, with some subsistence agriculture and livestock. New Zealand's temperate climate and abundant precipitation supports a productive livestock industry and little else besides tourism—which is an important economic element throughout the remainder of the region as well.

-167-

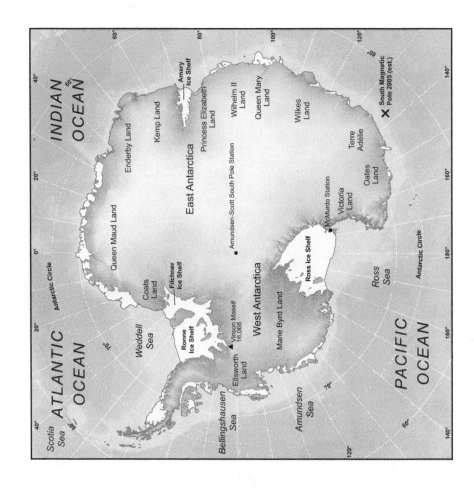

Map 142   Antarctica

INDIAN OCEAN

Amery Ice Shelf

Enderby Land

Kemp Land

Princess Elizabeth Land

Wilhelm II Land

Queen Mary Land

Wilkes Land

East Antarctica

Amundsen-Scott South Pole Station

Queen Maud Land

Terre Adélie

X   South Magnetic Pole 2005 (est.)

McMurdo Station

Victoria Land

Oates Land

Antarctic Circle

Ross Sea

Antarctic Circle

Coats Land

Filchner Ice Shelf

Ross Ice Shelf

ATLANTIC OCEAN

Weddell Sea

Ronne Ice Shelf

Vinson Massif 16,066

West Antarctica

Marie Byrd Land

PACIFIC OCEAN

Ellsworth Land

Bellingshausen Sea

Amundsen Sea

Scotia Sea

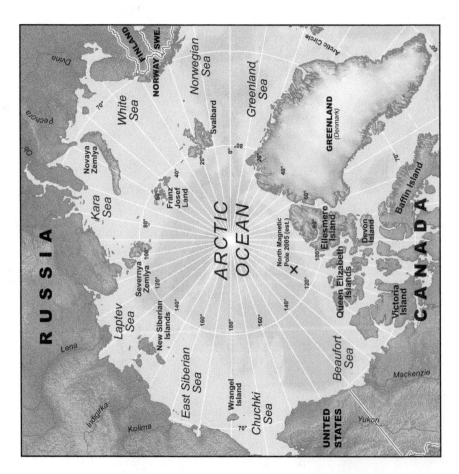

Map 141   The Arctic

RUSSIA

Dvina

FINLAND

NORWAY   SWE.

Norwegian Sea

Greenland Sea

Arctic Circle

White Sea

Svalbard

GREENLAND (Denmark)

Pechora

Ob

Novaya Zemlya

Kara Sea

Franz Josef Land

Baffin Island

Severnaya Zemlya

North Magnetic Pole 2005 (est.)

X

ARCTIC OCEAN

Ellesmere Island

Devon Island

Laptev Sea

Queen Elizabeth Islands

Lena

New Siberian Islands

Victoria Island

CANADA

Indigirka

East Siberian Sea

Wrangel Island

Beaufort Sea

Mackenzie

Kolima

Chuchki Sea

UNITED STATES

Yukon

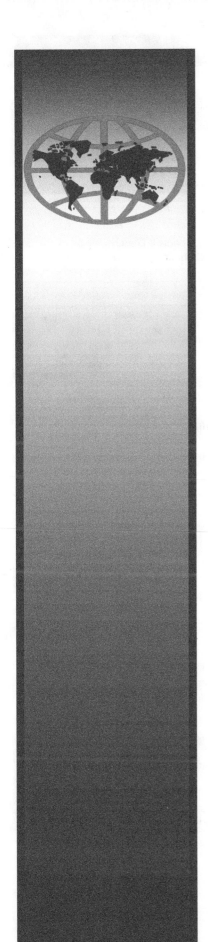

Unit VIII

Country and Dependency Profiles

Country and Dependency Profiles

Afghanistan

Afghanestan

Official Name: Islamic Republic of Afghanistan
Capital: Kabul
Area: 250,001 sq mi (647,500 sq km)
Population: 28,395,716
Major Language(s): Dari, Pashto
Major Religion(s): Sunni Islam
Currency: afghani

Albania

Shqiperia

Official Name: Republic of Albania
Capital: Tirana
Area: 11,100 sq mi (28,748 sq km)
Population: 3,639,453
Major Language(s): Albanian
Major Religion(s): Sunni Islam
Currency: lek

Algeria

Al Jaza'ir

Official Name: People's Democratic Republic of Algeria
Capital: Algiers
Area: 919,595 sq mi (2,381,740 sq km)
Population: 34,178,188
Major Language(s): Arabic, French, Berber dialects
Major Religion(s): Sunni Islam
Currency: Algerian dinar

American Samoa

(territory of the United States)

Official Name: Territory of American Samoa
Capital: Pago Pago
Area: 77 sq mi (199 sq km)
Population: 65,628
Major Language(s): Samoan
Major Religion(s): Protestant Christianity
Currency: U.S. dollar

Andorra

Official Name: Principality of Andorra
Capital: Andorra la Vella
Area: 181 sq mi (468 sq km)
Population: 83,888
Major Language(s): Catalan, Spanish, French
Major Religion(s): Roman Catholic Christianity
Currency: euro

Angola

Official Name: Republic of Angola
Capital: Luanda
Area: 481,354 sq mi (1,246,700 sq km)
Population: 12,799,293
Major Language(s): Portuguese, Bantu languages
Major Religion(s): Indigenous beliefs, Christianity
Currency: kwanza

Anguilla

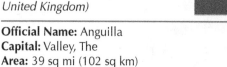

(overseas territory of the United Kingdom)

Official Name: Anguilla
Capital: Valley, The
Area: 39 sq mi (102 sq km)
Population: 14,436
Major Language(s): English
Major Religion(s): Protestant Christianity
Currency: East Caribbean dollar

Antigua and Barbuda

Official Name: Antigua and Barbuda
Capital: Saint John's
Area: 171 sq mi (443 sq km)
Population: 85,632
Major Language(s): English
Major Religion(s): Protestant Christianity
Currency: East Caribbean dollar

Argentina

Official Name: Argentine Republic
Capital: Buenos Aires
Area: 1,068,302 sq mi (2,766,890 sq km)
Population: 40,913,584
Major Language(s): Spanish
Major Religion(s): Roman Catholic Christianity
Currency: Argentine peso

Austria

Oesterreich

Official Name: Republic of Austria
Capital: Vienna
Area: 32,382 sq mi (83,870 sq km)
Population: 8,210,281
Major Language(s): German
Major Religion(s): Roman Catholic Christianity
Currency: euro

Armenia

Hayastan

Official Name: Republic of Armenia
Capital: Yerevan
Area: 11,484 sq mi (29,743 sq km)
Population: 2,967,004
Major Language(s): Armenian
Major Religion(s): Armenian Apostolic Christianity
Currency: dram

Azerbaijan

Azarbaycan

Official Name: Republic of Azerbaijan
Capital: Baku
Area: 33,436 sq mi (86,600 sq km)
Population: 8,238,672
Major Language(s): Azerbaijani
Major Religion(s): Shia Islam
Currency: manats

Aruba

(part of the Kingdom of the Netherlands)

Official Name: Aruba
Capital: Oranjestad
Area: 75 sq mi (193 sq km)
Population: 103,065
Major Language(s): Papiamento, Dutch
Major Religion(s): Roman Catholic Christianity
Currency: Arubian guilder/florin

Bahamas, The

Official Name: Commonwealth of the Bahamas
Capital: Nassau
Area: 5,382 sq mi (13,940 sq km)
Population: 307,552
Major Language(s): English
Major Religion(s): Protestant Christianity
Currency: Bahamian dollar

Australia

Official Name: Commonwealth of Australia
Capital: Canberra
Area: 2,967,909 sq mi (7,686,850 sq km)
Population: 21,262,641
Major Language(s): English, Aboriginal languages
Major Religion(s): Christianity
Currency: Australian dollar

Bahrain

Al Bahrayn

Official Name: Kingdom of Bahrain
Capital: Manama
Area: 257 sq mi (665 sq km)
Population: 728,709
Major Language(s): Arabic, English
Major Religion(s): Sunni Islam
Currency: Bahraini dollar

Country and Dependency Profiles

Bangladesh

Banladesh

Official Name: People's Republic of Bangladesh
Capital: Dhaka
Area: 55,599 sq mi (144,000 sq km)
Population: 156,050,883
Major Language(s): Bangla, English
Major Religion(s): Sunni Islam
Currency: taka

Belize

Official Name: Belize
Capital: Belmopan
Area: 8,867 sq mi (22,966 sq km)
Population: 307,899
Major Language(s): Spanish, Creole, English
Major Religion(s): Roman Catholic Christianity
Currency: Belizian dollar

Barbados

Official Name: Barbados
Capital: Bridgetown
Area: 166 sq mi (431 sq km)
Population: 284,589
Major Language(s): English
Major Religion(s): Protestant Christianity
Currency: Barbadian dollar

Benin

Official Name: Republic of Benin
Capital: Porto-Novo
Area: 43,483 sq mi (112,620 sq km)
Population: 8,791,832
Major Language(s): French, Fon, Yoruba, other African languages
Major Religion(s): Indigenous beliefs, Christianity
Currency: CFA franc

Belarus

Byelarus'

Official Name: Republic of Belarus
Capital: Minsk
Area: 80,155 sq mi (207,600 sq km)
Population: 9,648,533
Major Language(s): Belarusian, Russian
Major Religion(s): Eastern Orthodox Christianity
Currency: Belarusian ruble

Bermuda

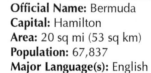

(overseas territory of the United Kingdom)

Official Name: Bermuda
Capital: Hamilton
Area: 20 sq mi (53 sq km)
Population: 67,837
Major Language(s): English
Major Religion(s): Protestant Christianity
Currency: Bermudian dollar

Belgium

Belgique/Belgie

Official Name: Kingdom of Belgium
Capital: Brussels
Area: 11,787 sq mi (30,528 sq km)
Population: 10,414,336
Major Language(s): Dutch, French, German
Major Religion(s): Roman Catholic Christianity
Currency: euro

Bhutan

Druk Yul

Official Name: Kingdom of Bhutan
Capital: Thimphu
Area: 18,147 sq mi (47,000 sq km)
Population: 691,141
Major Language(s): Dzongkha, Tibetan dialects, Nepalese dialects
Major Religion(s): Buddhism
Currency: ngultrum

Bolivia

Official Name: Plurinational State of Bolivia
Capital: La Paz (administrative), Sucre (constitutional)
Area: 424,164 sq mi (1,098,580 sq km)
Population: 9,775,246
Major Language(s): Spanish, Quechua, Aymara
Major Religion(s): Roman Catholic Christianity
Currency: boliviano

British Virgin Islands

*Overseas territory of the
United Kingdom*

Official Name: British Virgin Islands
Capital: Road Town
Area: 58 sq mi (151 sq km)
Population: 25,383
Major Language(s): English
Major Religion(s): Protestant Christianity
Currency: U.S. dollar

Bosnia and Herzegovina

Bosna i Hercegovina

Official Name: Bosnia and Herzegovina
Capital: Sarajevo
Area: 19,772 sq mi (51,209 sq km)
Population: 4,613,414
Major Language(s): Bosnian, Croatian, Serbian
Major Religion(s): Christianity, Islam
Currency: konvertibilna mark

Brunei

Official Name: Brunei Darussalam
Capital: Bandar Seri Begawan
Area: 2,228 sq mi (5,770 sq km)
Population: 388,190
Major Language(s): Malay, English
Major Religion(s): Sunni Islam
Currency: Bruneian dollar

Botswana

Official Name: Republic of Botswana
Capital: Gaborone
Area: 231,804 sq mi (600,370 sq km)
Population: 1,990,876
Major Language(s): Setswana, Kalanga, English
Major Religion(s): Christianity
Currency: pula

Bulgaria

Balgariya

Official Name: Republic of Bulgaria
Capital: Sofia
Area: 42,823 sq mi (110,910 sq km)
Population: 7,204,687
Major Language(s): Bulgarian
Major Religion(s): Eastern Orthodox Christianity
Currency: leva

Brazil

Brasil

Official Name: Federative Republic of Brazil
Capital: Brasilia
Area: 3,286,488 sq mi (8,511,965 sq km)
Population: 198,739,269
Major Language(s): Portuguese, many Amerindian languages
Major Religion(s): Roman Catholic Christianity
Currency: real

Burkina Faso

Official Name: Burkina Faso
Capital: Ouagadougou
Area: 105,869 sq mi (274,200 sq km)
Population: 15,746,232
Major Language(s): French, many African languages
Major Religion(s): Sunni Islam
Currency: CFA franc

Country and Dependency Profiles

Burma (Myanmar)

Myanma Naingngandaw

Official Name: Union of Burma
Capital: Rangoon
Area: 261,970 sq mi (678,500 sq km)
Population: 48,137,741
Major Language(s): Burmese
Major Religion(s): Buddhism
Currency: kyat

Canada

Official Name: Canada
Capital: Ottawa
Area: 3,855,103 sq mi (9,984,670 sq km)
Population: 33,487,208
Major Language(s): English, French, many Amerindian languages
Major Religion(s): Roman Catholic Christianity
Currency: Canadian dollar

Burundi

Official Name: Republic of Burundi
Capital: Bujumbura
Area: 10,745 sq mi (27,830 sq km)
Population: 9,511,330
Major Language(s): Kirundi, French, Swahili
Major Religion(s): Roman Catholic Christianity
Currency: Burundi franc

Cape Verde

Cabo Verde

Official Name: Republic of Cape Verde
Capital: Praia
Area: 1,557 sq mi (4,033 sq km)
Population: 429,474
Major Language(s): Portuguese
Major Religion(s): Roman Catholic Christianity
Currency: escudo

Cambodia

Kampuchea

Official Name: Kingdom of Cambodia
Capital: Phnom Penh
Area: 69,900 sq mi (181,040 sq km)
Population: 14,494,293
Major Language(s): Khmer
Major Religion(s): Buddhism
Currency: riel

Cayman Islands

(overseas territory of the United Kingdom)

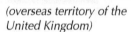

Official Name: Cayman Islands
Capital: George Town
Area: 101 sq mi (262 sq km)
Population: 49,035
Major Language(s): English
Major Religion(s): Christianity
Currency: Caymanian dollar

Cameroon

Cameroun

Official Name: Republic of Cameroon
Capital: Yaounde
Area: 183,568 sq mi (475,440 sq km)
Population: 18,879,301
Major Language(s): English, French, many African languages
Major Religion(s): Indigenous beliefs, Christianity
Currency: CFA franc

Central African Republic

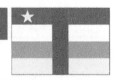

Official Name: Central African Republic
Capital: Bangui
Area: 240,535 sq mi (622,984 sq km)
Population: 4,511,488
Major Language(s): French, Sangho
Major Religion(s): Indigenous beliefs, Christianity
Currency: CFA franc

Chad

Tchad/Tshad

Official Name: Republic of Chad
Capital: N'Djamena
Area: 495,755 sq mi (1,284,000 sq km)
Population: 10,329,208
Major Language(s): French, Arabic, many African languages
Major Religion(s): Sunni Islam
Currency: CFA franc

Comoros

Komori/Comores/Juzur al Qamar

Official Name: Union of the Comoros
Capital: Moroni
Area: 838 sq mi (2,170 sq km)
Population: 752,438
Major Language(s): Arabic, French
Major Religion(s): Sunni Islam
Currency: Comoran franc

Chile

Official Name: Republic of Chile
Capital: Santiago
Area: 292,260 sq mi (756,950 sq km)
Population: 16,601,707
Major Language(s): Spanish
Major Religion(s): Roman Catholic Christianity
Currency: Chilean peso

Congo, Democratic Republic of

Congo (Kinshasa)

Official Name: Democratic Republic of the Congo
Capital: Kinshasa
Area: 905,345 sq mi (2,344,858 sq km)
Population: 68,692,542
Major Language(s): French, Lingala, Kingwana
Major Religion(s): Christianity, Islam, Indigenous beliefs
Currency: Congolese franc

China

Zhongguo

Official Name: People's Republic of China
Capital: Beijing
Area: 3,705,407 sq mi (9,596,960 sq km)
Population: 1,338,612,968
Major Language(s): Chinese (Mandarin), Yue (Cantonese), many other dialects
Major Religion(s): Officially atheist
Currency: Renminbi yuan

Congo, Republic of

Congo (Brazzaville)

Official Name: Republic of the Congo
Capital: Brazzaville
Area: 132,047 sq mi (342,000 sq km)
Population: 4,012,809
Major Language(s): French, Lingala, Monokutuba
Major Religion(s): Christianity, Animist
Currency: Congolese franc

Colombia

Official Name: Republic of Colombia
Capital: Bogotá
Area: 439,736 sq mi (1,138,910 sq km)
Population: 45,644,023
Major Language(s): Spanish
Major Religion(s): Roman Catholic Christianity
Currency: Colombian peso

Costa Rica

Official Name: Republic of Costa Rica
Capital: San Jose
Area: 19,730 sq mi (51,100 sq km)
Population: 4,253,877
Major Language(s): Spanish
Major Religion(s): Roman Catholic Christianity
Currency: colón

Country and Dependency Profiles

Côte d'Ivoire

Official Name: Republic of Côte d'Ivoire
Capital: Yamoussoukro
Area: 124,503 sq mi (322,460 sq km)
Population: 20,617,068
Major Language(s): French, many African languages
Major Religion(s): Sunni Islam, Christianity
Currency: CFA franc

Cyprus
Kypros/Kibris

Official Name: Republic of Cyprus
Capital: Nicosia
Area: 3,571 sq mi (9,250 sq km)
Population: 796,740
Major Language(s): Greek, Turkish
Major Religion(s): Eastern Orthodox Christianity
Currency: euro

Croatia
Hrvatska

Official Name: Republic of Croatia
Capital: Zagreb
Area: 21,831 sq mi (56,542 sq km)
Population: 4,489,409
Major Language(s): Croatian
Major Religion(s): Roman Catholic Christianity
Currency: kuna

Czechia (Czech Republic)
Cesko

Official Name: Czech Republic
Capital: Prague
Area: 30,450 sq mi (78,866 sq km)
Population: 10,211,904
Major Language(s): Czech
Major Religion(s): Roman Catholic Christianity
Currency: koruny

Cuba

Official Name: Republic of Cuba
Capital: Havana
Area: 42,803 sq mi (110,860 sq km)
Population: 11,451,652
Major Language(s): Spanish
Major Religion(s): Roman Catholic Christianity
Currency: Cuban peso

Denmark
Danmark
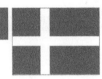

Official Name: Kingdom of Denmark
Capital: Copenhagen
Area: 16,639 sq mi (43,094 sq km)
Population: 5,500,510
Major Language(s): Danish
Major Religion(s): Protestant Christianity
Currency: Danish kroner

Curaçao
Constituent country within the Kingdom of the Netherlands
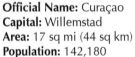

Official Name: Curaçao
Capital: Willemstad
Area: 17 sq mi (44 sq km)
Population: 142,180
Major Language(s): Papiamentu, Dutch
Major Religion(s): Roman Catholic Christianity
Currency: Netherlands Antilles guilder

Djibouti
Jibuti

Official Name: Republic of Djibouti
Capital: Djibouti
Area: 8,880 sq mi (23,000 sq km)
Population: 516,055
Major Language(s): French, Arabic
Major Religion(s): Sunni Islam
Currency: Djiboutian franc

Dominica

Official Name: Commonwealth of Dominica
Capital: Roseau
Area: 291 sq mi (754 sq km)
Population: 72,660
Major Language(s): English
Major Religion(s): Roman Catholic Christianity
Currency: East Caribbean dollar

El Salvador

Official Name: Republic of El Salvador
Capital: San Salvador
Area: 8,124 sq mi (21,040 sq km)
Population: 7,185,218
Major Language(s): Spanish
Major Religion(s): Roman Catholic Christianity
Currency: U.S. dollar

Dominican Republic

La Dominicana

Official Name: Dominican Republic
Capital: Santo Domingo
Area: 18,815 sq mi (48,730 sq km)
Population: 9,650,054
Major Language(s): Spanish
Major Religion(s): Roman Catholic Christianity
Currency: Dominican peso

Equatorial Guinea

Guinea Ecuatorial/Guinee equatoriale

Official Name: Republic of Equatorial Guinea
Capital: Malabo
Area: 10,831 sq mi (28,051 sq km)
Population: 633,441
Major Language(s): Spanish, French, Fang, Bubi
Major Religion(s): Roman Catholic Christianity
Currency: CFA franc

Ecuador

Official Name: Republic of Ecuador
Capital: Quito
Area: 109,483 sq mi (283,560 sq km)
Population: 14,573,101
Major Language(s): Spanish, many Amerindian languages
Major Religion(s): Roman Catholic Christianity
Currency: U.S. dollar

Eritrea

Ertra

Official Name: State of Eritrea
Capital: Asmara
Area: 46,842 sq mi (121,320 sq km)
Population: 5,647,168
Major Language(s): Tigrinya, Arabic
Major Religion(s): Sunni Islam, Christianity
Currency: nakfa

Egypt

Misr

Official Name: Arab Republic of Egypt
Capital: Cairo
Area: 386,662 sq mi (1,001,450 sq km)
Population: 83,082,869
Major Language(s): Arabic
Major Religion(s): Sunni Islam
Currency: Egyptian pound

Estonia

Eesti

Official Name: Republic of Estonia
Capital: Tallinn
Area: 17,462 sq mi (45,226 sq km)
Population: 1,299,371
Major Language(s): Estonian, Russian
Major Religion(s): Protestant Christianity
Currency: euro

Country and Dependency Profiles

Ethiopia

Ityop'iya

Official Name: Federal Democratic Republic of Ethiopia
Capital: Addis Ababa
Area: 435,186 sq mi (1,127,127 sq km)
Population: 85,237,338
Major Language(s): Amarigna, Oromigna, English
Major Religion(s): Ethiopian Orthodox Christianity, Islam
Currency: birr

Falkland Islands (Islas Malvinas)

(overseas territory of the United Kingdom, claimed by Argentina)

Official Name: Falkland Islands (Islas Malvinas)
Capital: Stanley
Area: 4,700 sq mi (12,173 sq km)
Population: 3,140
Major Language(s): English
Major Religion(s): Christianity
Currency: British pound

Faroe Islands

Foroyar
(part of the Kingdom of Denmark)

Official Name: Faroe Islands
Capital: Torshavn
Area: 540 sq mi (1,399 sq km)
Population: 48,856
Major Language(s): Faroese
Major Religion(s): Protestant Christianity
Currency: Danish kroner

Fiji

Fiji/Viti

Official Name: Republic of Fiji
Capital: Suva
Area: 7,054 sq mi (18,270 sq km)
Population: 944,720
Major Language(s): English, Fijian
Major Religion(s): Christianity
Currency: Fijian dollar

Finland

Suomi/Finland

Official Name: Republic of Finland
Capital: Helsinki
Area: 130,559 sq mi (338,145 sq km)
Population: 5,250,275
Major Language(s): Finnish
Major Religion(s): Protestant Christianity
Currency: euro

France

Official Name: French Republic
Capital: Paris
Area: 248,429 sq mi (643,427 sq km)
Population: 64,057,792
Major Language(s): French
Major Religion(s): Roman Catholic Christianity
Currency: euro

Gabon

Official Name: Gabonese Republic
Capital: Libreville
Area: 103,347 sq mi (267,667 sq km)
Population: 1,514,993
Major Language(s): French, Fang
Major Religion(s): Christianity
Currency: CFA franc

Gambia, The
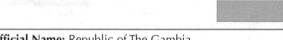

Official Name: Republic of The Gambia
Capital: Banjul
Area: 4,363 sq mi (11,300 sq km)
Population: 1,782,893
Major Language(s): English, Mandinka, Wolof, Fula
Major Religion(s): Sunni Islam
Currency: dalasis

Georgia

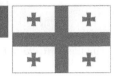

Sak'art'velo

Official Name: Georgia
Capital: T'bilisi
Area: 26,911 sq mi (69,700 sq km)
Population: 4,615,807
Major Language(s): Georgian, Russian
Major Religion(s): Eastern Orthodox Christianity
Currency: laris

Greenland

Kalaallit Nunaat
(part of the Kingdom of Denmark)

Official Name: Greenland
Capital: Nuuk
Area: 836,330 sq mi (2,166,086 sq km)
Population: 57,600
Major Language(s): Greenlandic, Danish, English
Major Religion(s): Protestant Christianity
Currency: Danish kroner

Germany

Deutschland

Official Name: Federal Republic of Germany
Capital: Berlin
Area: 137,847 sq mi (357,021 sq km)
Population: 82,329,758
Major Language(s): German
Major Religion(s): Christianity
Currency: euro

Grenada

Official Name: Grenada
Capital: Saint George's
Area: 133 sq mi (344 sq km)
Population: 90,739
Major Language(s): English, French patois
Major Religion(s): Roman Catholic Christianity
Currency: East Caribbean dollar

Ghana

Official Name: Republic of Ghana
Capital: Accra
Area: 92,456 sq mi (239,460 sq km)
Population: 23,832,495
Major Language(s): English, many African languages
Major Religion(s): Christianity
Currency: cedi

Guatemala

Official Name: Republic of Guatemala
Capital: Guatemala
Area: 42,043 sq mi (108,890 sq km)
Population: 13,276,517
Major Language(s): Spanish, many Amerindian languages
Major Religion(s): Roman Catholic Christianity
Currency: quetzal

Greece

Ellas or Ellada

Official Name: Hellenic Republic
Capital: Athens
Area: 50,942 sq mi (131,940 sq km)
Population: 10,737,428
Major Language(s): Greek
Major Religion(s): Eastern Orthodox Christianity
Currency: euro

Guernsey

(British crown dependency)

Official Name: Bailiwick of Guernsey
Capital: Saint Peter Port
Area: 30 sq mi (78 sq km)
Population: 65,870
Major Language(s): English
Major Religion(s): Protestant Christianity
Currency: British pound

Country and Dependency Profiles

Guinea

Guinee

Official Name: Republic of Guinea
Capital: Conakry
Area: 94,926 sq mi (245,857 sq km)
Population: 10,057,975
Major Language(s): French, many African languages
Major Religion(s): Sunni Islam
Currency: Guinean franc

Holy See (Vatican City)

Santa Sede (Citta del Vaticano)

Official Name: The Holy See (State of the Vatican City)
Capital: Vatican City
Area: 0.4 sq mi (1.1 sq km)
Population: 826
Major Language(s): Italian, Latin
Major Religion(s): Roman Catholic Christianity
Currency: euro

Guinea-Bissau

Guine-Bissau

Official Name: Republic of Guinea-Bissau
Capital: Bissau
Area: 13,946 sq mi (36,120 sq km)
Population: 1,533,964
Major Language(s): Portuguese, Crioulo
Major Religion(s): Sunni Islam, Indigenous beliefs
Currency: CFA franc

Honduras

Official Name: Republic of Honduras
Capital: Tegucigalpa
Area: 43,278 sq mi (112,090 sq km)
Population: 7,833,696
Major Language(s): Spanish, many Amerindian languages
Major Religion(s): Roman Catholic Christianity
Currency: lempira

Guyana

Official Name: Cooperative Republic of Guyana
Capital: Georgetown
Area: 83,000 sq mi (214,970 sq km)
Population: 772,298
Major Language(s): English, many Amerindian languages
Major Religion(s): Hinduism, Christianity
Currency: Guyanese dollar

Hungary

Magyarorszag

Official Name: Republic of Hungary
Capital: Budapest
Area: 35,919 sq mi (93,030 sq km)
Population: 9,905,596
Major Language(s): Hungarian
Major Religion(s): Roman Catholic Christianity
Currency: forint

Haiti

Haiti/Ayiti

Official Name: Republic of Haiti
Capital: Port-au-Prince
Area: 10,714 sq mi (27,750 sq km)
Population: 9,035,536
Major Language(s): French, Creole
Major Religion(s): Roman Catholic Christianity
Currency: gourde

Iceland

Island

Official Name: Republic of Iceland
Capital: Reykjavik
Area: 39,769 sq mi (103,000 sq km)
Population: 306,694
Major Language(s): Icelandic
Major Religion(s): Protestant Christianity
Currency: kronur

India

India/Bharat

Official Name: Republic of India
Capital: New Delhi
Area: 1,269,346 sq mi (3,287,590 sq km)
Population: 1,166,079,217
Major Language(s): Hindi, English, 17 other languages
Major Religion(s): Hinduism, Sunni Islam
Currency: Indian rupee

Indonesia

Official Name: Republic of Indonesia
Capital: Jakarta
Area: 741,100 sq mi (1,919,440 sq km)
Population: 240,271,522
Major Language(s): Bahasa Indonesia, many local dialects
Major Religion(s): Sunni Islam
Currency: rupiah

Iran

Official Name: Islamic Republic of Iran
Capital: Tehran
Area: 636,296 sq mi (1,648,000 sq km)
Population: 66,429,284
Major Language(s): Persian, Turkic dialects, Kurdish
Major Religion(s): Shia Islam
Currency: Iranian rial

Iraq

Al Iraq

Official Name: Republic of Iraq
Capital: Baghdad
Area: 168,754 sq mi (437,072 sq km)
Population: 28,945,657
Major Language(s): Arabic, Kurdish
Major Religion(s): Shia and Sunni Islam
Currency: New Iraqi dinar

Ireland

Eire

Official Name: Ireland
Capital: Dublin
Area: 27,135 sq mi (70,280 sq km)
Population: 4,203,200
Major Language(s): English, Irish
Major Religion(s): Roman Catholic Christianity
Currency: euro

Israel

Yisra'el

Official Name: State of Israel
Capital: Jerusalem (proclaimed), Tel Aviv (de facto)
Area: 8,019 sq mi (20,770 sq km)
Population: 7,233,701
Major Language(s): Hebrew, Arabic
Major Religion(s): Judaism
Currency: Israeli new shekel

Italy

Italia

Official Name: Italian Republic
Capital: Rome
Area: 116,306 sq mi (301,230 sq km)
Population: 58,126,212
Major Language(s): Italian, German, French
Major Religion(s): Roman Catholic Christianity
Currency: euro

Jamaica

Official Name: Jamaica
Capital: Kingston
Area: 4,244 sq mi (10,991 sq km)
Population: 2,825,928
Major Language(s): English, English patois
Major Religion(s): Protestant Christianity
Currency: Jamaica dollar

Country and Dependency Profiles

Japan

Nihon/Nippon

Official Name: Japan
Capital: Tokyo
Area: 145,883 sq mi (377,835 sq km)
Population: 127,078,679
Major Language(s): Japanese
Major Religion(s): Shintoism
Currency: yen

Kenya

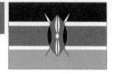

Official Name: Republic of Kenya
Capital: Nairobi
Area: 224,962 sq mi (582,650 sq km)
Population: 39,002,772
Major Language(s): English, Kiswahili
Major Religion(s): Christianity
Currency: Kenyan shilling

Jersey

(British crown dependency)

Official Name: Bailiwick of Jersey
Capital: Saint Helier
Area: 45 sq mi (116 sq km)
Population: 91,626
Major Language(s): English
Major Religion(s): Protestant Christianity
Currency: British pound

Kiribati

Official Name: Republic of Kiribati
Capital: Taraw
Area: 313 sq mi (811 sq km)
Population: 112,850
Major Language(s): I-Kiribati, English
Major Religion(s): Roman Catholic Christianity
Currency: Australian dollar

Jordan

Al Urdun

Official Name: Hashemite Kingdom of Jordan
Capital: Amman
Area: 35,637 sq mi (92,300 sq km)
Population: 6,342,948
Major Language(s): Arabic
Major Religion(s): Sunni Islam
Currency: Jordanian dinar

Korea, North

Choson

Official Name: Democratic People's Republic of Korea
Capital: P'yongyang
Area: 46,541 sq mi (120,540 sq km)
Population: 22,665,345
Major Language(s): Korean
Major Religion(s): Buddhism
Currency: North Korean won

Kazakhstan

Astana

Official Name: Republic of Kazakhstan
Capital: Almaty
Area: 1,049,155 sq mi (2,717,300 sq km)
Population: 15,399,437
Major Language(s): Kazakh, Russian
Major Religion(s): Sunni Islam, Eastern Orthodox Christianity
Currency: tenge

Korea, South

Han'guk

Official Name: Republic of Korea
Capital: Seoul
Area: 38,023 sq mi (98,480 sq km)
Population: 48,508,972
Major Language(s): Korean
Major Religion(s): Buddhism
Currency: South Korean won

Kosovo

Kosova

Official Name: Republic of Kosovo
Capital: Pristina
Area: 4,203 sq mi (10,887 sq km)
Population: 1,804,838
Major Language(s): Albanian, Serbian
Major Religion(s): Sunni Islam
Currency: euro

Latvia

Latvija

Official Name: Republic of Latvia
Capital: Riga
Area: 24,938 sq mi (64,589 sq km)
Population: 2,231,503
Major Language(s): Latvian, Russian
Major Religion(s): Protestant Christianity
Currency: lati

Kuwait

Al Kuwayt

Official Name: State of Kuwait
Capital: Kuwait
Area: 6,880 sq mi (17,820 sq km)
Population: 2,691,158
Major Language(s): Arabic
Major Religion(s): Sunni Islam
Currency: Kuwaiti dinar

Lebanon

Lubnan

Official Name: Lebanese Republic
Capital: Beirut
Area: 4,015 sq mi (10,400 sq km)
Population: 4,017,095
Major Language(s): Arabic, French, English, Armenian
Major Religion(s): Islam, Christianity
Currency: Lebanese pound

Kyrgyzstan

Official Name: Kyrgyz Republic
Capital: Bishkek
Area: 76,641 sq mi (198,500 sq km)
Population: 5,431,747
Major Language(s): Kyrgyz, Uzbek, Russian
Major Religion(s): Sunni Islam, Eastern Orthodox Christianity
Currency: som

Lesotho

Official Name: Kingdom of Lesotho
Capital: Maseru
Area: 11,720 sq mi (30,355 sq km)
Population: 2,130,819
Major Language(s): Sesotho, English, Zulu, Xhosa
Major Religion(s): Christianity, Indigenous beliefs
Currency: maloti

Laos

Pathet Lao

Official Name: Lao People's Democratic Republic
Capital: Vientiane
Area: 91,429 sq mi (236,800 sq km)
Population: 6,834,942
Major Language(s): Lao, French, English
Major Religion(s): Buddhism
Currency: kip

Liberia

Official Name: Republic of Liberia
Capital: Monrovia
Area: 43,000 sq mi (111,370 sq km)
Population: 3,441,790
Major Language(s): English, many African languages
Major Religion(s): Christianity, Indigenous beliefs
Currency: Liberian dollar

Country and Dependency Profiles

Libya

Ar-Libya

Official Name: Great Socialist People's Libyan Arab Jamahiriya
Capital: Tripoli
Area: 679,362 sq mi (1,759,540 sq km)
Population: 6,310,434
Major Language(s): Arabic
Major Religion(s): Sunni Islam
Currency: Libyan dinar

Macedonia

Makedonija

Official Name: Republic of Macedonia
Capital: Skopje
Area: 9,781 sq mi (25,333 sq km)
Population: 2,066,718
Major Language(s): Macedonian, Albanian
Major Religion(s): Eastern Orthodox Christianity, Sunni Islam
Currency: Macedonian denar

Liechtenstein

Official Name: Principality of Liechtenstein
Capital: Vaduz
Area: 62 sq mi (160 sq km)
Population: 34,761
Major Language(s): German
Major Religion(s): Roman Catholic Christianity
Currency: Swiss franc

Madagascar

Madagascar/Madagasikara

Official Name: Republic of Madagascar
Capital: Antananarivo
Area: 226,657 sq mi (587,040 sq km)
Population: 20,653,556
Major Language(s): English, French, Malagasy
Major Religion(s): Indigenous beliefs, Christianity
Currency: ariary

Lithuania

Lietuva

Official Name: Republic of Lithuania
Capital: Vilnius
Area: 25,212 sq mi (65,300 sq km)
Population: 3,555,179
Major Language(s): Lithuanian, Russian
Major Religion(s): Roman Catholic Christianity
Currency: litai

Malawi

Official Name: Republic of Malawi
Capital: Lilongwe
Area: 45,745 sq mi (118,480 sq km)
Population: 15,028,757
Major Language(s): Chichewa, Chinyanja, other African languages
Major Religion(s): Christianity, Islam
Currency: Malawian kwacha

Luxembourg

Official Name: Grand Duchy of Luxembourg
Capital: Luxembourg
Area: 998 sq mi (2,586 sq km)
Population: 491,775
Major Language(s): Luxembourgish, German, French
Major Religion(s): Roman Catholic Christianity
Currency: euro

Malaysia

Official Name: Malaysia
Capital: Kuala Lumpur
Area: 127,317 sq mi (329,750 sq km)
Population: 25,715,819
Major Language(s): Bahasa Malaysia, Chinese, Tamil
Major Religion(s): Islam, Buddhism
Currency: ringgit

Maldives

Dhivehi Raajje

Official Name: Republic of Maldives
Capital: Male
Area: 116 sq mi (300 sq km)
Population: 396,334
Major Language(s): Maldivian Dhivehi
Major Religion(s): Sunni Islam
Currency: rufiyaa

Mauritania

Muritaniyah

Official Name: Islamic Republic of Mauritania
Capital: Nouakchott
Area: 397,955 sq mi (1,030,700 sq km)
Population: 3,129,486
Major Language(s): Arabic, Pulaar, Soninke, Wolof, French
Major Religion(s): Sunni Islam
Currency: ouguiya

Mali

Official Name: Republic of Mali
Capital: Bamako
Area: 478,767 sq mi (1,240,000 sq km)
Population: 12,666,987
Major Language(s): Bambara, French, many African languages
Major Religion(s): Sunni Islam
Currency: CFA franc

Mauritius

Official Name: Republic of Mauritius
Capital: Port Louis
Area: 788 sq mi (2,040 sq km)
Population: 1,284,264
Major Language(s): Creole, Bhojpuri, French
Major Religion(s): Hinduism
Currency: Mauritian rupee

Malta

Official Name: Republic of Malta
Capital: Valletta
Area: 122 sq mi (316 sq km)
Population: 405,165
Major Language(s): Maltese
Major Religion(s): Roman Catholic Christianity
Currency: euro

Mayotte

(territorial overseas collectivity of France)

Official Name: Territorial Collectivity of Mayotte
Capital: Mamoutzou
Area: 144 sq mi (374 sq km)
Population: 223,765
Major Language(s): Mahorian, French
Major Religion(s): Sunni Islam
Currency: euro

Marshall Islands

Official Name: Republic of the Marshall Islands
Capital: Majuro
Area: 70 sq mi (181 sq km)
Population: 64,522
Major Language(s): Marshallese
Major Religion(s): Protestant Christianity
Currency: U.S. dollar

Mexico

Official Name: United Mexican States
Capital: Mexico City
Area: 761,606 sq mi (1,972,550 sq km)
Population: 111,211,789
Major Language(s): Spanish, many Amerindian languages
Major Religion(s): Roman Catholic Christianity
Currency: Mexican peso

Country and Dependency Profiles

Micronesia

Official Name: Federated States of Micronesia
Capital: Palikir
Area: 271 sq mi (702 sq km)
Population: 107,434
Major Language(s): English
Major Religion(s): Roman Catholic Christianity
Currency: U.S. dollar

Moldova

Official Name: Republic of Moldova
Capital: Chisinau
Area: 13,067 sq mi (33,843 sq km)
Population: 4,320,748
Major Language(s): Moldovan, Russian
Major Religion(s): Eastern Orthodox Christianity
Currency: lei

Monaco

Official Name: Principality of Monaco
Capital: Monaco
Area: 1 sq mi (2 sq km)
Population: 32,965
Major Language(s): French, English, Italian, Monegasque
Major Religion(s): Roman Catholic Christianity
Currency: euro

Mongolia

Mongol Uls

Official Name: Mongolia
Capital: Ulaanbaatar
Area: 603,909 sq mi (1,564,116 sq km)
Population: 3,041,142
Major Language(s): Khalkha Mongol
Major Religion(s): Buddhism
Currency: tögrög

Montenegro

Crna Gora

Official Name: Montenegro
Capital: Cetinje
Area: 5,415 sq mi (14,026 sq km)
Population: 672,180
Major Language(s): Montenegrin, Serbian
Major Religion(s): Eastern Orthodox Christianity, Sunni Islam
Currency: euro

Montserrat

(overseas territory of the United Kingdom)

Official Name: Montserrat
Capital: Plymouth
Area: 39 sq mi (102 sq km)
Population: 5,097
Major Language(s): English
Major Religion(s): Protestant Christianity
Currency: East Caribbean dollar

Morocco

Al Maghrib

Official Name: Kingdom of Morocco
Capital: Rabat
Area: 172,414 sq mi (446,550 sq km)
Population: 34,859,364
Major Language(s): Arabic, French, Berber dialects
Major Religion(s): Sunni Islam
Currency: Moroccan dirham

Mozambique

Moçambique

Official Name: Republic of Mozambique
Capital: Maputo
Area: 309,496 sq mi (801,590 sq km)
Population: 21,669,278
Major Language(s): Emakhuwa, Xichangana, Portuguese
Major Religion(s): Christianity, Sunni Islam
Currency: metical

Namibia

Official Name: Republic of Namibia
Capital: Windhoek
Area: 318,696 sq mi (825,418 sq km)
Population: 2,108,665
Major Language(s): Afrikaans, English, German
Major Religion(s): Christianity, Indigenous beliefs
Currency: Namibian dollar

New Zealand

Official Name: New Zealand
Capital: Wellington
Area: 103,738 sq mi (268,680 sq km)
Population: 4,213,418
Major Language(s): English, Maori
Major Religion(s): Christianity
Currency: New Zealand dollar

Nepal

Official Name: Federal Democratic Republic of Nepal
Capital: Kathmandu
Area: 56,827 sq mi (147,181 sq km)
Population: 28,563,377
Major Language(s): Nepali, Maithali, Bhojpuri
Major Religion(s): Hinduism, Buddhism
Currency: Nepalese rupee

Nicaragua

Official Name: Republic of Nicaragua
Capital: Managua
Area: 49,998 sq mi (129,494 sq km)
Population: 5,891,199
Major Language(s): Spanish
Major Religion(s): Roman Catholic Christianity
Currency: cordoba

Netherlands

Nederland

Official Name: Kingdom of the Netherlands
Capital: Amsterdam
Area: 16,033 sq mi (41,526 sq km)
Population: 16,715,999
Major Language(s): Dutch, Frisian
Major Religion(s): Christianity
Currency: euro

Niger

Official Name: Republic of Niger
Capital: Niamey
Area: 489,191 sq mi (1,267,000 sq km)
Population: 15,306,252
Major Language(s): French, Hausa, Djerma
Major Religion(s): Sunni Islam
Currency: CFA franc

New Caledonia

Nouvelle-Caledonie
(self-governing territory of France)

Official Name: Territory of New Caledonia and Dependencies
Capital: Noumea
Area: 7,359 sq mi (19,060 sq km)
Population: 227,436
Major Language(s): French, many Melanesian-Polynesian
dialects
Major Religion(s): Roman Catholic Christianity
Currency: CFP franc

Nigeria

Official Name: Federal Republic of Nigeria
Capital: Abuja
Area: 356,669 sq mi (923,768 sq km)
Population: 149,229,090
Major Language(s): English, Hausa, Yoruba, Igbo, Fulani
Major Religion(s): Sunni Islam, Christianity
Currency: naira

Country and Dependency Profiles

Niue

(self-governing territory in free association with New Zealand)

Official Name: Niue
Capital: Alofi
Area: 100 sq mi (260 sq km)
Population: 1,398
Major Language(s): Niuean, English
Major Religion(s): Protestant Christianity
Currency: New Zealand dollar

Norfolk Island

(self-governing territory of Australia)

Official Name: Territory of Norfolk Island
Capital: Kingston
Area: 14 sq mi (35 sq km)
Population: 2,141
Major Language(s): English
Major Religion(s): Protestant Christianity
Currency: Australian dollar

Norway

Norge

Official Name: Kingdom of Norway
Capital: Oslo
Area: 125,021 sq mi (323,802 sq km)
Population: 4,660,539
Major Language(s): Norwegian
Major Religion(s): Protestant Christianity
Currency: Norwegian kroner

Oman

Uman

Official Name: Sultanate of Oman
Capital: Muscat
Area: 82,031 sq mi (212,460 sq km)
Population: 3,418,085
Major Language(s): Arabic
Major Religion(s): Sunni Islam
Currency: Omani rial

Pakistan

Official Name: Islamic Republic of Pakistan
Capital: Islamabad
Area: 310,403 sq mi (803,940 sq km)
Population: 176,242,949
Major Language(s): Punjabi, Sindhi, Siraiki, Pashtu, Urdu
Major Religion(s): Sunni Islam
Currency: Pakistani rupee

Palau

Belau

Official Name: Republic of Palau
Capital: Koror
Area: 177 sq mi (458 sq km)
Population: 20,796
Major Language(s): Palauan, Tobi, English
Major Religion(s): Christianity
Currency: U.S. dollar

Panama

Official Name: Republic of Panama
Capital: Panama
Area: 30,193 sq mi (78,200 sq km)
Population: 3,360,474
Major Language(s): Spanish, English
Major Religion(s): Roman Catholic Christianity
Currency: balboa

Papua New Guinea

Papuaniugini

Official Name: Independent State of Papua New Guinea
Capital: Port Moresby
Area: 178,704 sq mi (462,840 sq km)
Population: 6,057,263
Major Language(s): Tok Pisin, English, Hiri Motu
Major Religion(s): Protestant Christianity
Currency: kina

Paraguay

Official Name: Republic of Paraguay
Capital: Asuncion
Area: 157,047 sq mi (406,750 sq km)
Population: 6,995,655
Major Language(s): Spanish, Guarani
Major Religion(s): Roman Catholic Christianity
Currency: guaraní

Poland
Polska

Official Name: Republic of Poland
Capital: Warsaw
Area: 120,726 sq mi (312,679 sq km)
Population: 38,482,919
Major Language(s): Polish
Major Religion(s): Roman Catholic Christianity
Currency: zloty

Peru

Official Name: Republic of Peru
Capital: Lima
Area: 496,226 sq mi (1,285,220 sq km)
Population: 29,546,963
Major Language(s): Spanish, Quechua, Aymara
Major Religion(s): Roman Catholic Christianity
Currency: nuevo sol

Portugal

Official Name: Portuguese Republic
Capital: Lisbon
Area: 35,672 sq mi (92,391 sq km)
Population: 10,707,924
Major Language(s): Portuguese
Major Religion(s): Roman Catholic Christianity
Currency: euro

Philippines
Pilipinas

Official Name: Republic of the Philippines
Capital: Manila
Area: 115,831 sq mi (300,000 sq km)
Population: 97,976,603
Major Language(s): Filipino, Tagalog, English
Major Religion(s): Roman Catholic Christianity
Currency: Philippine peso

Puerto Rico
(territory of the United States with commonwealth status)

Official Name: Commonwealth of Puerto Rico
Capital: San Juan
Area: 5,324 sq mi (13,790 sq km)
Population: 3,971,020
Major Language(s): Spanish, English
Major Religion(s): Roman Catholic Christianity
Currency: U.S. dollar

Pitcairn Islands
(overseas territory of the United Kingdom)

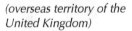

Official Name: Pitcairn, Henderson, Ducie, and Oeno Islands
Capital: Adamstown
Area: 18 sq mi (47 sq km)
Population: 48
Major Language(s): English
Major Religion(s): Protestant Christianity
Currency: New Zealand dollar

Qatar

Official Name: State of Qatar
Capital: Doha
Area: 4,416 sq mi (11,437 sq km)
Population: 833,285
Major Language(s): Arabic
Major Religion(s): Sunni Islam
Currency: Qatari rial

Country and Dependency Profiles

Romania

Official Name: Romania
Capital: Bucharest
Area: 91,699 sq mi (237,500 sq km)
Population: 22,215,421
Major Language(s): Romanian, Hungarian
Major Religion(s): Eastern Orthodox Christianity
Currency: lei

Russia

Rossiya

Official Name: Russian Federation
Capital: Moscow
Area: 6,592,772 sq mi (17,075,200 sq km)
Population: 140,041,247
Major Language(s): Russian, many minority languages
Major Religion(s): Russian Orthodox, Muslim
Currency: Russian ruble

Rwanda

Official Name: Republic of Rwanda
Capital: Kigali
Area: 10,169 sq mi (26,338 sq km)
Population: 10,746,311
Major Language(s): Kinyarwanda, French, English
Major Religion(s): Roman Catholic Christianity
Currency: Rwandan franc

Saint Barthélemy

Territorial overseas collectivity of France

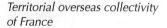

Official Name: Overseas Collectivity of Saint Barthélemy
Capital: Gustavia
Area: 8 sq mi (21 sq km)
Population: 7,367
Major Language(s): French, English
Major Religion(s): Roman Catholic Christianity
Currency: euro

Saint Helena

(overseas territory of the United Kingdom)

Official Name: Saint Helena
Capital: Jamestown
Area: 159 sq mi (413 sq km)
Population: 7,637
Major Language(s): English
Major Religion(s): Protestant Christianity
Currency: Saint Helenanian pound

Saint Kitts and Nevis

Official Name: Federation of Saint Kitts and Nevis
Capital: Basseterre
Area: 101 sq mi (261 sq km)
Population: 40,131
Major Language(s): English
Major Religion(s): Protestant Christianity
Currency: East Caribbean dollar

Saint Lucia

Official Name: Saint Lucia
Capital: Castries
Area: 238 sq mi (616 sq km)
Population: 160,267
Major Language(s): English, French patois
Major Religion(s): Roman Catholic Christianity
Currency: East Caribbean dollar

Saint Martin

Territorial overseas collectivity of France

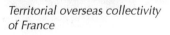

Official Name: Overseas Collectivity of Saint Martin
Capital: Marigot
Area: 21 sq mi (54 sq km)
Population: 30,615
Major Language(s): French, English
Major Religion(s): Roman Catholic Christianity
Currency: euro

Saint Pierre and Miquelon

Saint-Pierre et Miquelon
(territorial overseas collectivity of France)

Official Name: Territorial Collectivity of Saint Pierre and Miquelon
Capital: Saint-Pierre
Area: 93 sq mi (242 sq km)
Population: 7,051
Major Language(s): French
Major Religion(s): Roman Catholic Christianity
Currency: euro

São Tomé and Príncipe

São Tomé e Príncipe

Official Name: Democratic Republic of São Tomé and Príncipe
Capital: São Tomé
Area: 386 sq mi (1,001 sq km)
Population: 212,679
Major Language(s): Portuguese
Major Religion(s): Roman Catholic Christianity
Currency: dobra

Saint Vincent and the Grenadines

Official Name: Saint Vincent and the Grenadines
Capital: Kingstown
Area: 150 sq mi (389 sq km)
Population: 104,574
Major Language(s): English, French patois
Major Religion(s): Protestant Christianity
Currency: East Caribbean dollar

Saudi Arabia

Al Arabiyah as Suudiyah

Official Name: Kingdom of Saudi Arabia
Capital: Riyadh
Area: 830,000 sq mi (2,149,690 sq km)
Population: 28,686,633
Major Language(s): Arabic
Major Religion(s): Sunni Islam
Currency: Saudi riyal

Samoa

Official Name: Independent State of Samoa
Capital: Apia
Area: 1,137 sq mi (2,944 sq km)
Population: 219,998
Major Language(s): Samoan, English
Major Religion(s): Protestant Christianity
Currency: tala

Senegal

Official Name: Republic of Senegal
Capital: Dakar
Area: 75,749 sq mi (196,190 sq km)
Population: 13,711,597
Major Language(s): French, Wolof, Pulaar, Jola, Mandinka
Major Religion(s): Sunni Islam
Currency: CFA franc

San Marino

Official Name: Republic of San Marino
Capital: San Marino
Area: 24 sq mi (61 sq km)
Population: 30,324
Major Language(s): Italian
Major Religion(s): Roman Catholic Christianity
Currency: euro

Serbia

Srbija

Official Name: Republic of Serbia
Capital: Belgrade
Area: 29,913 sq mi (77,474 sq km)
Population: 7,379,339
Major Language(s): Serbian
Major Religion(s): Eastern Orthodox Christianity
Currency: Serbian dinal

Country and Dependency Profiles

Seychelles

Official Name: Republic of Seychelles
Capital: Victoria
Area: 176 sq mi (455 sq km)
Population: 87,476
Major Language(s): Creole
Major Religion(s): Roman Catholic Christianity
Currency: Seychelles rupee

Slovakia

Slovensko

Official Name: Slovak Republic
Capital: Bratislava
Area: 18,859 sq mi (48,845 sq km)
Population: 5,463,046
Major Language(s): Slovak, Hungarian
Major Religion(s): Roman Catholic Christianity
Currency: euro

Sierra Leone

Official Name: Republic of Sierra Leone
Capital: Freetown
Area: 27,699 sq mi (71,740 sq km)
Population: 6,440,053
Major Language(s): Mende, Temne, English, Krio
Major Religion(s): Sunni Islam
Currency: leone

Slovenia

Slovenija

Official Name: Republic of Slovenia
Capital: Ljubljana
Area: 7,827 sq mi (20,273 sq km)
Population: 2,005,692
Major Language(s): Slovenian
Major Religion(s): Roman Catholic Christianity
Currency: euro

Singapore

Official Name: Republic of Singapore
Capital: Singapore
Area: 268 sq mi (693 sq km)
Population: 4,657,542
Major Language(s): Chinese (Mandarin), English, Malay, Hokkien
Major Religion(s): Buddhism, Sunni Islam
Currency: Singapore dollar

Solomon Islands

Official Name: Solomon Islands
Capital: Honiara
Area: 10,985 sq mi (28,450 sq km)
Population: 595,613
Major Language(s): English, many indigenous languages
Major Religion(s): Protestant Christianity
Currency: Solomon Islands dollar

Sint Maarten

Constituent country within the Kingdom of the Netherlands

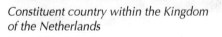
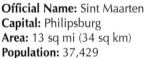

Official Name: Sint Maarten
Capital: Philipsburg
Area: 13 sq mi (34 sq km)
Population: 37,429
Major Language(s): English, Spanish, Creole
Major Religion(s): Roman Catholic Christianity
Currency: Netherlands Antilles guilder

Somalia

Soomaaliya

Official Name: Somalia
Capital: Mogadishu
Area: 246,201 sq mi (637,657 sq km)
Population: 9,832,017
Major Language(s): Somali, Arabic, Italian
Major Religion(s): Sunni Islam
Currency: Somali shilling

South Africa

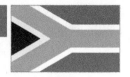

Official Name: Republic of South Africa
Capital: Bloemfontein (judicial), Cape Town (legislative)
Area: 471,011 sq mi (1,219,912 sq km)
Population: 49,052,489
Major Language(s): Zulu, Xhosa, Afrikaans, Sepedi, English, Setswana, Sesotho
Major Religion(s): Protestant Christianity
Currency: rand

Sudan

As-Sudan

Official Name: Republic of the Sudan
Capital: Khartoum
Area: 718,724 sq mi (1,861,484 sq km)
Population: 36,787,012
Major Language(s): Arabic, English
Major Religion(s): Sunni Islam
Currency: Sudanese pound

South Sudan

Official Name: Republic of South Sudan
Capital: Juba
Area: 24,838 sq mi (64,329 sq km)
Population: 8,260,490
Major Language(s): Arabic, English
Major Religion(s): Christianity, Animist
Currency: South Sudan pound

Suriname

Official Name: Republic of Suriname
Capital: Paramaribo
Area: 63,039 sq mi (163,270 sq km)
Population: 481,267
Major Language(s): Dutch, English
Major Religion(s): Hinduism, Christianity
Currency: Surinamese dollar

Spain

España

Official Name: Kingdom of Spain
Capital: Madrid
Area: 194,897 sq mi (504,782 sq km)
Population: 40,525,002
Major Language(s): Spanish, Catalan, Galician, Basque
Major Religion(s): Roman Catholic Christianity
Currency: euro

Swaziland

eSwatini

Official Name: Kingdom of Swaziland
Capital: Mbabane
Area: 6,704 sq mi (17,363 sq km)
Population: 1,337,186
Major Language(s): English, siSwati
Major Religion(s): Christianity, Indigenous beliefs
Currency: emalangeni

Sri Lanka

Shri Lamka/Ilankai

Official Name: Democratic Socialist Republic of Sri Lanka
Capital: Colombo
Area: 25,332 sq mi (65,610 sq km)
Population: 21,324,791
Major Language(s): Sinhala, Tamil
Major Religion(s): Buddhism
Currency: Sri Lankan rupee

Sweden

Sverige

Official Name: Kingdom of Sweden
Capital: Stockholm
Area: 173,732 sq mi (449,964 sq km)
Population: 9,059,651
Major Language(s): Swedish
Major Religion(s): Protestant Christianity
Currency: Swedish kronor

Country and Dependency Profiles

Switzerland

Schweiz/Suisse/Svizzera/Svizra

Official Name: Swiss Confederation
Capital: Bern
Area: 15,942 sq mi (41,290 sq km)
Population: 7,604,467
Major Language(s): German, French, Italian, Romansch
Major Religion(s): Christianity
Currency: Swiss franc

Tanzania

Official Name: United Republic of Tanzania
Capital: Dodoma
Area: 364,900 sq mi (945,087 sq km)
Population: 41,048,532
Major Language(s): Swahili, English
Major Religion(s): Sunni Islam, Christianity
Currency: Tanzanian shilling

Syria

Suriyah

Official Name: Syrian Arab Republic
Capital: Damascus
Area: 71,498 sq mi (185,180 sq km)
Population: 20,178,485
Major Language(s): Arabic
Major Religion(s): Sunni Islam
Currency: Syrian pound

Thailand

Prathet Thai

Official Name: Kingdom of Thailand
Capital: Bangkok
Area: 198,457 sq mi (514,000 sq km)
Population: 65,998,436
Major Language(s): Thai
Major Religion(s): Buddhism
Currency: baht

Taiwan

T'ai-wan
(unresolved status; has limited international recognition as the legitimate representative of China)

Official Name: Taiwan
Capital: Taipei
Area: 13,892 sq mi (35,980 sq km)
Population: 22,974,347
Major Language(s): Chinese (Mandarin), Taiwanese
Major Religion(s): Buddhism
Currency: New Taiwan dollar

Timor-Leste

Timor Lorosa'e/Timor-Leste

Official Name: Democratic Republic of Timor-Leste
Capital: Dili
Area: 5,794 sq mi (15,007 sq km)
Population: 1,131,612
Major Language(s): Tetum, Portuguese, Indonesian
Major Religion(s): Roman Catholic Christianity
Currency: U.S. dollar

Tajikistan

Tojikiston

Official Name: Republic of Tajikistan
Capital: Dushanbe
Area: 55,251 sq mi (143,100 sq km)
Population: 7,349,145
Major Language(s): Tajik, Russian
Major Religion(s): Sunni Islam
Currency: somoni

Togo

Official Name: Togolese Republic
Capital: Lome
Area: 21,925 sq mi (56,785 sq km)
Population: 6,031,808
Major Language(s): French, many African languages
Major Religion(s): Indigenous beliefs, Christianity
Currency: CFA franc

Tonga

Official Name: Kingdom of Tonga
Capital: Nuku'alofa
Area: 289 sq mi (748 sq km)
Population: 120,898
Major Language(s): Tongan, English
Major Religion(s): Protestant Christianity
Currency: pa'anga

Turkmenistan

Official Name: Turkmenistan
Capital: Ashgabat
Area: 188,456 sq mi (488,100 sq km)
Population: 4,884,887
Major Language(s): Turkmen, Russian, Uzbek
Major Religion(s): Sunni Islam
Currency: manats

Trinidad and Tobago

Official Name: Republic of Trinidad and Tobago
Capital: Port-of-Spain
Area: 1,980 sq mi (5,128 sq km)
Population: 1,229,953
Major Language(s): English, French, Spanish
Major Religion(s): Roman Catholic Christianity, Hinduism
Currency: Trinidad and Tobago dollar

Turks and Caicos Islands

*(overseas territory of the
United Kingdom)*

Official Name: Turks and Caicos Islands
Capital: Grand Turk
Area: 166 sq mi (430 sq km)
Population: 22,942
Major Language(s): English
Major Religion(s): Protestant Christianity
Currency: U.S. dollar

Tunisia

Tunis

Official Name: Tunisian Republic
Capital: Tunis
Area: 63,170 sq mi (163,610 sq km)
Population: 10,486,339
Major Language(s): Arabic, French
Major Religion(s): Sunni Islam
Currency: Tunisian dinar

Tuvalu

Official Name: Tuvalu
Capital: Funafuti
Area: 10 sq mi (26 sq km)
Population: 12,373
Major Language(s): Tuvaluan, English, Samoan
Major Religion(s): Protestant Christianity
Currency: Tuvaluan dollar

Turkey

Turkiye

Official Name: Republic of Turkey
Capital: Ankara
Area: 301,384 sq mi (780,580 sq km)
Population: 76,805,524
Major Language(s): Turkish, Kurdish
Major Religion(s): Sunni Islam
Currency: lira

Uganda

Official Name: Republic of Uganda
Capital: Kampala
Area: 91,136 sq mi (236,040 sq km)
Population: 32,369,558
Major Language(s): English, Ganda, Swahili, other African
languages
Major Religion(s): Christianity
Currency: Ugandan shilling

Country and Dependency Profiles

Ukraine

Ukrayina

Official Name: Ukraine
Capital: Kyiv
Area: 233,090 sq mi (603,700 sq km)
Population: 45,700,395
Major Language(s): Ukrainian, Russian
Major Religion(s): Eastern Orthodox Christianity
Currency: hryvnia

Uruguay

Official Name: Oriental Republic of Uruguay
Capital: Montevideo
Area: 68,039 sq mi (176,220 sq km)
Population: 3,494,382
Major Language(s): Spanish
Major Religion(s): Christianity
Currency: Uruguayan peso

United Arab Emirates

Al Imarat al Arabiyah al Muttahidah

Official Name: United Arab Emirates
Capital: Abu Dhabi
Area: 32,278 sq mi (83,600 sq km)
Population: 4,798,491
Major Language(s): Arabic
Major Religion(s): Sunni Islam
Currency: Emirati dirham

Uzbekistan

Ozbekiston

Official Name: Republic of Uzbekistan
Capital: Tashkent
Area: 172,742 sq mi (447,400 sq km)
Population: 27,606,007
Major Language(s): Uzbek, Russian
Major Religion(s): Sunni Islam
Currency: soum

United Kingdom

Official Name: United Kingdom of Great Britain and Northern Ireland
Capital: London
Area: 94,526 sq mi (244,820 sq km)
Population: 61,113,205
Major Language(s): English, Welsh, Scottish Gaelic
Major Religion(s): Christianity
Currency: British pound

Vanuatu

Official Name: Republic of Vanuatu
Capital: Port-Vila
Area: 4,710 sq mi (12,200 sq km)
Population: 218,519
Major Language(s): Many local languages
Major Religion(s): Protestant Christianity
Currency: vatu

United States

Official Name: United States of America
Capital: Washington, D.C.
Area: 3,794,083 sq mi (9,826,630 sq km)
Population: 307,212,123
Major Language(s): English, Spanish
Major Religion(s): Christianity
Currency: U.S. dollar

Venezuela

Official Name: Bolivarian Republic of Venezuela
Capital: Caracas
Area: 352,144 sq mi (912,050 sq km)
Population: 26,814,843
Major Language(s): Spanish, many Amerindian languages
Major Religion(s): Roman Catholic Christianity
Currency: bolivar

Vietnam

Viet Nam

Official Name: Socialist Republic of Vietnam
Capital: Hanoi
Area: 127,244 sq mi (329,560 sq km)
Population: 86,967,524
Major Language(s): Vietnamese, French, Chinese
Major Religion(s): Non-religious beliefs dominate
Currency: dong

Yemen

Al Yaman

Official Name: Republic of Yemen
Capital: Sanaa
Area: 203,850 sq mi (527,970 sq km)
Population: 23,822,783
Major Language(s): Arabic
Major Religion(s): Sunni Islam
Currency: Yemeni rial

Virgin Islands

(territory of the United States)

Official Name: United States Virgin Islands
Capital: Charlotte Amalie
Area: 737 sq mi (1,910 sq km)
Population: 109,825
Major Language(s): English, Spanish
Major Religion(s): Christianity
Currency: U.S. dollar

Zambia

Official Name: Republic of Zambia
Capital: Lusaka
Area: 290,586 sq mi (752,614 sq km)
Population: 11,862,740
Major Language(s): English, many African (Bantu) languages
Major Religion(s): Christianity, Islam
Currency: Zambian kwacha

Wallis and Futuna

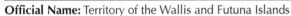

Wallis et Futuna
(overseas collectivity of France)

Official Name: Territory of the Wallis and Futuna Islands
Capital: Mata-Utu
Area: 106 sq mi (274 sq km)
Population: 15,289
Major Language(s): Wallisian, Futunian, French
Major Religion(s): Roman Catholic Christianity
Currency: CFP franc

Zimbabwe

Official Name: Republic of Zimbabwe
Capital: Harare
Area: 150,804 sq mi (390,580 sq km)
Population: 11,392,629
Major Language(s): English, many African (Bantu) languages
Major Religion(s): Christianity, Indigenous beliefs
Currency: Zimbabwean dollar

Unit IX

Geographic Index

GEOGRAPHIC INDEX

The geographic index contains approximately 1,250 names of cities, states, countries, rivers, lakes, mountain ranges, oceans, capes, bays, and other geographic features. The name of each geographical feature in the index is accompanied by a geographical coordinate (latitude and longitude) in degrees and by the page number of the primary map on which the geographical feature appears. Where the geographical coordinates are for specific places or points, such as a city or a mountain peak, the latitude and longitude figures give the location of the map symbol denoting that point. Thus, Los Angeles, California, is at 34.1°N and 118.3°W and the location of Mt. Everest is 28.0°N and 86.9°E.

The coordinates for political features (countries or states) or physical features (oceans, deserts) that are areas rather than points are given according to the location of the name of the feature on the map, except in those cases where the name of the feature is separated from the feature (such as a country's name appearing over an adjacent ocean area because of space requirements). In such cases, the feature's coordinates will indicate the location of the center of the feature. The coordinates for the Sahara Desert will lead the reader to the place name "Sahara Desert" on the map; the coordinates for North Carolina will show the center location of the state since the name appears over the adjacent Atlantic Ocean. Finally, the coordinates for geographical features that are lines rather than points or areas will also appear near the center of the text identifying the geographical feature.

Alphabetizing follows general conventions; the names of physical features such as lakes, rivers, and mountains are given as: proper name, followed by the generic name. Thus "Mount Everest" is listed as "Everest, Mt." Where an article such as "the," "le," or "al" appears in a geographic name, the name is alphabetized according to the article. Hence, "La Paz" is found under "L" and not under "P."

GEOGRAPHIC INDEX

NAME/DESCRIPTION	LATITUDE & LONGITUDE	PAGE	NAME/DESCRIPTION	LATITUDE & LONGITUDE	PAGE
Asuncion (nat. capital, Paraguay)	25.3°S, 57.7°W	154	Beaufort Sea (sea, Arctic Ocean)	73.0°N, 140.0°W	150
Atacama Desert (desert, Chile)	23.0°S, 70.2°W	153	Beijing (nat. capital, China)	39.9°N, 116.4°E	160
Athabasca, Lake (lake, Canada)	59.3°N, 107.5°W	150	Beirut (nat. capital, Lebanon)	33.9°N, 35.5°E	160
Athens (nat. capital, Greece)	38.0°N, 23.7°E	157	Belarus (country, Europe)	53.0°N, 28.0°E	157
Atlanta, GA (state capital, U.S.)	33.8°N, 84.4°W	151	Belgium (country, Europe)	50.8°N, 4.0°E	157
Atlantic-Indian Ridge (ridge, Atlantic Ocean)	50.0°S, 20.0°E	4	Belgrade (nat. capital, Serbia)	44.8°N, 20.5°E	157
Atlas Mountains (mountains, Morocco)	31.0°N, 8.0°E	162	Belize (country, North America)	17.3°N, 88.8°W	151
Auckland (city, New Zealand)	36.9°S, 174.8°E	166	Bellingshausen Sea (sea, Southern Ocean)	71.0°S, 85.0°W	168
Augusta, ME (state capital, U.S.)	44.3°N, 69.8°W	151	Belmopan (nat. capital, Belize)	17.3°N, 88.8°W	151
Austin, TX (state capital, U.S.)	30.3°N, 97.8°W	151	Belo Horizonte (city, Brazil)	19.9°S, 43.9°W	154
Australia (country, Oceania)	24.0°S, 135.0°E	166	Bengal, Bay of (bay, Indian Ocean)	15.0°N, 90.0°E	159
Australian Capital Territory (territory, Australia)	35.3°S, 149.1°E	166	Benghazi (city, Libya)	32.1°N, 20.1°E	163
Austria (country, Europe)	47.3°N, 13.3°E	157	Benin (country, Africa)	9.5°N, 2.3°E	163
Azerbaijan (country, Asia)	40.5°N, 47.5°E	160	Benin City (city, Nigeria)	6.3°N, 5.6°E	163
Azores Islands (islands, Atlantic Ocean)	38.5°N, 28.0°W	4	Benue (river, Africa)	8.6°N, 10.4°E	162
Azov, Sea of (sea, Atlantic Ocean)	46.0°N, 37.0°E	156	Bering Sea (sea, Pacific Ocean)	60.0°N, 175.0°W	150
Baffin Bay (bay, Arctic Ocean)	73.0°N, 66.0°W	150	Berlin (nat. capital, Germany)	52.5°N, 13.4°E	157
Baffin Island (island, Canada)	68.0°N, 70.0°W	150	Bermuda (island, North America)	32.3°N, 64.8°W	150
Baghdad (nat. capital, Iraq)	33.4°N, 44.4°E	160	Bern (nat. capital, Switzerland)	47.0°N, 7.4°E	157
Bahamas, The (country, North America)	25.1°N, 77.3°W	151	Bhopal (city, India)	23.3°N, 77.4°E	160
Bahrain (country, Asia)	26.0°N, 50.6°E	160	Bhutan (country, Asia)	27.5°N, 90.5°E	160
Baikal, Lake (lake, Russia)	53.5°N, 108.0°E	159	Birmingham (city, U.K.)	52.5°N, 1.9°W	157
Baja California (peninsula, Mexico)	28.0°N, 113.5°W	150	Biscay, Bay of (bay, Atlantic Ocean)	44.0°N, 4.0°W	156
Baja California (state, Mexico)	30.0°N, 113.0°W	151	Bishkek (nat. capital, Kyrgyzstan)	42.9°N, 74.6°E	160
Baja California Sur (state, Mexico)	25.9°N, 112.0°W	151	Bismarck, ND (state capital, U.S.)	46.8°N, 100.8°W	151
Baku (nat. capital, Azerbaijan)	40.4°N, 49.9°E	160	Bissau (nat. capital, Guinea-Bissau)	11.9°N, 15.6°W	163
Balearic Islands (islands, Spain)	39.5°N, 3.0°E	156	Black Sea (sea, Atlantic Ocean)	43.0°N, 35.0°E	156
Balkan Peninsula (peninsula, Europe)	40.0°N, 22.0°E	4	Blanc, Cape (cape, Western Sahara)	20.5°N, 17.0°E	162
Balkhash, Lake (lake, Kazakhstan)	46.2°N, 74.3°E	159	Blanc, Mont 15,771 (peak, Europe)	45.8°N, 6.9°E	156
Baltic Sea (sea, Atlantic Ocean)	57.0°N, 19.0°E	156	Bloemfontein (judicial capital, South Africa)	29.2°S, 26.1°E	163
Baltimore, MD (city, U.S.)	37.3°N, 76.6°W	151	Blue Nile (river, Africa)	11.0°N, 35.2°E	162
Bamako (nat. capital, Mali)	12.7°N, 8.0°W	163	Bo Hai (gulf, Pacific Ocean)	38.0°N, 120.0°E	159
Banda Sea (sea, Pacific Ocean)	5.0°S, 128.0°E	165	Boa Vista (city, Brazil)	2.8°N, 60.7°W	154
Bandar Seri Begawan (nat. capital, Brunei)	4.9°N, 114.9°E	160	Bogotá (nat. capital, Colombia)	4.6°N, 74.1°W	154
Bangalore (city, India)	16.0°N, 77.6°E	160	Boise, ID (state capital, U.S.)	43.6°N, 116.2°W	151
Bangkok (nat. capital, Thailand)	13.8°N, 100.5°E	160	Bolivia (country, South America)	17.0°S, 65.0°W	154
Bangladesh (country, Asia)	24.0°N, 90.0°E	160	Bordeaux (city, France)	44.8°N, 0.6°W	157
Bangui (nat. capital, Central African Republic)	4.4°N, 18.6°E	163	Borneo (island, Indonesia)	0.5°N, 114.0°E	159
Banjul (nat. capital, Gambia)	13.5°N, 16.7°W	163	Bosnia & Herzegovina (country, Europe)	44.0°N, 18.0°E	157
Banks Island (island, Canada)	75.3°N, 121.5°W	150	Boston, MA (state capital, U.S.)	42.4°N, 71.1°W	151
Baotou (city, China)	40.7°N, 109.8°E	160	Bothnia, Gulf of (gulf, Atlantic Ocean)	63.0°N, 20.0°E	156
Barbados (country, North America)	13.2°S, 59.6°W	154	Botswana (country, Africa)	22.0°S, 24.0°E	163
Barcelona (city, Spain)	41.4°N, 2.2°E	157	Brahmaputra (river, Asia)	28.0°N, 90.0°E	159
Barents Sea (sea, Arctic Ocean)	74.0°N, 36.0°E	156	Brasília (nat. capital, Brazil)	15.8°S, 47.9°W	154
Basra (city, Iraq)	30.5°N, 47.8°E	160	Bratislava (nat. capital, Slovakia)	48.2°N, 17.1°E	157
Bass Strait (strait, Pacific Ocean)	39.3°S, 145.5°E	165	Brazil (country, South America)	8.0°S, 53.0°W	154
Baton Rouge, LA (state capital, U.S.)	30.5°N, 91.1°W	151	Brazilian Highlands (plateau, Brazil)	21.0°S, 47.0°W	153
Bay of Plenty (bay, New Zealand)	37.3°S, 176.8°E	165	Brazzaville (nat. capital, Congo Rep.)	4.3°S, 15.3°E	163

GEOGRAPHIC INDEX

GEOGRAPHIC INDEX

NAME/DESCRIPTION	LATITUDE & LONGITUDE	PAGE
Conakry (nat. capital, Guinea)	9.5°N, 13.7°W	163
Concord, NH (state capital, U.S.)	43.2°N, 71.5°W	151
Congo (river, Africa)	1.0°N, 24.0°E	162
Congo, Democratic Republic of (country, Africa)	5.0°S, 25.0°E	163
Congo, Republic of (country, Africa)	0.7°S, 15.0°E	163
Connecticut (state, U.S.)	41.6°N, 72.7°W	151
Copenhagen (nat. capital, Denmark)	55.7°N, 12.6°E	157
Coral Sea (sea, Pacific Ocean)	15.0°S, 150.0°E	165
Cordoba (city, Brazil)	31.4°S, 63.2°W	154
Corsica (island, France)	0.9°N, 9.3°E	156
Costa Rica (country, North America)	10.0°N, 84.1°W	151
Côte d'Ivoire (country, Africa)	8.0°N, 5.0°W	163
Crete (island, Greece)	35.3°N, 24.8°E	156
Croatia (country, Europe)	45.2°N, 15.5°E	157
Cuba (country, North America)	22.0°N, 79.5°W	151
Cuiabá (city, Brazil)	15.6°S, 56.1°W	154
Culiacán (state capital, Mexico)	24.8°N, 107.4°W	151
Curitiba (city, Brazil)	25.4°S, 49.3°W	154
Cyprus (country, Europe)	35.0°N, 33.0°E	157
Czechia (country, Europe)	49.8°N, 15.5°E	157
Dakar (nat. capital, Senegal)	14.7°N, 17.4°W	163
Dallas (city, U.S.)	32.8°N, 96.8°W	151
Damascus (nat. capital, Syria)	33.5°N, 36.3°E	160
Danube (river, Europe)	48.0°N, 8.5°E	156
Dar es Salaam (city, Tanzania)	6.8°S, 39.3°E	163
Darling (river, Australia)	31.0°S, 145.0°E	165
Darwin (city, Australia)	12.5°S, 130.8°E	166
Dasht-e Lut (desert, Asia)	30.6°N, 59.1°E	159
Deccan Plateau (plateau, India)	17.0°N, 77.0°E	159
Delaware (state, U.S.)	39.0°N, 75.5°W	151
Denmark (country, Europe)	56.0°N, 10.0°E	157
Denver, CO (state capital, U.S.)	39.7°N, 105.0°W	151
Des Moines, IA (state capital, U.S.)	41.6°N, 93.6°W	151
Detroit (city, U.S.)	42.3°N, 83.1°W	151
Devon Island (island, Canada)	75.1°N, 87.9°W	168
Dhaka (nat. capital, Bangladesh)	23.7°N, 90.4°E	160
Dili (nat. capital, Timor-Leste)	8.6°S, 125.6°E	160
Djibouti (country, Africa)	11.5°N, 43.0°E	163
Djibouti (nat. capital, Djibouti)	11.5°N, 43.3°E	163
Dnieper (river, Europe)	46.5°N, 32.3°E	156
Dnipropetrovsk (city, Ukraine)	48.5°N, 35.0°E	157
Dodoma (nat. capital, Tanzania)	6.2°S, 35.8°E	163
Doha (nat. capital, Qatar)	25.3°N, 51.5°E	160
Dominican Republic (country, North America)	19.0°N, 70.7°W	151
Donetsk (city, Ukraine)	48.0°N, 37.8°E	157
Dover, DE (state capital, U.S.)	39.2°N, 75.5°W	151
Drake Passage (sea, Atlantic Ocean)	60.0°S, 60.0°W	153
Drakensburg (mountains, South Africa)	31.5°S, 27.0°E	162

NAME/DESCRIPTION	LATITUDE & LONGITUDE	PAGE
Dubai (city, U.A.E.)	25.3°N, 55.3°E	160
Dublin (nat. capital, Ireland)	53.3°N, 6.3°W	157
Dunedin (city, New Zealand)	45.9°S, 170.5°E	166
Durango (state capital, Mexico)	24.0°N, 104.7°W	151
Durango (state, Mexico)	24.9°N, 104.9°W	151
Durban (city, South Africa)	29.9°S, 31.0°E	163
Dushanbe (nat. capital, Tajikistan)	38.6°N, 68.8°E	160
Dvina (river, Europe)	55.8°N, 27.8°E	156
Dzhugdzhur Range (mountains, Asia)	58.0°N, 136.0°E	159
East Antarctica (region, Antarctica)	80.0°S, 80.0°E	168
East China Sea (sea, Pacific Ocean)	30.0°N, 126.0°E	159
East Pacific Rise (ridge, Pacific Ocean)	40.0°S, 110.0°W	4
East Siberian Sea (sea, Arctic Ocean)	74.0°N, 166.0°E	159
Eastern Ghats (mountains, India)	20.0°N, 85.0°E	159
Ebro (river, Spain)	41.5°N, 2.2°E	156
Ecuador (country, South America)	2.0°S, 78.0°W	154
Edmonton, AB (prov. capital, Canada)	53.5°N, 113.5°W	151
Egypt (country, Africa)	27.0°N, 30.0°E	163
El Paso (city, U.S.)	31.8°N, 106.4°W	151
El Salvador (country, North America)	14.0°N, 89.0°W	151
Elbe (river, Europe)	51.5°N, 11.5°E	156
Elbert, Mt. 14,440 (peak, U.S.)	39.1°N, 106.4°W	150
Elbrus, Mt. 18,510 (peak, Asia)	43.4°N, 42.4°E	159
Elburz (mountains, Asia)	36.1°N, 51.8°E	159
Ellesmere Island (island, Canada)	81.0°N, 80.0°W	150
Ellsworth Land (region, Antarctica)	75.5°S, 80.0°W	168
Enderby Land (region, Antarctica)	67.5°S, 53.0°E	168
Equatorial Guinea (country, Africa)	2.0°N, 10.0°E	163
Erg Chech (desert, Africa)	3.0°W, 26.0°N	4
Erie, Lake (lake, North America)	42.5°N, 81.0°W	150
Eritrea (country, Africa)	15.0°N, 39.0°E	163
Estonia (country, Europe)	59.0°N, 26.0°E	157
Ethiopia (country, Africa)	8.0°N, 38.0°E	163
Ethiopian Highlands (mountains, Ethiopia)	12.5°N, 41.4°E	162
Euphrates (river, Asia)	32.0°N, 50.0°E	159
Everest, Mt. 29,028 (peak, Asia)	28.0°N, 86.9°E	159
Fairbanks (city, U.S.)	64.8°N, 147.7°W	151
Falkland Islands (islands, U.K.)	51.8°S, 59.0°W	153
Faroe Islands (islands, Denmark)	62.0°N, 7.0°W	156
Fes (city, Morocco)	34.0°N, 5.0°W	163
Fiji (country, Oceania)	18.0°S, 179.0°E	166
Filchner Ice Shelf (ice shelf, Antarctica)	77.9°S, 61.3°W	168
Finland (country, Europe)	64.0°N, 26.0°E	157
Flores Sea (sea, Pacific Ocean)	7.7°S, 119.8°E	159
Florida (state, U.S.)	28.1°N, 81.6°W	151
Formosa (city, Brazil)	15.5°S, 47.3°W	154
Fort Worth (city, U.S.)	32.8°N, 97.3°W	151
Fortaleza (city, Brazil)	3.8°S, 38.5°W	154

GEOGRAPHIC INDEX

NAME/DESCRIPTION	LATITUDE & LONGITUDE	PAGE	NAME/DESCRIPTION	LATITUDE & LONGITUDE	PAGE
Foxe Basin (basin, Atlantic Ocean)	67.0°N, 78.0°W	150	Greenland (dependency, North America)	72.0°N, 40.0°W	151
France (country, Europe)	46.0°N, 2.0°E	157	Greenland Sea (sea, Atlantic Ocean)	79.0°N, 5.0°W	156
Frankfort (state capital, U.S.)	50.1°N, 8.7°E	151	Grenada (country, North America)	12.1°N, 61.8°W	154
Franz Josef Land (islands, Russia)	81.0°N, 55.0°E	168	Guadalajara (state capital, Mexico)	20.7°N, 103.4°W	151
Fredericton, NB (prov. capital, Canada)	46.0°N, 66.7°W	151	Guanajuato (state, Mexico)	21.0°N, 101.3°W	151
Freetown (nat. capital, Sierra Leone)	8.5°N, 13.3°W	163	Guanajuato (state capital, Mexico)	21.0°N, 101.3°W	151
French Guiana (country, South America)	4.0°N, 53.0°W	154	Guangzhou (city, China)	23.2°N, 113.4°E	160
Fria, Cape (cape, Namibia)	18.1°S, 11.8°E	162	Guatemala (nat. capital, Guatemala)	14.6°N, 90.5°W	151
Fuji, Mt. 12,388 (peak, Asia)	35.4°N, 138.7°E	159	Guatemala (country, North America)	14.6°N, 90.5°W	151
Funafuti (nat. capital, Tuvalu)	8.5°S, 179.2°E	166	Guayaquil (city, Ecuador)	2.2°S, 79.9°W	154
Fuzhou (city, China)	26.1°N, 119.3°E	160	Guerrero (state, Mexico)	17.6°N, 100.0°W	151
Gabon (country, Africa)	1.0°S, 11.8°E	163	Guiana Shield (plateau, South America)	4.0°N, 62.0°W	153
Gaborone (nat. capital, Botswana)	24.8°S, 25.9°E	163	Guinea (country, Africa)	11.0°N, 10.0°W	163
Galapagos Islands (islands, Ecuador)	0.7°S, 90.6°W	153	Guinea, Gulf of (gulf, Atlantic Ocean)	3.0°N, 2.5°E	162
Gambia, The (country, Africa)	13.5°N, 15.5°W	163	Guinea-Bissau (country, Africa)	12.0°N, 15.0°W	163
Ganges (river, India)	25.0°N, 81.0°E	159	Guyana (country, South America)	5.0°N, 59.0°W	154
Georgetown (nat. capital, Guyana)	6.8°N, 58.2°W	154	Hainan (island, China)	19.0°N, 109.5°E	159
Georgia (country, Asia)	42.0°N, 43.5°E	160	Haiti (country, North America)	18.5°N, 72.0°W	151
Georgia (state, U.S.)	33.0°N, 83.5°W	151	Halifax, NS (prov. capital, Canada)	44.7°N, 63.6°W	151
Germany (country, Europe)	51.0°N, 9.0°E	157	Halmahera (island, Indonesia)	0.6°N, 127.9°E	165
Ghana (country, Africa)	8.0°N, 2.0°W	163	Hamburg (city, Germany)	53.6°N, 10.0°E	157
Gibraltar, Strait of (strait, Atlantic Ocean)	36.0°N, 5.6°W	162	Hangzhou (city, China)	30.3°N, 120.2°E	160
Gibson Desert (desert, Australia)	23.0°S, 125.0°E	165	Hanoi (nat. capital, Vietnam)	21.0°N, 105.9°E	160
Gila (river, U.S.)	32.7°N, 114.6°W	150	Harare (nat. capital, Zimbabwe)	17.8°S, 31.1°E	163
Glasgow (city, U.K.)	55.9°N, 4.3°E	157	Harbin (city, China)	45.8°N, 126.6°E	160
Gobi Desert (desert, Asia)	42.5°N, 107.0°E	159	Harrisburg, PA (state capital, U.S.)	40.3°N, 76.9°W	151
Godavari (river, India)	20.0°N, 77.0°E	159	Hartford, CT (state capital, U.S.)	41.8°N, 72.7°W	151
Goiânia (city, Brazil)	16.7°S, 49.3°W	154	Hatteras, Cape (cape, U.S.)	35.3°N, 75.5°W	150
Gold Coast (city, Australia)	28.0°S, 153.4°E	166	Havana (nat. capital, Cuba)	23.1°N, 82.4°W	151
Good Hope, Cape of (cape, South Africa)	34.4°S, 18.5°E	162	Hawaii (island, U.S.)	19.8°N, 155.8°W	150 Inset
Gran Chaco (region, South America)	24.0°S, 60.0°W	153	Hawaii (state, U.S.)	21.3°N, 157.8°W	151 Inset
Grand Erg Occidental (desert, Algeria)	30.7°N, 0.0°W	162	Hawaiian Ridge (ridge, Pacific Ocean)	20.0°N, 160.0°W	4
Grand Erg Oriental (desert, Africa)	29.0°N, 8.0°E	162	Hefei (city, China)	31.9°N, 117.3°E	160
Great Artesian Basin (basin, Australia)	25.0°S, 144.0°E	165	Helena, MT (state capital, U.S.)	47.0°N, 112.0°W	151
Great Australian Bight (gulf, Indian Ocean)	35.0°S, 130.0°E	165	Helsinki (nat. capital, Finland)	60.2°N, 25.0°E	157
Great Barrier Reef (reef, Australia)	18.0°S, 148.0°E	165	Hermosillo (state capital, Mexico)	29.1°N, 111.0°W	151
Great Basin (basin, U.S.)	40.7°N, 117.7°W	150	Hidalgo (state, Mexico)	20.5°N, 95.9°W	151
Great Bear Lake (lake, Canada)	66.0°N, 121.0°W	150	Himalayas (mountains, Asia)	28.0°N, 82.0°E	159
Great Dividing Range (mountains, Australia)	31.0°S, 151.0°E	165	Hiroshima (city, Japan)	34.4°N, 132.5°E	160
Great Indian Desert (desert, India)	27.0°N, 71.0°E	159	Ho Chi Minh City (city, Vietnam)	10.8°N, 106.7°E	160
Great Plains (plain, North America)	37.0°N, 97.0°W	150	Hobart (city, Australia)	42.9°S, 147.3°E	166
Great Salt Lake (lake, U.S.)	41.2°N, 112.6°W	150	Hokkaido (island, Japan)	44.0°N, 143.0°E	159
Great Sandy Desert (desert, Australia)	20.0°S, 125.0°E	165	Honduras (country, North America)	15.0°N, 87.0°W	151
Great Slave Lake (lake, Canada)	61.7°N, 114.0°W	150	Hong Kong (sp. admin. reg., China)	22.3°N, 114.2°E	160
Great Victoria Desert (desert, Australia)	29.0°S, 129.0°E	165	Honiara (nat. capital, Solomon Islands)	9.4°S, 160.0°E	166
Greater Khingan Range (mountains, Asia)	49.4°N, 123.2°E	159	Honolulu (city, U.S.)	21.3°N, 157.8°W	151 Inset
Greece (country, Europe)	38.0°N, 22.0°E	157	Honshu (island, Japan)	36.0°N, 138.0°E	159
Greenland (island, North America)	72.0°N, 40.0°W	150	Horn, Cape (cape, Argentina)	56.0°S, 67.3°W	153

GEOGRAPHIC INDEX

GEOGRAPHIC INDEX

GEOGRAPHIC INDEX

NAME/DESCRIPTION	LATITUDE & LONGITUDE	PAGE	NAME/DESCRIPTION	LATITUDE & LONGITUDE	PAGE
Maseru (nat. capital, Lesotho)	29.5°S, 27.5°E	163	Molokai (island, U.S.)	21.1°N, 157.0°W	150 Inset
Massachusetts (state, U.S.)	42.3°N, 71.8°W	151	Monaco (country, Europe)	43.7°N, 7.4°E	157
Mato Grosso, Planalto do (plateau, Brazil)	15.0°S, 52.0°W	153	Mongol Altai (mountains, Mongolia)	49.0°N, 89.0°E	159
Maui (island, U.S.)	20.8°N, 156.3°W	150 Inset	Mongolia (country, Asia)	46.0°N, 105.0°E	160
Mauritania (country, Africa)	20.0°N, 12.0°W	163	Monrovia (nat. capital, Liberia)	6.3°N, 10.8°W	163
Mbabane (nat. capital, Swaziland)	26.3°S, 31.1°E	163	Montana (state, U.S.)	47.0°N, 110.0°W	151
Mbuji-Mayi (city, D.R. Congo)	6.2°S, 23.6°E	163	Montenegro (country, Europe)	42.8°N, 19.5°E	157
McKinley, Mt. 20,327 (peak, U.S.)	63.1°N, 151.0°W	150	Monterrey (state capital, Mexico)	25.7°N, 100.3°W	151
McMurdo Station (Antarctica)	77.9°S, 166.7°E	168	Montevideo (nat. capital, Uruguay)	34.9°S, 56.2°W	154
Medellin (city, Colombia)	6.2°N, 75.6°W	154	Montgomery, AL (state capital, U.S.)	32.4°N, 86.3°W	151
Medina (city, Saudi Arabia)	24.5°N, 39.6°E	160	Montpelier, VT (state capital, U.S.)	44.3°N, 72.6°W	151
Mediterranean Sea (sea, Atlantic Ocean)	36.0°N, 15.0°E	156	Montreal (city, Canada)	45.5°N, 73.6°W	151
Mekong (river, Asia)	22.0°N, 100.0°E	159	Morelia (state capital, Mexico)	19.8°N, 101.2°W	151
Melanesia (islands, Oceania)	4.0°S, 155.0°E	165	Morocco (country, Africa)	32.0°N, 5.0°W	163
Melbourne (city, Australia)	37.8°S, 145.0°E	166	Moroni (nat. capital, Comoros)	11.7°S, 43.3°E	163
Melekeok (nat. capital, Palau)	7.5°N, 134.6°E	166	Moscow (nat. capital, Russia)	55.8°N, 37.6°E	157
Memphis (city, U.S.)	35.1°N, 90.0°W	151	Mosul (city, Iraq)	36.3°N, 43.1°E	160
Mendocino, Cape (cape, U.S.)	40.4°N, 124.4°W	150	Mozambique (country, Africa)	18.3°S, 35.0°E	163
Mendoza (city, Argentina)	32.9°S, 68.8°W	154	Mozambique Channel (channel, Indian Ocean)	19.0°S, 41.0°E	162
Merida (state capital, Mexico)	21.0°N, 89.6°W	151	Mumbai (city, India)	19.0°N, 72.8°E	160
Meuse (river, Europe)	50.5°N, 5.0°E	156	Munich (city, Germany)	48.1°N, 11.6°E	157
Mexicali (state capital, Mexico)	32.7°N, 115.5°W	151	Murray (river, Australia)	36.0°S, 145.0°E	165
Mexico (state, Mexico)	19.4°N, 99.6°W	151	Muscat (nat. capital, Oman)	23.6°N, 58.6°E	160
Mexico (country, North America)	20.0°N, 100.0°W	151	Myanmar (Burma) (country, Asia)	22.0°N, 98.0°E	160
Mexico City (nat. capital, Mexico)	19.4°N, 99.2°W	151	Nagoya (city, Japan)	35.2°N, 136.9°E	160
Mexico, Gulf of (gulf, Atlantic Ocean)	25.0°N, 90.0°W	150	Nairobi (nat. capital, Kenya)	1.3°S, 36.8°E	163
Miami (city, U.S.)	25.8°N, 80.2°W	151	Namib Desert (desert, Namibia)	24.0°S, 15.0°E	162
Mianyang (city, China)	31.5°N, 104.7°E	160	Namibia (country, Africa)	22.0°S, 17.0°E	163
Michigan (state, U.S.)	44.3°N, 85.6°W	151	Nanchang (city, China)	28.7°N, 115.9°E	160
Michigan, Lake (lake, North America)	43.5°N, 87.5°W	150	Nanjing (city, China)	32.1°N, 118.8°E	160
Michoacán (state, Mexico)	19.2°N, 101.9°W	151	Nanning (city, China)	22.8°N, 108.3°E	160
Micronesia (islands, Oceania)	8.0°N, 155.0°E	165	Nanyang (city, China)	33.0°N, 112.5°E	160
Micronesia, Fed. States of (country, Oceania)	7.0°N, 158.0°E	166	Naples (city, Italy)	40.9°N, 14.3°E	157
Mid-Atlantic Ridge (ridge, Atlantic Ocean)	10.0°N, 40.0°W	4	Nashville (city, U.S.)	36.2°N, 86.8°W	151
Middle America Trench (trench, Pacific Ocean)	15.0°N, 100.0°W	4	Nassau (nat. capital, Bahamas)	25.1°N, 77.4°W	151
Mid-Indian Ridge (ridge, Indian Ocean)	5.0°S, 65.0°E	4	Nauru (country, Oceania)	0.5°S, 166.9°E	166
Milan (city, Italy)	45.5°N, 9.2°E	157	Nayarit (state, Mexico)	21.8°N, 105.2°W	151
Milwaukee (city, U.S.)	43.1°N, 88.0°W	151	Naypyitaw (nat. capital, Myanmar (Burma))	19.8°N, 96.1°E	160
Mindanao (island, Philippines)	8.0°N, 125.0°E	159	Nazca Ridge (ridge, Pacific Ocean)	20.0°S, 80.0°E	4
Minneapolis (city, U.S.)	45.0°N, 93.3°W	151	N'Djamena (nat. capital, Chad)	12.1°N, 15.1°E	163
Minnesota (state, U.S.)	46.0°N, 94.0°W	151	Nebraska (state, U.S.)	41.5°N, 100.0°W	151
Minsk (nat. capital, Belarus)	53.9°N, 27.6°E	157	Negro (river, Argentina)	40.0°S, 65.0°W	153
Mississippi (river, U.S.)	29.2°N, 89.3°W	150	Negro (river, Brazil)	2.0°S, 62.0°W	153
Mississippi (state, U.S.)	33.0°N, 90.0°W	151	Nelson (river, Canada)	57.1°N, 92.5°W	150
Missouri (river, U.S.)	38.8°N, 90.1°W	150	Nepal (country, Asia)	27.7°N, 85.0°E	160
Missouri (state, U.S.)	38.5°N, 92.5°W	151	Netherlands (country, Europe)	52.5°N, 5.8°E	157
Mogadishu (nat. capital, Somalia)	2.1°N, 45.4°E	163	Neuquén (city, Argentina)	39.0°S, 68.2°W	154
Moldova (country, Europe)	49.0°N, 29.0°E	157	Nevada (state, U.S.)	39.0°N, 117.0°W	151

GEOGRAPHIC INDEX

NAME/DESCRIPTION	LATITUDE & LONGITUDE	PAGE	NAME/DESCRIPTION	LATITUDE & LONGITUDE	PAGE
New Britain (island, Papua New Guinea)	6.0°S, 150.0°E	165	Nubian Desert (desert, Africa)	20.5°N, 33.0°E	162
New Brunswick (province, Canada)	46.7°N, 66.1°W	151	Nuevo León (state, Mexico)	25.6°N, 100.0°W	151
New Caledonia (island, Oceania)	21.5°S, 165.5°E	165	Nuku'alofa (nat. capital, Tonga)	21.1°S, 175.2°W	166
New Delhi (nat. capital, India)	28.6°N, 77.2°E	160	Nullarbor Plain (plain, Australia)	31.0°S, 130.0°E	165
New Guinea (island, Oceania)	5.0°S, 140.0°E	165	Nunavut (territory, Canada)	73.0°N, 91.0°W	151
New Hampshire (state, U.S.)	44.0°N, 71.5°W	151	Nuuk (city, Greenland)	64.2°N, 51.7°W	151
New Hebrides (islands, Oceania)	16.0°S, 167.0°E	165	Nyasa, Lake (lake, Africa)	12.2°S, 34.4°E	162
New Jersey (state, U.S.)	40.0°N, 74.5°W	151	Oahu (island, U.S.)	21.5°N, 158.0°W	150 Inset
New Mexico (state, U.S.)	34.0°N, 106.0°W	151	Oates Land (region, Antarctica)	69.5°S, 159.0°E	168
New Orleans (city, U.S.)	30.0°N, 90.1°W	151	Oaxaca (state, Mexico)	16.9°N, 96.4°W	151
New Siberian Islands (islands, Russia)	75.0°N, 142.0°E	168	Oaxaca (state capital, Mexico)	17.1°N, 96.8°W	151
New South Wales (state, Australia)	32.0°S, 147.0°E	166	Ob (river, Russia)	65.0°N, 65.0°E	159
New York (city, U.S.)	40.7°N, 74.0°W	151	Oder (river, Europe)	51.2°N, 16.9°E	156
New York (state, U.S.)	43.0°N, 75.0°W	151	Odessa (city, Ukraine)	46.5°N, 30.7°E	157
New Zealand (country, Oceania)	42.0°S, 174.0°E	166	Ohio (river, U.S.)	37.0°N, 89.1°W	150
Newcastle (city, U.K.)	55.0°N, 1.6°W	157	Ohio (state, U.S.)	40.5°N, 82.5°W	151
Newfoundland (island, Canada)	52.0°N, 56.0°W	150	Okhotsk, Sea of (sea, Pacific Ocean)	53.0°N, 150.0°E	159
Newfoundland and Labrador (province, Canada)	52.6°N, 59.7°W	151	Oklahoma (state, U.S.)	65.5°N, 98.0°W	151
Niamey (nat. capital, Niger)	13.5°N, 2.1°E	163	Oklahoma City, OK (state capital, U.S.)	35.5°N, 97.5°W	151
Nicaragua (country, North America)	13.0°N, 85.0°W	151	Olympia, WA (state capital, U.S.)	47.0°N, 122.9°W	151
Nice (city, France)	43.7°N, 7.3°E	157	Omaha (city, U.S.)	41.3°N, 96.0°W	151
Nicosia (nat. capital, Cyprus)	35.2°N, 33.4°E	157	Oman (country, Asia)	21.0°N, 57.0°E	160
Niger (river, Africa)	14.0°N, 5.0°W	162	Oman, Gulf of (gulf, Indian Ocean)	24.5°N, 58.5°E	159
Niger (country, Africa)	17.0°N, 9.0°E	163	Omsk (city, Russia)	55.0°N, 73.4°E	160
Nigeria (country, Africa)	8.0°N, 9.0°E	163	Onega, Lake (lake, Russia)	61.7°N, 35.7°E	156
Niihau (island, U.S.)	21.9°N, 160.2°W	150 Inset	Ontario, Lake (lake, North America)	43.5°N, 78.0°W	150
Nile (river, Africa)	27.0°N, 31.5°E	162	Orange (river, South Africa)	29.6°S, 22.7°E	162
Ninety East Ridge (ridge, Indian Ocean)	10.0°S, 90.0°E	4	Oregon (state, U.S.)	44.0°N, 120.5°W	151
Niue (N.Z.) (dependency, Oceania)	19.1°S, 169.9°W	166	Orinoco (river, South America)	8.0°N, 63.0°W	153
Nizhny Novgorod (city, Russia)	56.3°N, 44.0°E	160	Orizaba, Pico de 18,491 (peak, Mexico)	19.0°N, 97.3°W	150
North Atlantic Ocean (ocean)	30.0°N, 45.0°W	4	Orlando (city, U.S.)	28.5°N, 81.4°W	151
North Carolina (state, U.S.)	35.5°N, 80.0°W	151	Osaka (city, Japan)	34.7°N, 135.5°E	160
North Dakota (state, U.S.)	47.5°N, 100.5°W	151	Oslo (nat. capital, Norway)	59.9°N, 10.8°E	157
North Dvina (river, Russia)	63.0°N, 44.0°E	159	Ottawa (nat. capital, Canada)	45.4°N, 75.7°W	151
North Island (island, New Zealand)	39.0°S, 176.0°E	165	Ouagadougou (nat. capital, Burkina Faso)	12.4°N, 1.5°W	163
North Korea (country, Asia)	40.0°N, 127.0°E	160	Ozark Plateau (plateau, U.S.)	37.2°N, 92.5°W	150
North Pacific Ocean (ocean)	30.0°N, 165.0°W	4	Pachuca (state capital, Mexico)	20.1°N, 98.7°W	151
North Saskatchewan (river, Canada)	53.2°N, 105.1°W	150	Pakistan (country, Asia)	30.0°N, 70.0°E	160
North Sea (sea, Atlantic Ocean)	56.0°N, 4.0°E	156	Palau (country, Oceania)	7.5°N, 134.5°E	166
Northern European Plain (plain, Europe)	54.0°N, 14.0°E	159	Palembang (city, Indonesia)	3.0°S, 104.8°E	160
Northern Territory (state, Australia)	20.0°S, 133.0°E	166	Palermo (city, Italy)	38.1°N, 13.4°E	157
Northwest Territories (territory, Canada)	64.3°N, 119.2°W	151	Palikir (nat. capital, Micronesia)	6.9°N, 158.1°E	166
Norway (country, Europe)	62.0°N, 10.0°E	157	Pampas (region, Argentina)	35.0°S, 63.0°W	153
Norwegian Sea (sea, Atlantic Ocean)	66.0°N, 6.0°E	156	Panama (country, North America)	9.0°N, 79.5°W	151
Nouakchott (nat. capital, Mauritania)	18.1°N, 16.0°W	163	Panama (nat. capital, Panama)	9.0°N, 79.5°W	151
Nova Scotia (province, Canada)	45.2°N, 62.7°W	151	Papua New Guinea (country, Oceania)	6.0°S, 144.0°E	166
Novaya Zemlya (islands, Russia)	74.0°N, 57.0°E	159	Papua, Gulf of (gulf, Papua New Guinea)	9.0°S, 145.0°E	165
Novosibirsk (city, Russia)	55.0°N, 82.9°E	160	Paraguay (river, South America)	23.0°S, 61.0°W	153

GEOGRAPHIC INDEX

NAME/DESCRIPTION	LATITUDE & LONGITUDE	PAGE
Paraguay (country, South America)	23.0°S, 58.0°W	154
Paramaribo (nat. capital, Suriname)	5.8°N, 55.2°W	154
Paraná (river, South America)	21.0°S, 52.0°W	153
Paris (nat. capital, France)	48.9°N, 2.3°E	157
Patagonia (region, Argentina)	48.0°S, 61.0°W	153
Peace (river, Canada)	59.0°N, 111.4°W	150
Pechora (river, Russia)	65.5°N, 52.0°E	159
Pennsylvania (state, U.S.)	41.0°N, 77.5°W	151
Perm (city, Russia)	58.0°N, 56.3°E	160
Persian Gulf (gulf, Indian Ocean)	27.0°N, 51.0°E	4
Perth (city, Australia)	31.9°S, 115.8°E	166
Peru (country, South America)	8.0°S, 76.0°W	154
Peru-Chile Trench (trench, Pacific Ocean)	23.0°S, 73.0°E	4
Philadelphia (city, U.S.)	40.0°N, 75.2°W	151
Philippine Sea (sea, Pacific Ocean)	20.0°N, 134.0°E	159
Philippines (country, Asia)	13.0°N, 122.0°E	160
Phnom Penh (nat. capital, Cambodia)	11.6°N, 104.9°E	160
Phoenix, AZ (state capital, U.S.)	33.5°N, 112.1°W	151
Pierre, SD (state capital, U.S.)	44.4°N, 100.3°W	151
Pittsburgh (city, U.S.)	40.4°N, 80.0°W	151
Po (river, Italy)	45.0°N, 10.0°E	156
Podgorica (nat. capital, Montenegro)	42.4°N, 19.3°E	157
Point Conception (cape, U.S.)	34.5°N, 120.5°W	150
Poland (country, Europe)	52.0°N, 20.0°E	157
Polynesia (islands, Oceania)	10.0°S, 170.0°E	165
Port Elizabeth (city, South Africa)	34.0°S, 25.6°E	163
Port Moresby (nat. capital, Papua New Guinea)	9.5°S, 147.2°E	166
Port-Au-Prince (nat. capital, Haiti)	18.5°N, 72.3°W	151
Port-Harcourt (city, Nigeria)	4.8°N, 7.0°E	163
Portland (city, U.S.)	45.5°N, 122.7°W	151
Porto (city, Portugal)	41.2°N, 8.6°W	157
Porto Allegre (city, Brazil)	30.0°S, 51.2°W	154
Porto-Novo (nat. capital, Benin)	6.5°N, 2.6°E	163
Portugal (country, Europe)	40.0°N, 8.0°E	157
Port-Vila (nat. capital, Vanuatu)	17.7°S, 168.3°E	166
Prague (nat. capital, Czechia)	50.1°N, 14.5°E	157
Pretoria (nat. capital, South Africa)	25.7°S, 28.2°E	163
Prince Edward Island (province, Canada)	46.3°N, 63.3°W	151
Princess Elizabeth Land (region, Antarctica)	80.0°S, 78.0°E	168
Pristina (nat. capital, Kosovo)	42.7°N, 21.2°E	157
Providence, RI (state capital, U.S.)	41.8°N, 71.4°W	151
Puebla (state, Mexico)	19.0°N, 97.9°W	151
Puebla (state capital, Mexico)	19.1°N, 98.2°W	151
Punta Lavapié (cape, Chile)	38.0°S, 73.0°W	153
Punta Negra (cape, Peru)	7.0°S, 81.5°W	153
P'yongyang (nat. capital, North Korea)	39.0°N, 125.8°E	160
Pyrenees (mountains, Europe)	42.5°N, 0.8°E	156
Qatar (country, Asia)	25.3°N, 51.5°E	160

NAME/DESCRIPTION	LATITUDE & LONGITUDE	PAGE
Qingdao (city, China)	36.1°N, 120.4°E	160
Qom (city, Iran)	34.6°N, 50.9°E	160
Québec (province, Canada)	53.8°N, 72.0°W	151
Québec, QC (prov. capital, Canada)	46.8°N, 71.3°W	151
Queen Charlotte Islands (islands, Canada)	53.0°N, 132.0°W	150
Queen Elizabeth Islands (islands, Canada)	78.0°N, 95.0°W	150
Queen Mary Land (region, Antarctica)	66.8°S, 96.0°E	168
Queen Maud Land (region, Antarctica)	73.5°S, 12.0°E	168
Queensland (state, Australia)	23.0°S, 143.0°E	166
Querétaro (state capital, Mexico)	20.6°N, 100.4°W	151
Querétaro (state, Mexico)	20.8°N, 99.9°W	151
Quintana Roo (state, Mexico)	19.6°N, 87.9°W	151
Quito (nat. capital, Ecuador)	0.2°S, 78.5°W	154
Rabat (nat. capital, Morocco)	34.0°N, 6.9°W	163
Rainier, Mt. 14,411 (peak, U.S.)	46.9°N, 121.8°W	150
Raleigh, NC (state capital, U.S.)	35.8°N, 78.7°W	151
Recife (city, Brazil)	8.1°S, 34.9°W	154
Red (river, U.S.)	31.0°N, 91.8°W	150
Red Sea (sea, Indian Ocean)	20.0°N, 38.0°E	159
Regina, SK (prov. capital, Canada)	50.5°N, 104.6°W	151
Reindeer Lake (lake, Canada)	57.6°N, 102.3°W	150
Reykjanes Ridge (ridge, Atlantic Ocean)	60.0°N, 30.0°W	4
Reykjavik (nat. capital, Iceland)	64.2°N, 22.0°W	157
Rhine (river, Europe)	50.4°N, 7.6°E	156
Rhode Island (state, U.S.)	41.7°N, 71.5°W	151
Rhône (river, France)	44.8°N, 4.8°E	156
Richmond, VA (state capital, U.S.)	37.5°N, 77.4°W	151
Riga (nat. capital, Latvia)	57.0°N, 24.1°E	157
Rio Branco (city, Brazil)	10.0°S, 67.8°W	154
Rio de Janeiro (city, Brazil)	22.9°S, 43.3°W	154
Rio Gallegos (city, Argentina)	51.6°S, 69.2°W	154
Rio Grande (river, North America)	26.0°N, 97.2°W	150
Riyadh (nat. capital, Saudi Arabia)	24.6°N, 46.7°E	160
Rocky Mountains (mountains, North America)	52.0°N, 110.0°W	150
Romania (country, Europe)	47.0°N, 25.0°E	157
Rome (nat. capital, Italy)	41.9°N, 12.5°E	157
Ronne Ice Shelf (ice shelf, Antarctica)	77.9°S, 61.3°W	168
Ross Ice Shelf (ice shelf, Antarctica)	81.5°S, 175.0°W	168
Ross Sea (sea, Antarctica)	76.0°S, 175.0°W	168
Rostov (city, Russia)	57.2°N, 39.4°E	157
Rotterdam (city, Netherlands)	51.9°N, 4.5°E	157
Rub Al Khali (desert, Saudi Arabia)	19.5°N, 49.0°E	159
Russia (country, Asia)	60.0°N, 100.0°E	160
Rwanda (country, Africa)	2.0°S, 30.0°E	163
Rybinsk Reservoir (lake, Russia)	58.4°N, 38.4°E	156
Ryukyu Islands (islands, Japan)	26.5°N, 128.0°E	159
Sable, Cape (cape, U.S.)	43.5°N, 63.6°W	150
Sacramento, CA (state capital, U.S.)	38.6°N, 121.5°W	151

GEOGRAPHIC INDEX

NAME/DESCRIPTION	LATITUDE & LONGITUDE	PAGE	NAME/DESCRIPTION	LATITUDE & LONGITUDE	PAGE
Sahara (desert, Africa)	23.0°N, 13.0°E	162	Seoul (nat. capital, South Korea)	37.6°N, 127.0°E	160
Sahel, The (region, Africa)	15.0°N, 8.0°W	162	Serbia (country, Europe)	44.8°N, 22.5°E	157
Sakhalin (island, Russia)	51.0°N, 143.0°E	159	Shanghai (city, China)	31.2°N, 121.5°E	160
Salem, OR (state capital, U.S.)	44.9°N, 123.0°W	151	Shantou (city, China)	23.4°N, 116.7°E	160
Salt Lake City, UT (state capital, U.S.)	40.8°N, 111.9°W	151	Shenyeng (city, China)	41.8°N, 123.4°E	160
Salta (city, Argentina)	24.8°S, 65.4°W	154	Shenzhen (city, China)	22.6°N, 114.1°E	160
Saltillo (state capital, Mexico)	25.4°N, 101.0°W	151	Shetland Islands (islands, U.K.)	60.5°N, 1.5°W	156
Salvador (city, Brazil)	13.0°S, 38.5°W	154	Shikoku (island, Japan)	33.8°N, 133.5°E	159
Samar (island, Philippines)	12.0°N, 125.0°E	159	Shiraz (city, Iran)	29.6°N, 52.5°E	160
Samara (city, Russia)	53.2°N, 50.2°E	160	Sichuan Basin (basin, China)	30.5°N, 105.5°E	159
Samoa (country, Oceania)	13.6°S, 172.3°W	166	Sicily (island, Italy)	37.5°N, 14.0°E	156
San Antonio (city, U.S.)	29.4°N, 98.5°W	151	Sierra Leone (country, Africa)	8.7°N, 12.0°W	163
San Diego (city, U.S.)	32.7°N, 117.2°W	151	Sierra Madre Occidental (mountains, Mexico)	23.0°N, 108.0°W	150
San Francisco (city, U.S.)	37.8°N, 122.4°W	151	Sierra Madre Oriental (mountains, Mexico)	23.0°N, 100.0°W	150
San Jose (nat. capital, Costa Rica)	9.9°N, 84.1°W	151	Sierra Nevada (mountains, U.S.)	38.0°N, 120.0°W	150
San Jose (city, U.S.)	37.3°N, 121.9°W	151	Sikhote-alin (mountains, Russia)	47.0°N, 137.0°E	159
San Juan (city, Argentina)	31.5°S, 68.5°W	154	Simpson Desert (desert, Australia)	24.5°S, 137.5°E	165
San Juan (city, Puerto Rico)	18.5°N, 66.1°W	151	Sinaloa (state, Mexico)	25.0°N, 107.5°W	151
San Lucas, Cabo (cape, Mexico)	22.9°N, 109.9°W	150	Singapore (country, Asia)	1.3°N, 103.9°E	160
San Luis (city, Argentina)	33.3°S, 66.3°W	154	Skagerrak (strait, Atlantic Ocean)	57.8°N, 9.0°E	156
San Luis Potosi (state capital, Mexico)	22.2°N, 100.9°W	151	Skopje (nat. capital, Macedonia)	42.0°N, 21.4°E	157
San Luis Potosi (state, Mexico)	22.6°N, 100.4°W	151	Slave (river, Canada)	61.3°N, 113.6°W	150
San Marino (country, Europe)	43.9°N, 12.4°E	157	Slovakia (country, Europe)	48.7°N, 19.5°E	157
San Salvador (nat. capital, El Salvador)	13.7°N, 89.2°W	151	Slovenia (country, Europe)	46.0°N, 15.0°E	157
Sanaa (nat. capital, Yemen)	15.4°N, 44.2°E	160	Snake (river, U.S.)	46.2°N, 119.0°W	150
Santa Cruz (city, Bolivia)	17.8°S, 63.2°W	154	Socotra (island, Yemen)	12.5°N, 54.0°E	159
Santa Fe (city, Argentina)	31.6°S, 60.7°W	151	Sofia (nat. capital, Bulgaria)	42.7°N, 23.3°E	157
Santa Fe (city, U.S.)	35.7°N, 106.0°W	154	Solomon Islands (country, Oceania)	8.0°S, 159.0°E	166
Santiago (nat. capital, Chile)	33.5°S, 70.7°W	154	Solomon Sea (sea, Pacific Ocean)	8.0°S, 153.0°E	165
Santo Domingo (nat. capital, Dominican Republic)	18.5°N, 69.9°W	151	Somalia (country, Africa)	5.5°N, 47.0°E	163
São Francisco (river, Brazil)	12.0°S, 42.0°W	153	Sonora (state, Mexico)	29.7°N, 110.9°W	151
São Luis (city, Brazil)	23.6°S, 46.7°W	154	South Africa (country, Africa)	30.0°S, 24.0°E	163
São Paulo (city, Brazil)	23.6°S, 46.6°W	154	South Atlantic Ocean (ocean)	30.0°S, 15.0°W	4
São Tomé (nat. capital, São Tomé and Príncipe)	0.3°N, 6.7°E	163	South Australia (state, Australia)	30.0°S, 135.0°E	166
São Tomé and Príncipe (country, Africa)	0.2°N, 6.7°E	163	South Carolina (state, U.S.)	34.0°N, 81.0°W	151
Sapporo (city, Japan)	43.1°N, 141.3°E	160	South China Sea (sea, Pacific Ocean)	10.0°N, 113.0°E	159
Sarajevo (nat. capital, Bosnia-Herzegovina)	43.9°N, 18.4°E	157	South Dakota (state, U.S.)	44.5°N, 100.0°W	151
Sardinia (island, Italy)	40.0°N, 9.0°E	156	South Georgia (island, U.K.)	54.3°S, 36.8°W	153
Saskatchewan (province, Canada)	54.5°N, 105.7°W	151	South Island (island, New Zealand)	43.0°S, 171.0°E	165
Saudi Arabia (country, Asia)	25.0°N, 45.0°E	160	South Korea (country, Asia)	37.0°N, 127.5°E	160
Sayan Mountains (mountains, Asia)	53.3°N, 95.0°E	159	South Pacific Ocean (ocean)	30.0°S, 130.0°W	4
Scandinavian Peninsula (peninsula, Europe)	63.0°N, 13.0°E	4	South Sandwich Trench (trench, Atlantic Ocean)	55.0°S, 20.0°W	4
Scotia Sea (sea, Atlantic Ocean)	56.0°S, 40.0°W	153	South Saskatchewan (river, Canada)	53.2°N, 105.1°W	150
Seattle (city, U.S.)	47.6°N, 122.3°W	151	South Sudan (country, Africa)	7.0°N, 30.0°E	163
Seine (river, France)	48.4°N, 3.0°E	156	Southern Alps (mountains, New Zealand)	43.5°S, 170.5°E	165
Sendai (city, Japan)	38.3°N, 140.9°E	160	Southwest Indian Ridge (ridge, Indian Ocean)	33.0°S, 55.0°E	4
Senegal (river, Africa)	16.5°N, 14.0°W	162	Spain (country, Europe)	40.0°N, 4.0°W	157
Senegal (country, Africa)	14.5°N, 15.0°W	163	Springfield, IL (state capital, U.S.)	39.8°N, 89.7°W	151

GEOGRAPHIC INDEX

GEOGRAPHIC INDEX

NAME/DESCRIPTION	LATITUDE & LONGITUDE	PAGE	NAME/DESCRIPTION	LATITUDE & LONGITUDE	PAGE
Tunisia (country, Africa)	35.0°N, 9.2°E	163	Virginia (state, U.S.)	37.5°N, 79.0°W	151
Turin (city, Italy)	45.1°N, 7.7°E	157	Virginia Beach (city, U.S.)	38.9°N, 76.0°W	151
Turkey (country, Asia)	39.0°N, 35.0°E	160	Vistula (river, Poland)	52.4°N, 20.9°E	156
Turkmenistan (country, Asia)	40.0°N, 60.0°E	160	Viti Levu (island, Fiji)	18.0°S, 178.0°E	165
Tuvalu (country, Oceania)	8.5°S, 179.2°E	166	Vitória (city, Brazil)	26.2°S, 51.1°W	154
Tuxtla Gutiérrez (state capital, Mexico)	16.8°N, 93.1°W	151	Volga (river, Russia)	52.0°N, 48.0°E	159
Tyrrhenian Sea (sea, Atlantic Ocean)	40.0°N, 12.0°E	156	Volgograd (city, Russia)	48.7°N, 44.5°E	160
Ubangi (river, Africa)	4.8°N, 20.2°E	162	Voronezh (city, Russia)	51.7°N, 39.2°E	157
Uganda (country, Africa)	1.5°N, 32.0°E	163	Vychegda (river, Russia)	62.0°N, 50.4°E	156
Ukraine (country, Europe)	49.0°N, 32.0°E	157	Wallis & Futuna (Fr.) (dependency, France)	13.3°S, 176.2°W	166
Ulaanbaatar (nat. capital, Mongolia)	47.9°N, 106.9°E	160	Walvis Ridge (ridge, Atlantic Ocean)	23.0°S, 8.0°E	4
Ulsan (city, South Korea)	35.6°N, 129.3°E	160	Warsaw (nat. capital, Poland)	52.3°N, 21.0°E	157
Uluru 2,831 (peak, Australia)	25.3°S, 131.0°E	165	Washington (state, U.S.)	45.7°N, 120.5°W	151
Ungava Peninsula (peninsula, Canada)	59.0°N, 74.0°W	150	Washington, DC (nat. capital, U.S.)	38.9°N, 77.0°W	151
United Arab Emirates (country, Asia)	24.0°N, 54.0°E	160	Weddell Sea (sea, Antarctica)	72.0°S, 45.0°W	168
United Kingdom (country, Europe)	54.0°N, 2.0°W	157	Wellington (nat. capital, New Zealand)	41.5°S, 174.9°E	166
United States (country, North America)	40.0°N, 100.0°W	151	West Antarctica (region, Antarctica)	60.0°N, 75.0°E	168
Ural (river, Russia)	52.0°N, 55.0°E	159	West Siberian Plain (plain, Russia)	62.0°N, 76.0°E	159
Ural Mountains (mountains, Russia)	60.0°N, 60.0°E	159	West Virginia (state, U.S.)	39.0°N, 80.5°W	151
Uruguay (country, South America)	33.0°S, 56.0°W	154	Western Australia (state, Australia)	26.0°S, 121.0°E	166
Ürümqi (city, China)	43.7°N, 87.6°E	160	Western Ghats (mountains, India)	13.7°N, 75.0°E	159
Utah (state, U.S.)	39.5°N, 111.5°W	151	Western Sahara (country, Africa)	24.5°N, 13.0°W	163
Uzbekistan (country, Asia)	41.0°N, 64.0°E	160	White Nile (river, Africa)	3.7°N, 31.3°E	162
Valencia (city, Spain)	39.5°N, 0.4°W	157	White Sea (sea, Arctic Ocean)	65.3°N, 38.0°E	156
Valparaiso (city, Chile)	33.1°S, 71.6°W	154	Whitehorse, YT (terr. capital, Canada)	60.7°N, 135.1°W	151
Vancouver (city, Canada)	49.3°N, 123.1°W	151	Whitney, Mt. 14,505 (peak, U.S.)	36.0°N, 118.3°W	150
Vancouver Island (island, Canada)	49.8°N, 126.0°W	150	Wilhelm II Land (region, Antarctica)	66.8°S, 89.2°E	168
Vanua Levu (island, Fiji)	16.6°S, 179.2°E	165	Wilhelm, Mt. 14,793 (peak, Papua New Guinea)	5.8°S, 145.0°E	165
Vanuatu (country, Oceania)	16.0°S, 167.0°E	166	Wilkes Land (region, Antarctica)	71.0°S, 120.0°E	168
Varanasi (city, India)	25.3°N, 83.0°E	160	Windhoek (nat. capital, Namibia)	22.6°S, 17.1°E	163
Vatican City (country, Europe)	41.9°N, 12.5°E	157	Winnipeg, Lake (lake, Canada)	52.1°N, 97.3°W	150
Venezuela (country, South America)	7.0°N, 67.0°W	154	Winnipeg, MB (prov. capital, Canada)	49.9°N, 97.2°W	151
Veracruz (state capital, Mexico)	19.2°N, 96.2°W	151	Wisconsin (state, U.S.)	44.5°N, 89.5°W	151
Veracruz (state, Mexico)	19.4°N, 96.4°W	151	Wrangel Island (island, Russia)	71.2°N, 179.6°W	168
Verkhoyansk Range (mountains, Russia)	67.0°N, 129.0°E	159	Wuhan (city, China)	30.6°N, 114.3°E	160
Vermont (state, U.S.)	44.0°N, 72.7°W	151	Wyoming (state, U.S.)	43.0°N, 107.5°W	151
Victoria (state, Australia)	37.0°S, 144.0°E	166	Xiamen (city, China)	24.5°N, 118.1°E	160
Victoria Island (island, Canada)	71.0°N, 110.0°W	150	Xian (city, China)	36.2°N, 108.9°E	160
Victoria Land (region, Antarctica)	72.0°S, 155.0°E	168	Yablonovy Range (mountains, Russia)	52.0°N, 133.5°E	159
Victoria, BC (prov. capital, Canada)	48.4°N, 123.4°W	151	Yakutsk (city, Russia)	62.0°N, 129.7°E	160
Victoria, Lake (lake, Africa)	1.0°S, 33.0°E	162	Yamoussoukro (nat. capital, Côte d'Ivoire)	6.8°N, 5.3°W	163
Viedma (city, Argentina)	40.8°S, 63.0°W	154	Yangon (city, Myanmar (Burma))	16.8°N, 96.2°E	160
Vienna (nat. capital, Austria)	48.2°N, 16.4°E	157	Yangtze (Chang) (river, China)	30.0°N, 112.0°E	159
Vientiane (nat. capital, Laos)	18.0°N, 102.6°E	160	Yaoundé (nat. capital, Cameroon)	3.9°N, 11.5°E	163
Vietnam (country, Asia)	16.0°N, 107.5°E	160	Yekaterinburg (city, Russia)	56.8°N, 60.7°E	160
Villahermosa (state capital, Mexico)	18.0°N, 92.9°W	151	Yellow Sea (sea, Pacific Ocean)	36.0°N, 123.0°E	159
Vilnius (nat. capital, Lithuania)	54.7°N, 25.3°E	157	Yellowknife, NT (terr. capital, Canada)	62.5°N, 114.4°W	151
Vinson Massif 16,066 (peak, Antarctica)	78.5°S, 85.6°W	168	Yemen (country, Asia)	15.0°N, 48.0°E	160

GEOGRAPHIC INDEX

Sources

Amnesty International. Online access at www.amnesty.org.

Asia-Pacific Economic Organization (APEC). Online access at www.apecsec.org.

Bercovitch, J., and R. Jackson. (1997). *International conflict: A chronological encyclopedia of conflicts and their management 1945–1995.* Washington, D.C.: Congressional Quarterly.

Boden, T., G. Marland, and R. J. Andrew (2009). *National CO_2 emissions from fossil-fuel burning, cement manufacture, and gas flaring: 1751–2006.* Carbon Dioxide Information Analysis Center. Oak Ridge National Laboratory. Online access at http://cdiac.ornl.gov.

BP Statistical Review of World Energy. Online access at www.bp.com/bpstats.

Canadian Forces College, Information Resources Centre. Online access at www.cfcsc.dnd.ca/links/wars/index.html.

Cohen, S. (2002). *Geopolitics of the world system.* Lanham, MD: Rowman & Littlefield.

Commonwealth of Independent States (CIS). Online access at www.cis.minsk.by/english.

Crabb, C. (1993, January). Soiling the planet. *Discover, 14* (1), 74–75.

de Blij, H. J., and P. O. Muller. *Geography: Realms, regions, and concepts,* 12th ed. Hoboken, NJ: John Wiley & Sons, Inc.

Domke, K. (1988). *War and the changing global system.* New Haven, CT: Yale University Press.

Economic Community of West African States (ECOWAS). Online access at www.state.gov.

European Free Trade Association (EFTA). Online access at www.efta.int.

The European Union (EU). Online access at www.europa.eu.int.

Food and Agricultural Organization of the United Nations (FAO). Online access at www.fao.org.

Freedom House. Online access at www.freedomhouse.org.

Goode's world atlas, 22nd ed. (2010). New York: Rand McNally.

The Greater Caribbean Community (CARICOM). Online access at www.caricom.org.

Gunnemark, E. V. (n.d., early 1990s). *Countries, peoples and their languages.* Gothenburg, Sweden: The Geolinguistic Handbook.

Hammond atlas of the world. (1993). Maplewood, NJ: Hammond.

Information please almanac, atlas, and yearbook 2002. (2002). Boston & New York: Houghton Mifflin.

International Energy Agency. (2001). *Key world energy statistics 2000.* Paris. Online access at www.iea.org/statist/keyworld/keystats.htm.

Johnson, D. (1977). *Population, society, and desertification.* New York: United Nations Conference on Desertification, United Nations Environment Programme.

Köppen, W., and R. Geiger (1954). *Klima der erde* [Climate of the earth]. Darmstadt, Germany: Justus Perthes.

Lindeman, M. (1990). *The United States and the Soviet Union: Choices for the 21st century.* Guilford, CT: Dushkin Publishing Group.

Murphy, R. E. (1968). Landforms of the world [Map supplement No. 9]. *Annals of the Association of American Geographers, 58* (1), 198–200.

National Oceanic and Atmospheric Administration. (1990–1992). Unpublished data. Washington, D.C.: NOAA.

New York Times. Online access at http://archives.nytimes.com/archives/.

North Atlantic Treaty Organization (NATO). Online access at www.nato.int.

The Peace Corps. Online access at www.peacecorps.gov.

Population Reference Bureau. (2010). *World Population Data Sheet.* Online access at http://www.prb.org/pdf10/10wpds_eng.pdf.

Rourke, J. T. (2003). *International politics on the world stage,* 9th ed. Guilford, CT: McGraw-Hill/Dushkin.

Southern African Development Community (SADC). Online access at www.sadc.int.

Southern Cone Common Market (MERCOSUR). Online access at www.infoplease.com/ce6/history/A0846059.html.

Spector, L. S. and J.R. Smith (1990). *Nuclear ambitions: The spread of nuclear weapons.* Boulder, CO: Westview Press.

The Times Atlas of World History. (1978). London: Times Books Limited.

United Nations Development Programme (UNDP). (2011). *Human Development 2011*. Online access at http://hdr.undp.org/en/media/HDR_2011_EN_Complete.pdf.

United Nations Food and Agriculture Organization. *FAOSTAT database*. Online access at http://apps.fao.org/page/collections?subset=agriculture.

United Nations High Commissioner for Refugees, Population Data Unit, Population and Geographic Data Section. (2009). Online access at www.unhcr.org/.

United Nations Department of Economic and Social Affairs, Population Division. *World Urbanization Prospects, The 2009 Revision*. Online access at http://esa.un.org/unpd/wpp/index.htm.

United Nations Statistics Division, Department of Economic and Social Affairs. (2001). *Social indicators*. Online access at www.un.org/depts/unsd/social/index.htm.

Uranium Institute. Online access at www.uilondon.org/safetab.htm.

U.S. Census Bureau. (2000). *International database, United States Census Bureau*. Online access at www.census.gov/ipc/www/idbnew.html.

U.S. Central Intelligence Agency. (2011). *The World Factbook 2011*. Washington, D.C.: Central Intelligence Agency. Online access at www.cia.gov/library/publications/the-world-factbook/.

USDA Forest Service. (1989). *Ecoregions of the continents*. Washington, D.C.: U.S. Government Printing Office.

U.S. Department of State. (1999). Undersecretary for Arms Control and International Security. *World military expenditures and arms transfers*. Online access at www.state.gov/www/global/arms/bureau_ac/wmeat98/wmeat98.html.

World Bank. (2011). *World development indicators, 2011*. Washington, D.C.: World Bank. Online access at data.worldbank.org.

World Health Organization. (1998). *World health statistics annual*. Geneva: World Health Organization.

World Resources Institute. (2000). *World resources 2000–2001: People and ecosystems: The fraying web of life*. Washington, D.C.: World Resources Institute. Online access at www.wri.org.

World Trade Organization (WTO). Online access at www.wto.org.

Wright, J. W., ed. (2003). *The New York Times almanac 2003*. New York: Penguin Reference.